OUR PEOPLE ARE WARLIKE

OUR PEOPLE ARE

★ ★ ★ ★ ★

WARLIKE

CIVIL WAR PITTSBURGH AND HOME-FRONT MOBILIZATION

ALLEN CHRISTOPHER YORK

The University of Tennessee Press
Knoxville

Library of Congress Cataloging-in-Publication Data

NAMES: York, Allen Christopher, 1977- author.
TITLE: Our people are warlike : Civil War Pittsburgh
and home-front mobilization / Allen Christopher York.
DESCRIPTION: First edition. | Knoxville : The University of Tennessee
Press, [2023] | Includes bibliographical references and index. |
SUMMARY: "While one of the most persistent underlying themes in the
historiography of the Civil War is the 'brother against brother' one, particularly
in states that were deeply divided, Pittsburgh and its citizenry provide an instance
of almost universal pro-Union ideological solidarity as the war approached and
overtook the country. The city achieved this unity despite forces that might
ordinarily tear it apart: an ethnically diverse population, including many new
immigrants, a complex industrial-economic situation, and an enormous
contribution of soldiers who died in combat. A study of local history during
a tumultuous time and of pro-Unionism in which different groups tried to outdo
one another in patriotic fervor, this book provides a wide-ranging look at
Pittsburgh during the war years"—Provided by publisher.
IDENTIFIERS: LCCN 2023031042 (print) | LCCN 2023031043 (ebook) |
ISBN 9781621908258 (hardcover) | ISBN 9781621908265 (pdf) | ISBN 9781621908272 (kindle edition)
SUBJECTS: LCSH: Pittsburgh (Pa.)—History. | Soldiers—Pennsylvania—Pittsburgh—History—
19th century. | United States—Armed Forces—Pennsylvania—Pittsburgh. | United States—
Armed Forces—Mobilization. | United States—History—Civil War, 1861–1865—
Social aspects. | United States—History—Civil War, 1861–1865—Civilian relief.
CLASSIFICATION: LCC F159.P657 Y67 2023 (print) | LCC F159.P657 (ebook) |
DDC 973.709748/86—dc23/eng/20230717

LC record available at https://lccn.loc.gov/2023031042
LC ebook record available at https://lccn.loc.gov/2023031043

★ ★ ★ ★ ★

I dedicate this book to my wife, Tina York.
Her unwavering support and dedication
are behind every accomplishment of mine.
If this work contains anything worthy of merit,
it is because she has always believed in me.

★ ★ ★ ★ ★

CONTENTS

ILLUSTRATIONS

Figures

Map

Tables

ACKNOWLEDGMENTS

Growing up in Pittsburgh fascinated with the Civil War, I had no idea of what a rich part of the story transpired on the very streets I saw every day. But as I investigated the city's experience in the war, it became clear that this story involved so much more than a community sending off its soldiers, waiting for news of their battles, then welcoming them home on its conclusion. It has been a tremendously rewarding experience to write this history of a great community.

There are a number of scholars who guided and encouraged me in the pursuit of this project. In the Department of History at the University of Tennessee, Daniel Feller was always accessible, frequently giving of his time to listen to my ideas and offer me candid feedback. Luke Harlow offered valuable recommendations on my initial draft that led to a more comprehensive work. Stephen Rockenbach read the manuscript and offered insightful and constructive feedback that corrected oversights and added breadth to the analysis. Most of all, Stephen Ash's professional and scholarly guidance throughout this project led me to explore topics and to ask questions that greatly enriched the depth and quality of this study. I will forever be indebted for his exceptional mentorship. Whatever shortcomings this project may have, the greatest is that I was unable to bring it to print before Steve's passing.

I am also grateful to the several archivists who introduced me to sources and directions of inquiry that otherwise would have been lost to this project. Particularly, the staff of the Senator John Heinz History Center in Pittsburgh shared with me their vast knowledge of local archival sources that added voices to this story that have not been heard from for generations.

As indebted as I am to the faculty who guided me, I owe even more to my family for their support. This project has been a part of their lives as much as it has my own. They have encouraged me when I needed a push and supported me when I needed a break.

INTRODUCTION

On October 9, 1910, more than forty-five years after the Civil War concluded, a week of public celebration commemorating the completion of the Soldiers and Sailors Memorial Hall in Pittsburgh began. On that Sunday morning, churches citywide held services with sermons all coordinated to honor the service and sacrifices of Allegheny County soldiers of the Union Army. For the past seven years, veterans and prominent citizens from Pittsburgh had endeavored through committees to erect a monument to the men of their county who lost their lives in the Civil War that would prove unlike any other in the nation. Rather than a pedestal and statue, this project would feature a functional hall that included grand rooms for veterans' groups to gather, featuring artifacts from the war and an elaborate auditorium seating twenty-three hundred people. The hall was built, said the *Pittsburgh Post-Gazette*, "in refutation of the theory that men forget." Following the religious services, the hall was opened to Civil War veterans from the community. The finished two-story structure on a three-acre plot honored the actions of soldiers and citizens alike in Civil War Pittsburgh. More than two thousand soldiers crowded into the auditorium that afternoon with the emblems of their former corps proudly pinned to their lapels. Many were disabled and required assistance from the ushers—all of whom were members of the local Sons of Veterans chapter.[1]

The celebrations continued on Tuesday, beginning with a large parade. Formations of Union veterans, organized by their local chapters of the Grand Army of the Republic, American Veterans of Foreign Service, and the Union

Veteran Legion, marched through the city streets to the adulation of cheering crowds. The city's veterans of the Spanish-American War and the Sons of Veterans organization marched with them. Union veterans not affiliated with a local post were gathered into their own formation after providing satisfactory evidence of their service. The grand marshal was escorted by the storied local militia company, the Washington Infantry, whose service dated back to the Mexican War. The day was declared a holiday, with businesses closing their doors for what the local press declared "the biggest day in the lives of many who fought for the preservation of the Union and on whom a grateful public is now showering material expressions of gratitude."[2] An estimated twenty-five hundred marched in the procession that ended at the hall for the official dedication, which began with commemorative speeches followed by a campfire that evening and then a Women's Day. Speakers for the dedication included Mayor W. A. Magee, Governor Edwin Sydney Stuart, and Congressman John Dalzell; they extolled the part played by Allegheny County in the war and the "women who were called on to see their loved ones go away and endure the agonizing battle of suspense." But the most sensational of the distinguished guests was General Daniel Sickles. At eighty-six, Sickles was the last living corps commander of the old Army of the Potomac. He spoke from his wheelchair, lauding the newly erected monument to the wartime experience of Pittsburgh: "Neither Rome nor Greece ever spent $1,500,000 on a monument to her soldier martyrs. No country of ancient or modern times ever did what Allegheny County has done, and this county stands before the world today as having lavished more money on a soldiers' memorial than any nation on earth."[3]

Before the Civil War even became a matter of history, Pittsburghers began to write a record of the city's prominent role in it, a role characterized by overwhelming support for the Union war effort. The more I researched the city's experience, the more it became clear that community leaders and patriotic citizens were highly successful at mobilizing Pittsburghers' efforts to sustain that cause. And while the Soldiers and Sailors Memorial was, in name, intended to honor the servicemen mobilized for that cause, it went well beyond, commemorating the actions and sacrifices of ordinary civilians, male and female. In speeches, monuments, and celebrations surrounding the new memorial, Home Guards, vigilance and bounty fund committees, benevolent organizations, and workers were honored alongside their loved ones who served in uniform.

This book is a study of the Pittsburgh home front during the Civil War. I focus primarily on the myriad ways by which Pittsburghers became connected with and manifested support for the Union war effort. What were the methods used by community leaders and organizers to inspire and sustain popular support for the war? What challenges did they face in their efforts to support the war and how did they overcome them? How did Pittsburghers' interpretations of the events of the war shape their actions on the home front? Finally, how did Pittsburgh's distinctive geography—human and physical—its economy, and its culture shape the ways in which its civilians experienced and connected with the war?

This study of the Pittsburgh home front contributes to the historiography of the Civil War in two important ways. First, it adds to the growing subfield of studies that advance our understandings of how the local and regional dynamics of communities shaped the experience of the Civil War in the North. Ginnette Aley and J. L. Anderson, in their edited collection of essays, *Union Heartland: The Midwestern Home Front During the Civil War*, argue that while historians of nineteenth-century America have succeeded in advancing a narrative of multiple Souths, the Civil War North continues to be portrayed as a single cohesive society. Union Heartland challenges the paradigm which portrays Eastern cities as representative of the whole of northern society. From its establishment as a frontier village, Pittsburgh evolved on a path divergent from the culture of both the Northeast and the towns that quickly emerged farther to the west. It was a community that entered the war with close economic ties to the East, West, and South, yet stood apart from each. It was a city whose population was too small to assume the characteristics of New York or Philadelphia that exacerbated class conflict, yet it was large enough to manifest the complex institutions and systems of an urban center. The story of this city—on the border between small town and urban metropolis, as well as between the geopolitical regions of East and Midwest—offers insight into one of the many diverse experiences that made up the Civil War home front.[4]

Since the publication of *Union Heartland*, a series of important works have answered the call for more regional studies of the northern home front. Edward L. Ayers's *In the Presence of Mine Enemies* endeavors to recapture the experiences of ordinary Americans during the Civil War, typically obscured by "generalizations, categories, and scattered quotes." Ayers, through the story of two communities along the Pennsylvania-Virginia border, demonstrates how studies of Civil War communities challenge those broad generalizations, revealing how people's actions were guided by the interplay of national and local events and motivations. Nichole Etcheson's *A Generation at War* localizes and personalizes national issues through an investigation of how the Civil War affected gender roles and race in Putnam County, Indiana. A series of subsequent studies seek to argue the commonalities of communities on both sides of the Ohio River Valley. Christopher Phillips in *The Rivers Ran Backward* views the Midwest as a cohesive region of familial, economic, cultural, and political ties. Stephen Rockenbach's *War upon Our Border* argues that the Ohio River existed not as much a hard boundary between slave states and free, but a conduit that sustained social and cultural ties. Matthew E. Stanley contends in *The Loyal West* that a distinctive regional, political, social, and racial culture developed in the southern parts of Ohio, Indiana, Illinois, and, to a lesser degree, Kentucky. According to Stanley, the Antebellum United States consisted of three sections rather than two: the South, Northeast, and old Northwest. A study of Pittsburgh, a physical, economic, and cultural junction of these diverse regions, offers a valuable addition to these important studies.[5]

The second historiographical matter that this study engages with is the question of support for the Union war effort in northern communities. While notable advances have been made in demonstrating the complexities of the northern home front in the Midwest, much of the scholarship on Pennsylvania emphasizes conflict over consensus, dissent over support. Pennsylvania played an indispensable role in the Union war effort, yet the most prominent scholarly works on the Keystone State focus on efforts to undermine rather than support that cause. Arnold Shankman, in *The Pennsylvania Antiwar Movement, 1861–1865*, examines political dissent in the state legislature, concluding that opposition to the war at the state government level was just as fervent in Pennsylvania as in the Midwest or New York. Grace Palladino's *Another Civil War: Labor, Capital, and the State in the Anthracite Regions of Pennsylvania, 1840–1868* looks at unrest among immigrant coal miners in eastern Pennsylvania and argues that the actions of these miners, while contrary to mobilization, did not represent opposition to the Union war effort but rather stemmed from longstanding labor disputes over pay and working conditions. In *Deserter Country: Civil War Opposition in the Pennsylvania Appalachians*, Robert M. Sandow also finds earlier roots of wartime unrest, in this case among farmers whose seasonal logging was threatened by economic changes in the 1850s and again during the war. In *Patriot Fires: Forging a New American Nationalism in the Civil War North*, Melinda Lawson demonstrates that the need for support from the home front required the cultivation of a new ideology of nationalism. Among the obstacles to this new nationalism, Lawson finds, were conflicting interests at the state and local level. She cites the loss of Southern markets and observes that those Northern regions affected were expected to suffer "in silence; for though the region might suffer, the nation came first."[6]

Studying popular support is in some ways more problematic than focusing on opposition. It opens the historian to criticisms of ignoring dissent and of being too celebratory. However, the fact remains that the Union victory in the Civil War involved enlarging an army of sixteen thousand to more than two million, sustaining that army predominantly through volunteers despite staggering losses, transforming industries to develop new technologies and systems, and instituting programs to care for soldiers and their families. The resources for all of this came not from the central government, but from communities. Therefore, if, as the scholarship has demonstrated, there is such a rich story of opposition in the North to the Union war effort, there must be an even more compelling story of support. The historiography is not completely devoid of arguments for the prevalence of support for the war in northern society. Earl J. Hess, in *Liberty, Virtue, and Progress: Northerners and Their War for the Union*, asks "what factors motivated Northerners to support the war to save the Union and then to sustain their war effort in the face of the unexpectedly high cost in battlefield suffering." He finds ideology and culture at the heart of the matter. A sense of moral purpose to preserve the world's best hope for free government enabled Northerners to endure the catastrophe of war. Certain cultural values provided "language that served to explain the Southern rebellion and why it was important for Unionists to crush it." J. Matthew Gallman in *The North Fights the Civil War: The Home Front* and Gary Gallagher in *The Union War* emphasize the importance of preserving the Union as the dominant ideology that motivated Northerners to fight. More recently, Bridget Ford argues that the bonds of Union served to bridge differences between white and black, Catholic and Protestant, and North and South for nineteenth century Americans. James Oakes counters that any explanation of wartime ideology that rests only on the preservation of the Union is inadequate, for it neglects the crucial role of antislavery sentiment. But while historians have written extensively on the ideology of support for the northern war effort, little was done to advance our understanding of the processes by which that ideology was transformed into action. In Pittsburgh, this ideology was so dominant that political rivals spent more time trying to outdo one another in mobilization than in debating the merits of the war.[7]

This book, therefore, specifically focuses on the mobilization of Pittsburghers in support of the Union war effort. It seeks to build on the work of historians Paul A. Cimbala and Randall M. Miller to increase our understanding of "the ways the Northern people engaged and understood the war."[8] This book is not a social or economic or political history of the city during the war, though all of those elements come into play. I do not directly engage in the debate among historians regarding the transformative effects of the war on northern society. Rather, I concern myself with understanding how Pittsburgh, through the actions of diverse groups of prominent and ordinary civilians, became one of the many communities that, in various and distinctive ways, enabled the North to achieve victory.

The scope of this study is confined to the people of Pittsburgh and its surrounding area and to the actors from outside of the area that interacted with the city. In referring to Pittsburgh, I include the adjacent city of Allegheny and the surrounding townships and boroughs that comprise the county of Allegheny, most of which rest within the city proper today. Where necessary, I distinguish between the nine wards of Pittsburgh in the Antebellum and Civil War years and specific municipalities on its outskirts.

A study of such narrow scope in both theme and geographic area creates significant challenges in terms of sources. This is compounded even more with a focus on a city of such modest population. I have endeavored to incorporate a variety of personal and official memoirs and correspondence and government records wherever possible. For many aspects of Pittsburgh's experience in the war, I have relied considerably on local newspapers. This may present a concern for some of my fellow historians. However, while newspaper accounts are often not reliable for the facts of historical events, they exist as valuable sources for understanding the positions taken by different groups on important debates and the messages that they propagated to shape those debates. As a great deal of this book centers on the efforts of community leaders to mobilize Pittsburghers, local newspapers are invaluable repositories of the positions and messages embraced in those efforts. I have done my best to convey this evidence for what it tells us: the perspectives, agendas, and ideas of those engaged in mobilizing the community.

One important story I have been limited in telling is that of the black community in Pittsburgh for which sources are greatly limited. The rich and thriving black community of Antebellum Pittsburgh diminished greatly in the decade preceding the war. In 1850, blacks in Allegheny County totaled 3,431, 2.5 percent of the total population. By 1860, the black population of the county declined by more than one-fifth to 2,725, now 1.5 percent, while the white population increased by 31 percent to 176,102. Throughout the Antebellum period the political climate in Allegheny County became increasingly tenuous for blacks. First came the 1838 revocation of black suffrage by the new state constitution, a right they would not regain until the Fifteenth Amendment in 1870. The passage of the Fugitive Slave Act of 1850 spurred a mass exodus of blacks from Pittsburgh to New England and Canada. The city directory in 1861 listed only 163 households and six churches as "colored." There were no black newspapers in Allegheny County during the war years and the only fraternal organization for blacks was an Odd Fellows chapter for which no records exist. The sources are largely silent on the black voices from Pittsburgh that certainly engaged in the robust debate amongst black Northerners on the subjects of emancipation and military service.[9]

I have chosen to organize this study thematically rather than chronologically. There is always an appeal to tell the story as experienced by those who lived through the events. However, given my central question of the myriad ways by which Pittsburghers became connected with and manifested support for the Union war effort, I found it more effective to organize my evidence and analysis around the categories of those myriad ways. I have made every effort to keep the chronology as clear as possible while striving first to answer that question in a compelling manner. I hope that this story still conveys the experience of the people who lived through these seminal times.

Finally, one of my key conclusions warrants some clarification. The strong influence of localism that I find in the mobilization of wartime support in Pittsburgh does not refer to a local distinctiveness compared to the mobilization of other communities. The wartime experience of Pittsburgh was, in many ways, distinctive; but it also mirrored the conditions and experiences of Northern society more broadly in many ways. A combination of local, regional, and national forces and ideas influenced wartime mobilization in Pittsburgh, and across Northern society. Localism, in my research conclusions, refers to the strong preference of Pittsburghers for their own community and the manifestation of that preference in efforts to outdo other Northern communities and to control perceptions of the city's loyalty to the Union.

In Pittsburgh, the process of mobilizing the community in support for the Union war effort began with the influence of prewar experiences and social conditions involving everything from the celebration of veterans of previous wars to the city's early riverine economy. As the Civil War drew nearer, proslavery and anti-protectionist measures at the federal level primed Pittsburgh for a strong initial reaction of indignation to secession. Pittsburghers perceived secession as treason, and community leaders drew on traditions of martial pageantry, benevolent work, and the community's manufacturing identity to mobilize the citizens. Sustaining that mobilization, as the war progressed with increasing costs and evolving objectives, was a complex process. Connecting the people to the war, in ideas and in actions, was accomplished by drawing on local pride, by fostering diverse methods for citizens to participate in the war, and by interpreting home-front events through a lens of frontline experiences.

In the chapters that follow, these themes are demonstrated through an exploration of Pittsburgh's reaction to the secession crisis of 1860–1861, the presence of soldiers and the threat of invasions, wartime industries, the introduction of conscription and emancipation to the war, the care of soldiers on the home front and front lines, and the devastating loss experienced throughout the war. In short, the story of Pittsburgh in the Civil War contributes in important ways to a more complete understanding of the Northern home front.

1

★ ★ ★ ★ ★

FOR THE VICTORY THAT MUST SOONER OR LATER CROWN THEIR EFFORTS

Pittsburgh on the Eve of War

Nature itself has conspired to render the Ohio hereabouts
a place of consequence and importance, and the rendezvous
of all the people of North America that are within reach of it.

—JOHN MITCHELL—

The Contest in America Between Great Britain and France (1757)

ivil War–era Pittsburgh was an urban center of moderate size. With 49,217 inhabitants in 1860, it ranked twentieth in population among American cities. Including the inhabitants of its sister city across the river, Allegheny, the population was 77,919, making the Pittsburgh-Allegheny district one of the most populous urban areas in the country. Still, Pittsburgh's small size allowed it to retain a rather close-knit community. The city had no large tenement buildings or slum districts like New York and Philadelphia. Pittsburgh comprised nine wards, ranging in population from about three thousand to nine thousand. The oldest and wealthiest wards sat at the confluence of the city's three rivers, with the rest radiating outward. The oldest wards, in the city center, housed the most prominent citizens and blacks primarily congregated in the Sixth and Seventh Wards. Every ward had a wide range of wealth. In each, the top 15 percent or so of families possessed personal estates valued at five hundred dollars or more. The city's foreign-born population, 37 percent of the whole, was widely dispersed throughout the nine wards, with about half the immigrants originating from Ireland and a third from Germany.[1]

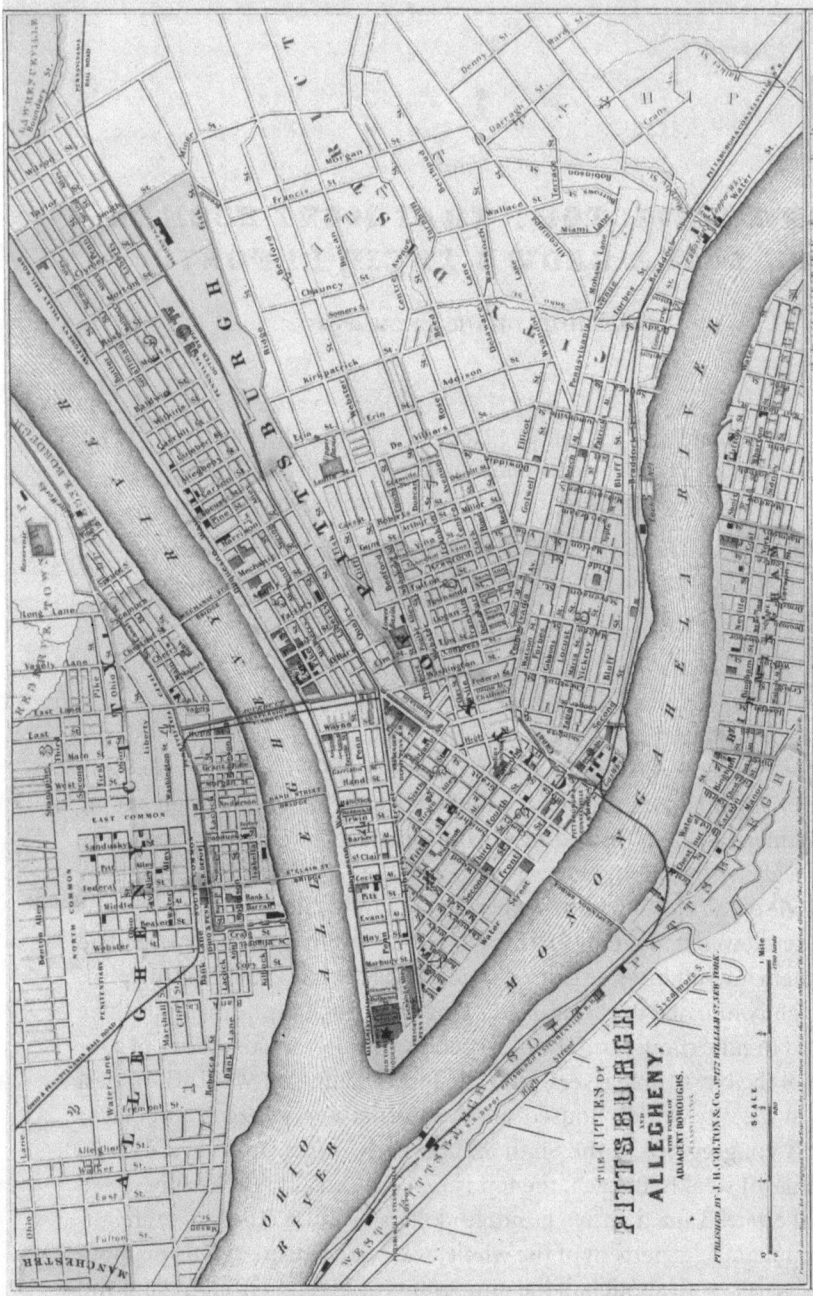

"Cities of Pittsburgh and Allegheny, with parts of adjacent boroughs, Pennsylvania, J. H. Colton & Co., 1855." —Darlington Digital Library, Special Collections, University Library System, University of Pittsburgh. Numerals indicate the wards of each city.

Pittsburgh's history extended back only about a century. Conceived out of military necessity, the city ultimately prospered through economic opportunity. The conditions that made this site an important frontier outpost during the Seven Years' War also made it a center of commerce and manufacturing. The strategic significance of the confluence of the Allegheny and Monongahela rivers forming the Ohio was apparent to both the French and British; control of the contested Ohio River Valley would necessitate a strong fort at that point. The British in 1758 captured Fort Duquesne, erected by the French to protect the fur trade and block enemy incursion, and replaced it two years later with Fort Pitt. However, while British authorities focused on the strategic importance of Fort Pitt, colonists quickly began to capitalize on the favorable geography of the area, establishing the region's first white settlement on the grounds surrounding the fort. By 1761, the new village had 464 settlers in 220 houses. That same year, the village employed a schoolmaster who provided instruction for twenty children and, in the absence of a local minister, also led religious services. In their earliest correspondence with government officials, British officers frequently used the term "Pitts-borough" or "Pittsburgh" interchangeably with Fort Pitt, reflecting the importance of the civilian settlement to the army garrison.[2]

However, Pittsburgh's growth did not began in earnest until after the Revolution. The threat of attacks from indigenous populations suppressed westward migration through the colonial era but, when the new United States government determined to pay Revolutionary War veterans with land grants, migrants from the east poured through Pittsburgh into the Northwest Territory and Kentucky. Roads previously established by military expeditions and widespread promotion of Pittsburgh in Eastern newspapers made the town a nexus of postwar westward migration. In 1784, Dr. Johann Schoepf, while travelling through western Pennsylvania, commented that Pittsburgh and the surrounding area were "incessantly and perceptibly increased by daily influxes of large numbers of men. The Pittsburghers derive much profit from the passage of these transients." Schoepf went on to predict that given its "advantageous situation, Pittsburgh cannot fail to become . . . an important post for inland trade." The *Pittsburgh Gazette* estimated that, between October 1786 and December 1788, some 16,203 migrants passed through the town along the Ohio River.[3]

By the beginning of the nineteenth century the truth of Schoepf's prediction was apparent. In 1802, Zadok Cramer wrote of Pittsburgh that "[n]o inland town can boast of a superior situation to this, both as to its beauty, as also with respect to the many advantages with which it is attended. . . .

The local situation of this town is so very commanding, that it has been emphatically called the key to the western country." He went on to describe the town's elegant houses and nascent manufactories and advised would-be emigrants and traders that Pittsburghers were certain to become "an opulent and happy people."[4]

The most ardent advocate for Pittsburgh's early growth was Hugh Henry Brackenridge, a writer and jurist who, seeing little chance of gaining prominence in Philadelphia, migrated in 1781 to Pittsburgh. There, he established the *Gazette*, the first newspaper west of the Allegheny Mountains, and subsequently used it to promote Pittsburgh to potential migrants. In 1786, the *Gazette* boasted that: "The town consists at present of about an [*sic*] hundred dwelling houses, with buildings appurtenant. More are daily added, and for some time past it has improved with an equal but continual pace. The inhabitants, children, men and women are about fifteen hundred; this number doubling almost every year from the accession of people from abroad and from those born in the town."[5] Nine years later, the paper claimed that "emigration to this country this fall surpasses that of any other season and we are informed that the banks of the Monongahela . . . are lined with people intending for the settlements on the Ohio and Kentucky."[6]

Historian Richard C. Wade argues that towns emerged quickly with the arrival of the earliest pioneers on the Ohio River Valley frontier: "towns were the spearheads by which the region was settled around, rather than the culmination of the settlement process." According to Wade, the newcomers recreated Eastern towns in founding their own. They brought to the frontier "established institutions and ways" from the urban East. However, from its earliest days, Pittsburgh existed as a town more closely tied to the developing Mississippi Valley than to the established cities of the Atlantic coast.[7]

Western Pennsylvania's relative isolation fostered in Pittsburgh a unique identity and the town identified more closely with the Midwest and Mississippi Valley than the East. Before the railroads came, transportation from the East over the Allegheny Mountains proved difficult. The roads were generally problematic for wagons, necessitating in the earliest years the use of pack-horse trains. With a maximum of 150 pounds per horse and twenty horses per train, the journey took twenty days to move one and a half tons over the old military supply route—the Braddock Road. Pittsburghers repeatedly petitioned the state legislature to fund better roads, but to no avail. This encouraged Pittsburgh's merchants to build closer ties with the West and encouraged western Pennsylvania settlers to look to Pittsburgh rather than the East for economic leadership. Thus, there emerged a distinct community that saw itself as separate in many respects from Eastern America while not wholly a part of the West.[8]

By the first decade of the nineteenth century, Pittsburgh was the preeminent link connecting East, West, and South. Farmers around Pittsburgh used the rivers to export their surplus products west to other frontier towns and also south to New Orleans, where they were generally sold and then transported by ship to markets on the eastern seaboard. Money earned from sales in New Orleans was, however, mostly spent by Pittsburghers purchasing manufactured goods from eastern cities, goods that generally came to them by way of New Orleans. No city was more important to Pittsburgh's early development than New Orleans.[9]

Pittsburgh's isolation from the East, its connection with markets in the West and South, the growing flood of immigrants passing through, the town's access to rivers, and the abundance of nearby raw materials all encouraged the rise of local manufacturing. Shipbuilding became one of Pittsburgh's earliest industries. The Louisiana Purchase greatly stimulated this enterprise, which experienced its zenith from 1803 to 1808. Merchants built crude vessels for their own use, while the government and larger trading firms contracted a handful of craftsmen to construct ships for their usage. Between 1798 and 1799, two ships of war, the *Adams* and the *Senator Ross*, were built on the Monongahela River near Pittsburgh for $80,000. In 1800, a consortium of local farmers commissioned the construction of *Monongahela Farmer*. However, by the end of 1808, shipbuilding in Pittsburgh had essentially disappeared, a casualty of the Embargo Act of 1807 among other factors.[10]

Emerging at the same time, however, was an industry that would come to define Pittsburgh for generations to come. In 1805, Joseph McClung established the first iron foundry in the city. There, he manufactured pots, kettles, stoves, grates, and plows for the growing community. Even before this milestone in local manufacturing, enterprising pioneers were establishing small-scale ironworks throughout the region. There was a heavy demand for iron on the frontier. Settlers needed horseshoes, wagon wheel rims, hardware, and many other items, but the transportation problems severely limited their importation from the East. As Pittsburgh grew, residents frequently resorted to burning abandoned structures to reclaim the nails as they built more permanent homes and businesses. Blacksmiths established the earliest ironworks in the rural districts surrounding Pittsburgh, close to the abundant iron deposits and the forests needed to fuel their forges. Their works were organized as plantations: self-sufficient complexes that included—in addition to the ironworks—the ironmasters' and workers' cabins, farmlands, sawmills, gristmills, and smithies to sustain the operation. At the close of the eighteenth century, no fewer than thirteen of these operations functioned in the area, with names such as Alliance Iron Works, the Laurel Furnace, and the Union Furnace and Forge.[11]

Local manufacturers greatly advanced the iron industry in Pittsburgh when they began to employ Henry Cort's technology of the puddling furnace and rolling mill. Developed in Britain in 1784, Cort's innovation crossed the Atlantic only years later, delayed by British legislation that prevented the export of industrial technology and the emigration of skilled laborers. The establishment of the first such foundry and rolling mill in Pittsburgh occurred in 1819. There were twenty-five by 1860.[12]

The trade disputes with Great Britain, beginning in 1803 and culminating in the War of 1812, boosted tremendously iron and other industries in Pittsburgh—shipbuilding aside. however, with the end of the war came a flood of foreign goods that crippled industry throughout the North. The value of goods manufactured annually in Pittsburgh declined dramatically from $2,617,833 in 1815 to $832,000 in 1819, causing many workers to be laid off. As a result, Pittsburgh became one of the most prominent centers of a growing Northern protectionist movement.[13]

Representative Henry Baldwin of Pittsburgh was named chairman of the House Committee on Manufactures, which he and other protectionists managed to split from the Committee on Agriculture and Manufactures. Baldwin was a Pittsburgh lawyer who, in 1816, was sent to Congress with the support of a consortium of local manufacturers whose businesses were struggling under the postwar conditions. Baldwin was to be their champion for a higher tariff. During the depression that followed the war and in the aftermath of the panic of 1819, the new committee became the wellspring for protectionist measures in Congress. Baldwin called for higher tariffs on the "national principle that we ought to feed, clothe, and be able to defend ourselves." He and his allies achieved some success with the tariff acts of 1824 and 1828, and by 1830 there were as many as thirty-four new furnaces in the city. As the Nullification crisis loomed and Southerners became more antagonistic toward what they saw as the special interest of the North, manufacturing became ever more a part of the economic aspirations of Pittsburghers, but with the compromise tariff of 1833, the protectionist issue waned and manufacturing in Pittsburgh continued to prosper.[14]

Thanks to the advent of iron hulls and improvements in steam engines, Pittsburgh saw a resurgence of its shipbuilding industry. The first iron-hulled vessel produced in the city, the *Valley Forge*, was launched in 1839. Pittsburgh builders pioneered the manufacturing of ironclad steam warships. In 1842, Secretary of the Navy Abel P. Upshur selected Pittsburgh as the site for developing this new technology. A year later, the firm of Stackhouse and Tomlinson completed the U.S.S. *Michigan* on the Allegheny River, subsequently transporting it by canal to Erie.[15]

Pittsburghers continued to experience cycles of prosperity and woe corresponding to the health of the city's manufacturing. The recession following a financial panic in 1837 significantly affected Pittsburgh. The Walker Tariff (which drastically lowered duties from the Whig Party's Tariff of 1842), the overproduction of iron products, and the bursting of the railroad speculation bubble caused a dramatic decline in manufacturing. One newspaper of the period estimated that four out of five ironworks in Allegheny County closed down in the space of a few months in 1849. Iron manufacturers held conventions in the city, calling for the government to again raise tariffs to protect domestic manufacturing.[16]

Pittsburgh's iron industry recovered rapidly, however. New plants opened all over the city, generating large profits for manufacturers. By 1850, 150 furnaces in western Pennsylvania supplied Pittsburgh with one hundred thousand tons of pig metal annually. With the exception of a brief period in the wake of the Panic of 1857, economic prosperity continued for manufacturers and their workers up to the Civil War, but Pittsburgh's economic experience prior to the Civil War established a strong sentiment of just how precarious that prosperity if manufacturing was threatened.[17]

In the early decades of the nineteenth century, community leaders were determined to establish Pittsburgh as the foremost trading center of the growing nation. They believed the city would continue to serve as the gateway between East, West, and South and would retain its economic importance to all three. However, by mid-century, the industrial manufacturing that distinguished Pittsburgh from its rivals came to supplant trade as the city's economic heart. Meanwhile, westward expansion enabled downriver cities to challenge Pittsburgh for commercial supremacy. The transportation revolution exacerbated competition between Pittsburgh and its rival communities. As canals and railroads were built in the early and middle nineteenth century, community leaders and legislators vied for bills and charters that would route new lines of transportation through their cities.[18]

Pittsburgh had rapidly outgrown its first main routes. By 1785, the old military roads over the Allegheny Mountains into western Pennsylvania could not accommodate the increased private traffic. The state legislature responded by funding the construction of Pennsylvania's share of the State

Road from Cumberland, Maryland to Pittsburgh. Opened for public use in 1791, this new route further encouraged westward migration. The Pittsburgh-Philadelphia Turnpike, which was completed in 1817, eventually replaced the State Road. Additionally, about that time, a stagecoach line was established running between the two cities.[19]

While the construction of the State Road brought much excitement and increased trade for Pittsburghers, plans for an even more significant road were already underway. In 1806, to ease westward migration and unify the expanding nation, Congress authorized the first federally funded highway to run from Cumberland to a point on the Ohio River. However, this National Road, or Cumberland Road, which was completed in 1818, proved a great disappointment to Pittsburghers for it met the Ohio River at Wheeling, Virginia, thus diverting a significant amount of East-West trade from Pittsburgh.[20]

A few years later, there came an even bigger blow to Pittsburgh's commercial aspirations. The Erie Canal, completed in 1825, spanned 363 miles from Buffalo on Lake Erie to Albany on the Hudson River, thus giving New York City easy and cheap access to the West. To compete with the Erie Canal for Western trade, the Pennsylvania State Works was constructed. Opened in 1834, this cumbersome hybrid system of transportation traversed 394 miles from Philadelphia to Pittsburgh. Traveling east, passengers and cargo covered the first 250 miles by a combination of horse-drawn railcars and canal boats until reaching the Allegheny Mountains. There, they transferred to the Allegheny Portage Railroad, a system of five steam-powered inclined planes that hauled canal boats thirty-six miles over the mountains to a canal that accommodated the boats for the remaining 104 miles to Pittsburgh.[21]

For a time, the State Works did elevate Pittsburgh's status as a nexus of interregional trade. Western agricultural products, Southern goods such as sugar, and foreign imports coming by way of New Orleans, including tea, coffee, and spices, passed through Pittsburgh's merchant houses to Eastern markets. Return trips brought Eastern merchandise to Pittsburgh, where much of it was passed on to Western markets, along with Pittsburgh-made glassware, iron, and machinery. The Works, furthermore, reduced travel time across the state from twenty-three to four and a half days, but the Works proved expensive and difficult to maintain. The complex system cost ten million dollars to build, required extensive maintenance, and proved unreliable in bad weather due to freezing and freshets. By the mid-forties, Pittsburgh's further decline in the competition for trade was apparent and that the Works was not living up to its promise.[22]

As Pittsburghers wrote off the State Works—and canals in general—they started to place their hope in a new, more exciting mode of transportation. On June 6, 1830, Pittsburgh Mayor M. B. Lowrie wrote to the Select and Common Council: "Gentlemen, I have this day seen the steam engine and railroad in miniature which is now exhibiting in this city. It is a complete and beautiful machine and exhibits the railroad system in full operation in a very clear and satisfactory manner. I would be glad that our whole community might be favored with a sight of this interesting machine." Lowrie requested that the owner be permitted to "exhibit this curiosity in Pittsburgh without the expense of a license," which the council quickly approved.[23]

Two years before this model engine was displayed in the city, Pittsburgh had found itself at the center of a rivalry between Philadelphia and Baltimore. By that time, Pittsburgh's population and manufacturing had made the city an attractive potential junction for the burgeoning system of railroads that would connect urban centers in the East with the rapidly growing markets in the West. That year, Baltimore obtained a charter from the Pennsylvania legislature to construct a line (the Baltimore and Ohio Railroad) through southwestern Pennsylvania. However, work on it moved slowly and, when in 1843 the charter expired with the line reaching only as far as Cumberland, the Philadelphia delegation in the legislature opposed granting an extension, desiring instead a Philadelphia-to-Pittsburgh line. Representatives from Pittsburgh, however argued fervently for its passage. The *Gazette* went so far as to urge the secession of western Pennsylvania from the state if the measure did not pass. Debate went on for more than two years until the measure's defeat in February 1846. Pittsburghers subsequently held a large public meeting to condemn the legislature's decision. One speaker remarked that "heretofore there has been too much legislation passed for the special benefit of the rich capitalists of Philadelphia aided by hosts of lobby members."[24]

The state legislature reacted to the Pittsburgh protest by reversing its decision and granting the charter extension, but at the same time, it authorized construction of the Pennsylvania Railroad to run from Philadelphia to Pittsburgh, in direct competition with the Baltimore and Ohio. Furthermore, the legislature made the continuation of the Baltimore and Ohio through Pittsburgh contingent on the Pennsylvania line's failure to meet certain financial and construction goals by July 30, 1847. Despite that, the goals were met by the deadline, whereupon Governor Francis R. Shunk declared the Baltimore and Ohio charter null and void.[25]

The Baltimore and Ohio Railroad went on to follow the route of the National Road, reaching the Ohio River at Wheeling in 1852. However, by that time, Pittsburghers were no longer concerned with the competition of opposing routes. The year prior, the Ohio and Pennsylvania Railroad had opened with its terminus in Allegheny, thereby linking Pittsburgh and the markets downriver. In the fall of 1854, the Pennsylvania Railroad was completed and, two years later, the Allegheny Valley Railroad opened and would soon transport oil from Titusville and Oil Creek. In 1858, a rail bridge between Allegheny and Pittsburgh was completed, connecting the Ohio and Pennsylvania Railroad with the Pennsylvania Railroad. Finally, the Pittsburgh and Lake Erie Railroad opened for operation in March 1860. So, by the time of the Civil War, four railroads connected Pittsburgh to markets in every direction. Railroads now followed the banks of all three of the city's rivers, reestablishing Pittsburgh as the primary commercial gateway between East and West.[26]

As Pittsburgh grew into a major manufacturing center, European immigrants flocked to the city in response to the demand for laborers. In 1861, the city directory listed twenty iron foundries, twenty-one iron manufacturers, and seventeen glass manufacturers. By that year, 37 percent of Pittsburgh's population was foreign-born. Already by 1850, more than ten thousand Irish immigrants had settled in Pittsburgh, but this migrant group differed from the destitute Irish of Boston who fled from famine, as depicted in Oscar Handlin's 1957 study. The Irish of Pittsburgh predominately originated from wealthier regions of independent rather than tenant farming. The greatest number established themselves in three areas of the city: a prosperous neighborhood just outside of the business district; a poorer area of the city's Hill district inhabited mostly by single male laborers; and an ethnically diverse neighborhood of Welsh, Scottish, English, and German immigrants amidst the iron and glass works of the lower Strip district along the banks of the Allegheny River.[27]

While German immigrants comprised a smaller percentage of the city's foreign-born population, more is known about their past. The first distinctively German community formed in eastern Allegheny City in what Pittsburghers called Dutchtown, a nickname that persists today in the North Shore neighborhood. Here, the distinctive ethnicity of the neighborhood was apparent through the small businesses and churches that dotted its streets, but most of Pittsburgh's Germans were dispersed in smaller groups in a wide array of the city's wards and surrounding townships. They owned no property. The men worked as manual laborers or craftsmen, while women were employed as domestic servants or laundresses. More than other immigrant groups, German Pittsburghers were fractured and divided by religion, class, homeland, and politics. Such divisions manifested throughout the mid-nineteenth century through important issues such as temperance and slavery and the endorsement of political parties and candidates.[28]

Chain migration, the process by which early immigrants enticed family members to follow with their favorable accounts of America, attributed much to the settlement of immigrants in Pittsburgh. Wilhelm Stille left his family farm in Westphalia for America in 1833. His letters home from Pittsburgh—filled with glowing reports of the climate, his pay, and the opportunities that the city and the surrounding area offered—led no fewer than eleven of his own family members and twelve of his sister's fiancé's to follow him.[29]

Some of the immigrants who ended up in Pittsburgh had planned to go farther west but had run out of money. The city contained so many destitute people by 1818, immigrants and natives, that the city's leaders reported spending three thousand dollars on assistance and decided to establish a poorhouse. By 1844, the problem of caring for the poor demanded not just a house but a farm. The Select and Common Councils of Pittsburgh and Allegheny worked together to fund the poor farm.[30]

Philanthropy for the poor continued as an important endeavor, but the first benevolent movement to truly energize Pittsburghers was temperance. The temperance movement exemplified the social forces behind all the antebellum reform and benevolent movements in Pittsburgh—strong grassroots sentiment guided and reinforced by community leaders. Two of the most influential clergymen in antebellum Pittsburgh, Francis Herron and Elisha P. Swift, regularly contributed to a temperance organ, the *Temperance Gem*. Editor J. S. Riddle of the *Daily Commercial Journal* and editor David N. White of the *Gazette* also strongly supported the movement and frequently warned their readers of the dangers of imbibing. Political leaders such as Judge William B. McClure and Alderman Thomas Steele also used their positions to advance the cause. These temperance leaders wielded a variety of arguments to appeal to people, ranging from the practical concerns of crime and health to moral and spiritual concerns, but they also cultivated the support of women in the community, recognizing the influence they exerted on men and children.[31]

The temperance movement in Pittsburgh began in 1830 when citizens became alarmed at the increasing number of drinking establishments in and around the city. In 1829, the authorities granted 129 permits to open taverns. 162 establishments were already spread across the county, amounting to one for every 123 people. Temperance activists in the city brought to the mayor's court that year a petition of protest with 1,116 signatures. City hall responded by reducing the number of permits for the following year by only six, prompting concerned citizens to establish, in 1832, the Pittsburgh Temperance Society.[32]

Pennsylvania's temperance societies pressured the legislature into enacting, in March 1834, a law prohibiting an innkeeper from extending credit for liquor and from bringing suit for a liquor bill. Two years later it became illegal to serve anyone identified as a drunkard. On November 6, 1839, Pittsburgh hosted a great temperance convention with delegates from societies across the region. Allegheny County alone had representatives from forty-one local societies in attendance.[33]

The temperance organization that gained the greatest following in Pittsburgh was the Washingtonian Society. Formed in Baltimore in 1840, it advocated complete abstinence from alcohol. To achieve this, it created a sponsorship system whereby alcoholics shared their stories and supported one another. The movement swept Pittsburgh in 1841; in a two-week period in July, thirty-six hundred people signed a pledge of abstinence. That month, the *Gazette* estimated that there were ten thousand Washingtonians in the Pittsburgh-Allegheny area, predominantly people of the working class. On October 20–21, Pittsburgh hosted another large, statewide convention, after which Temperance Hall was erected in Allegheny.[34]

A second type of temperance organization—the fraternal society—appeared in Pittsburgh about the same time as the Washingtonians. The Sons of Temperance, established in 1842, resembled a social lodge, with secret rituals and passwords. The organization endeavored to involve the entire family through auxiliary societies such as the Daughters of Temperance, which concentrated on enlisting the influence of women to bring more men into the ranks. On September 15, 1848, Pittsburgh was the site of a large Sons of Temperance convention and a parade with fifteen hundred marchers. The Allegheny chapter published the *Temperance Gem* weekly beginning in 1851; it offered news from temperance societies across the North as well as poems, short stories, and articles that aimed to educate women and children. In October 1851, the *Gem* reported a following of twenty-five hundred temperance men in Allegheny County.[35]

Temperance reformers in Pittsburgh attempted to stamp out liquor through legislation as early as 1838, when they failed to convince the state legislature to vote for prohibition. In 1846, however, they persuaded the legislature to enact a law that authorized eighteen counties, including Allegheny, to determine "whether vinous and spirituous liquors shall be continued." In the subsequent referendum in 1847, Pittsburgh and the surrounding area voted in favor of prohibition by a majority of two thousand, but the state supreme court overturned the law the next year. In July 1848, an Allegheny grand jury investigating the issue reported that "Drunkeness, gambling, rioting, and other crimes are engendered in these dens of infamy, and the sooner the public are rid of them the better."[36]

The debate over temperance in Pennsylvania continued through the early 1850s and culminated in a statewide referendum in October 1854. As the date approached, an Allegheny County grand jury declared that "[t]he great demoralizing agency at work in our community seems to be the traffic in intoxicating drinks." Prohibition was ultimately defeated, however, despite the 71 percent majority vote for it in Allegheny County.[37]

Though temperance reformers in Pittsburgh were ultimately unsuccessful, many gained experience and provided useful examples for the benevolent work and community mobilization that came during the Civil War. In striving to eliminate alcohol from their community, local organizers developed organizations, rallied the people around a cause, and petitioned lawmakers to enact policies favorable to them. The temperance movement in Pittsburgh was valuable training for those who would lead the community during the war.

Amid the temperance debate, Pittsburgh suffered a tragedy that would also serve to prepare its citizens for the trials of war. Around noon on April 10, 1845, a woman started a fire in the backyard of her modest rented home at the corner of Second and Ferry Streets. Because she carelessly disregarded the dry conditions and high winds that day, the flames quickly spread, igniting a nearby icehouse. The houses along Second, all wooden, also burned. The fire soon jumped across Second and in moments the cotton factory of Colonel James Woods was ablaze. Firemen and citizens struggled to put out the flames threatening the Third Presbyterian Church; their efforts saved not only the church but all of the city east of Ferry Street. Onlookers watched anxiously as the flames neared the grand building of the Bank of Pittsburgh, purportedly fireproof. If the bank held, the spread of the fire would be arrested, but the intense heat melted the zinc roof, igniting the interior of the bank.[38]

People looked on as building after building was consumed. William Brackenridge recalled that "the air was filled with flying pieces of wood in a state of combustion, for a piece of shingle as large as my hand, still blazing, fell at my feet, and was crushed out by me. . . . The fire broke out in so many places, and its irresistible progress became so evident, that every man hurried home to save what he could." Houses, offices, government buildings, and warehouses were engulfed. Many important establishments were destroyed: two hotels, the Monongahela and the Merchant's; the Baptist church on Grant

Street and the Associate Reformed Church on Fourth; and Western Pennsylvania University, along with its valuable library. By the time the fire burned out, fifty-six acres, one-third of the city's area, had been devastated. An estimated twelve hundred people became homeless, even though only two deaths were recorded, and two-thirds of the community's wealth was obliterated.[39]

In the aftermath of the fire, Pittsburgh, Allegheny, and the surrounding countryside teemed with refuge-seekers. Witnesses described the strange scene of hundreds sleeping in the open air the night of the fire. Some seized the opportunity to loot the belongings that so many had risked their lives to drag out of their homes, but far more citizens came to the aid of the displaced. The courthouse and other public buildings took in the homeless and the proprietors of surviving warehouses opened their doors to provide shelter as well. Across the city, those with rooms available for rent took in families at no charge. The community mobilized to begin repairs. Only two days after the fire, a visitor from Cincinnati wrote that "in many places the rubbish is not yet cleared away, yet the sufferers are at work repairing their losses, rebuilding their dwellings and stores, with an energy and industry that cannot be too highly commended." Monetary assistance came from private donors and the state legislature. President James K. Polk sent a hundred dollars and John Quincy Adams fifty. Historian Charles F. C. Arensberg has observed that great conflagrations have a galvanizing effect on urban populations. What initially appeared to be ruinous for a community often proved to bring "a more rapid growth and a greater prosperity." This was certainly true for Pittsburgh. The city rebuilt and rebounded quickly. The fire of 1845 evoked the benevolent impulses of many in the city and the resiliency of the community became a source of pride; it helped prepare Pittsburghers for the trials to come in the war.[40]

Pittsburghers' activism in the sectional debate over slavery would also bear fruit during the war. Slavery was a fact of life in Pittsburgh's early years. The census of 1790 counted 878 enslaved individuals in the five counties of southwestern Pennsylvania, one for every eighty-seven free persons. Nearly all of Pittsburgh's early citizens who had the means participated in slavery. However, responding to the post-Revolutionary currents that favored the expansion of liberty, the Pennsylvania legislature enacted in 1780 a measure for the gradual emancipation of the enslaved. It provided that all enslaved persons born in the state after its passage were to be freed at age twenty-eight. It also called for the registration of slaves and slaveholders in the state, and it prohibited Pennsylvanians from providing "any relief or shelter to any absconding or runaway negro or mulatto slave, or servant who has absented himself, from his or her owner, master or mistress, residing in any other state."[41]

Pittsburgh's racial climate—tolerant compared to that of other Northern cities close to the Mason-Dixon Line—attracted many freed and free-born blacks. From 1830 to 1850, the black population of the city rose from 472 to 1,959. Throughout the antebellum era, a number of organizations dedicated to the needs of the city's blacks were established through the collaboration of abolitionists, white and black. In 1832, the African Education Society and Theban Literary Society formed. Two years later, the Young Men's Moral Reform Society was founded and, in 1839, the Philanthropic Society for the protection of local blacks and assistance to fleeing enslaved. However, while these activists worked to advance the station of Pittsburgh's black population, racial tensions were evident. On at least two occasions, in 1834 and 1839, Pittsburgh experienced race riots. While there existed efforts of these societies to educate them, blacks in Pittsburgh continued to remain mostly confined to menial services on the waterfront and in hotels, demonstrating the pervasiveness of white supremacy undergirding the rising currents for the advancement of black rights.[42]

A remarkable document from Pittsburgh's black community illustrates its sophistication in the early nineteenth century, as well as the efforts of local activists to advance equality. In 1837, black Pennsylvanians were threatened with disfranchisement. The state's constitution was silent on the issue of race and black male taxpayers in Pittsburgh had always enjoyed the right to vote. However, in 1837, racial prejudice and recent race riots in the Philadelphia area prompted many legislators to try amending the constitution to prohibit blacks from voting. When news of the proposed amendment reached Pittsburgh, blacks organized a mass meeting on June 13, 1837, to consider the issue and draft a petition. The result of their deliberations was the *Memorial of the Free Citizens of Color in Pittsburgh and Its Vicinity Relative to the Right of Suffrage* or, as it came to be known, the Pittsburgh Memorial. This document called on the lawmakers to preserve the black franchise and justified this request with a detailed survey of the economic and social conditions of blacks in Pittsburgh, lauding "the stand that has been taken in the useful pursuits of life, in the requisition of property, and the efforts made to ameliorate the condition of our race." This effort seemed to achieve victory at first. When the state constitutional convention considering the amendment received the petition, the architect of the amendment, John Sterigere, withdrew it for the time being. However, when the convention reconvened in the fall, the

measure was passed and, in October 1838, the new constitution was rati-
fied by a close statewide vote of 113,971 to 112, 759. Allegheny County voted
against ratification, although with a margin of only 5,049 to 4,460. Despite
having failed to defend its franchise, however, Pittsburgh's black community
had spoken out loudly and shown its resolve in the struggle for equality.[43]

Pittsburgh had a vigorous abolitionist movement considering its distance
from the main centers of abolitionism and its close economic ties with the
South. The earliest recorded abolitionist organization in the city was the
Pittsburgh Anti-slavery Society, which held its first meeting in the home of
its founder, John Bathan Vashon, in 1833. It advocated gradual abolition and
the resettlement of freed slaves in Africa. Vashon was born in Virginia in
1792 to George Vashon, a white slaveholder's son, and an enslaved woman
named Fanny. John Vashon served in the War of 1812 and, having at some
point been freed, moved to Pittsburgh in 1829. He opened the city's first
bathhouse and became a highly successful entrepreneur and leader of the
growing black community. Vashon served as trustee of the African Methodist Episcopal Church and was cofounder with the Reverend Lewis Woodson
of the African Educational Society. Woodson arrived in Pittsburgh in 1831
and immediately set to work building up the black community. That year,
he founded the Bethel African Methodist Church and, the next year, the
African Educational Society. He also actively spirited fugitive slaves through
Pittsburgh. While he argued for the absolute freedom of blacks, Woodson
was an ardent separatist who wanted blacks to settle in their own farming
communities, a cause he promoted through his paper *The Colored American*.[44]

Another prominent black abolitionist, one inspired by the work of Vashon
and Woodson, was the Reverend Charles Avery, who moved to Pittsburgh
in 1812 and became a successful businessman and one of the wealthiest men
in southwestern Pennsylvania. Avery became deeply involved in the anti-
slavery movement, advocating education as the key to blacks' freedom and
independence. He founded the Avery Trade School for Colored Youth in
March 1849; later known as Avery College, it was one of the nation's earliest
vocational schools for blacks. Avery was also active with the Underground
Railroad in Allegheny County, offering his Avery Mission Church as a station with ready access to a canal and the Allegheny River.[45]

The most famous Pittsburgh abolitionist was the Reverend Martin R.
Delany. Born free in Charlestown, Virginia, Delany walked 150 miles to Pittsburgh at the age of nineteen to seek a better life. Arriving in 1831, he immediately enrolled in Lewis Woodson's African Educational Society. Taken on

as a protégé of both Woodson and Vashon, Delany established the Theban
Literary Society, a "club for young black men who desired to study and debate." He also cofounded, with his two mentors, the Philanthropic Society
to assist fugitive slaves in Pittsburgh. When Pennsylvania revoked black
suffrage in 1838, Delany lobbied to have it restored. He is also credited with
establishing one of the first abolitionist newspapers west of the Alleghenies.
For a time, he practiced medicine in Pittsburgh after apprenticing under the
prominent white local physician and community leader Joseph P. Gazzam.
Delany even studied briefly at Harvard Medical School but was forced out
by student protests. Although Delany was a supporter of black colonization
and even moved his family to Canada in the late 1850s, he returned when the
Civil War rekindled his hope for black liberty in the United States. He was
the first black army officer commissioned by Abraham Lincoln and spent
the war recruiting black soldiers.[46]

There was considerable resistance at first to the abolition movement in
Pittsburgh. As the sectional crisis grew, many in the city became concerned
with the threat to business interests. This opposition did not challenge the
justness of abolition, but rather questioned its prudence for the good of
the nation. One group dedicated to the integrity of the Union warned that
abolitionists were "as capable of evil as effectual as the worst enemies of the
Republic could wish" and that abolitionism "had sown wide the dragon teeth
of discord, disunion, and civil war."[47]

Efforts to defend fugitive slaves from slavery and free local blacks from capture strengthened the cohesiveness of the black community in Pittsburgh and
its solidarity with its white supporters. On numerous occasions, community
leaders and agents of abolition organizations resisted Southern slave catchers
hunting fugitives in Pittsburgh. Daniel Lockhart, born enslaved in Virginia,
escaped to Pittsburgh sometime in the 1840s and took work as a laborer. In
March 1847, the state legislature passed a law prohibiting the kidnapping of
free blacks and barring justices of the peace and aldermen from enforcing
the federal Fugitive Slave Act of 1793 and implemented other measures that
inhibited slave-catchers' ability to operate in Pennsylvania. One month after
the law's passage, Lockhart was working as a laborer when he was hired by a
stranger to transport a trunk to the Monongahela House. When he arrived
at the room, his owner with two constables from Virginia seized him. In the
ensuing struggle, the resistance that started with the hotel's black workers
grew until a large crowd of blacks "converged on the slave catchers" and freed
Lockhart. The slave-catchers were charged under the new law and brought

before Judge Walter Hodge Lowrie, but he dismissed the charges, insisting that the federal law must be respected: "We must not at least, while claiming the benefits of union, refuse the performance of the duties arising from it."[48]

In June 1850, Allegheny County congressman Moses Hampton criticized interference with slave-catchers, declaring that "we acknowledge the obligation imposed by the Constitution, and are willing to fulfill those obligations." Three months later, Congress passed a new Fugitive Slave Act that granted even greater protection for slave-catchers and required Northerners to assist them. The reaction in Pittsburgh was resounding indignation. Meetings held throughout the Pittsburgh area protested the act. Every candidate but one in the upcoming congressional election attended the largest of them, held September 28. At that gathering, congressional candidate Thomas M. Howe told the crowd that "[o]ur Constitution otherwise so perfect contains one blot, and we should not allow ourselves to be turned into slave-catchers." Charles Avery called on the community to shun anyone who accepted a commission to enforce the law "as though he was a leper." Resolutions passed calling for repeal of the law, the defeat of any candidate who did not actively oppose it, and publication in newspapers of the names of those who accepted positions as commissioners. The assembly further condemned all Pennsylvania congressmen who had voted for the act. On September 30, another meeting was held in the Allegheny Market House. Mayor Hugh S. Fleming made a powerful speech calling for repeal and further stirring the people's opposition to the law. The *Commercial Journal* declared that "[w]e have never seen a larger or more enthusiastic meeting in Allegheny. The demonstration is proof that the indignation of the people is deeply aroused."[49]

The black community in Pittsburgh reacted quickly to the new Fugitive Slave Act. Within one week after passing, more than a hundred blacks fled the city for Canada; by October, the number had grown to nearly three hundred. One hotel reportedly lost every one of its waiters. The census of 1860 showed that the number of blacks in Pittsburgh had dropped by eight hundred since 1850 and in Allegheny by 706.[50]

Not until early 1851 did the fears of those who fled began to be realized. On March 13, the first Pittsburgh fugitive-slave case under the new law came before Judge Thomas Irwin. A Mrs. Byers from Kentucky claimed that a man in the city named Woodson was her slave who had escaped two years prior. When Judge Irwin decided in favor of Byers, a large crowd attempted to block the extradition of Woodson but was dispersed by police. The *Post* reported on Woodson's departure the next day: "Contrary to the expectations of many persons, the case was determined without the slightest effort being made to resist the law of the land. . . . [T]he citizens of Pittsburgh are not disposed to follow the example of the fanatics of Boston and other places in a treasonable opposition to the law." Less than a month later, Pittsburghers raised six hundred dollars to purchase Woodson's freedom. The remarks of the *Post* and the people's reliance on a legal resolution revealed the prevailing sentiment in Pittsburgh. Despite the public's disdain for the Fugitive Slave Act, loyalty to the Constitution and the United States prevailed.[51]

In the decade between the passage of the Fugitive Slave Act and the beginning of the Civil War, there were numerous attempts made to free enslaved individuals traveling through the city. On the same day that the Woodson case was decided, slaveowner Leonard Boyd was traveling through Pittsburgh with his wife and a young enslaved woman. While they stayed at the St. Charles Hotel, some of the black employees attempted to free the girl but the police thwarted them. Boyd, fearing for the loss of his property, departed immediately by steamboat. As he made his way out of the city, more attempts were made to liberate the girl, resulting in a riotous struggle that again the police had to quell. The next day, the *Post* remarked that "The character of this city should not be stained, nor its business injured by negro mobs." In May 1853, J. Lindey of the Pennsylvania Abolition Society in Philadelphia sent a letter to Pittsburghers warning them of a Thomas Adams of Nashville who would arrive in the city on the Pennsylvania Railroad with a black youth named Alexander. The boy reportedly had emigrated from Jamaica and had lived in California when Adams, intent on selling him into slavery, lured him with the promise of riches. Pittsburgh abolitionists gathered a large crowd, met the train, and liberated the boy. In August of that year, Pittsburgh blacks were again warned by telegraph of another man en route to the city, traveling with an enslaved woman and three children. Arriving from Ohio at the station in Allegheny, the four blacks were seized and taken to the mayor's office. The man fled the city amid charges of kidnapping and threats from local blacks to tar and feather him. In March 1854, the *Post* warned that these events threatened the city's economy. The paper reminded Pittsburghers of the millions invested in the railroads, canals, and river improvements "to bring through ou[r] city and state a large share of the travel and trade of the South and West. These efforts to increase our prosperity will be useless if travelers are to be assailed by lawless mobs. . . . Shall our prosperity and reputation as a community be given over to the control of an irresponsible mob of negroes who do little for prosperity of the city themselves[?]"[52]

Pittsburgh abolitionists also acted to protect local blacks from slave-catchers. In July 1855, Pittsburgher George Ferris traveled with a band of singers to St. Louis. There, Mr. Shaw, a professional slave-catcher, captured Ferris and returned him to his enslaver. A short time later, Shaw was arrested in Pittsburgh while trying to seize Ferris's three-year-old child. That same month, antislavery activist H. B. Northup was mistaken for a slave-catcher and was apprehended in Pittsburgh. On his arrival in the city, Northup inquired about the local federal marshal, raising suspicions that he was there to retrieve a self-liberated refugee from slavery. Northup, who had labored for years in the cause of enslaved persons and had freed Solomon Northup, the noted author of *Twelve Years a Slave*, was indignant at first but ultimately praised Pittsburghers for their zeal. The *Gazette* agreed with him: "the prompt action taken by our anti-slavery friends, shows that the mass of our citizens are sound on the slavery question, and are fully resolved that no fugitive slave shall be taken from this city without an effort to resist it."[53]

As the sectional crisis unfolded, the Republican *Gazette* both reflected and stoked Pittsburghers' growing contempt for white Southerners, condemning not so much the institution of slavery but rather the Southerners' perceived nefarious means of pursuing their political objectives. The paper vilified the disloyalty of Southerners while extolling Northerners' virtuous adherence to the rule of law. After the Fugitive Slave Act of 1850, no other event leading up to the Civil War more alarmed the people of Pittsburgh than the Kansas-Nebraska Act of 1854. The *Gazette* began that year with the pronouncement that "the bill and the report from the committee on the territories must be a signal for the reopening of the slavery agitation. . . . [Southerners] are as treacherous, crafty and dishonest, in policy, as they are bold and unscrupulous in action." Ten days later, in response to Kentucky Senator Archibald Dixon's call for repeal of the Missouri Compromise, the *Gazette* declared in exasperation: "This need excite no surprise. No exhibition of treachery, craft or audacity, ought to surprise the country after what has happened during the past five years." In May, when the bill passed, the paper took aim at the Northern congressmen who voted for it, denouncing them as "forty-four traitors to the rights, interests and honor of the North."[54]

Opponents of proslavery measures continued to challenge Northern politicians to resist these affronts. When South Carolina Congressman Preston Brooks assaulted Massachusetts Senator Charles Sumner on the Senate floor in 1856, the *Gazette* called for retaliation: "Is there no free state man in Washington with arms strong enough to chastise properly such a brutal miscreant as this? If not, it is time that Northern constituencies should be looking out for fighting men for Representatives."[55]

The Dred Scott decision the following year prompted further determined responses to the provocation of the proslavery forces. "If there is left one spark of manliness among the freemen of Pennsylvania and of the free North," the *Gazette* declared, "they will address themselves anew to the battle and gird on their armor for the victory that must sooner or later crown their efforts." However, with the Supreme Court essentially striking the death blow to Northern efforts to arrest the spread of slavery into new territories, the *Gazette* appealed for restraint: "A good citizen should advocate a law-abiding disposition and a respect for constitutional authorities. . . . The decisions of the Supreme Court of the United States have hitherto been regarded, by all conservative men, with respect and confidence. Democratic demagogues, however . . . have always repudiated its decisions when they came athwart their partizan [*sic*] views."[56]

The debate culminated with the presidential election in 1860. In May that same year, Republicans in Pittsburgh celebrated Lincoln's nomination as the candidate of their party. On the hills surrounding the city, citizens fired cannons and enthusiastic demonstrators packed city hall. Over the next six months, a well-organized Republican political machine enlisted overwhelming support for Lincoln, including Pittsburghers of every sort. When the general election came in November, no major city gave a greater majority to Lincoln than Pittsburgh. The *Gazette* proclaimed that "the majority given by our glorious old county is indeed beautiful to contemplate." Republicans declared that Allegheny "has nobly earned the title of Banner County." A few days after the election, however, as the initial excitement began to wane, the *Gazette* pondered what lay ahead for the nation. What would Southerners do now that the outcome they so dreaded had come to pass? Would their "loud rants of resistance" prove to be nothing more than "simple boastings"? "Will they submit . . . or will they fulfill their threat of seceding from the Union[?]"[57]

2

★ ★ ★ ★ ★

NOT ONLY BY EXPRESSIONS OF SENTIMENT, BUT BY THE EXERCISE OF PHYSICAL FORCE

Reactions to Rebellion

Every great historical event reverberates in a very remarkable
manner through the fortunes of a multitude of private and even
secluded individuals. No volcano erupts without stirring the
existence of the mountain's mice.

–J. W. DE FOREST–

Miss Ravenel's Conversion from Secession to Loyalty (1867)

On December 24, 1860, as Northerners learned of South Carolina's break with the United States, news of a recent order from the War Department to the Allegheny Arsenal in Pittsburgh quickly spread through the city. The instructions to the commanding officer, Major John Symington, would send 124 cannons to forts in Texas and Louisiana. The community was outraged by what it perceived as "the treasonable purpose of the administration." How, asked Pittsburgh judge William Wilkins, could the federal government arm a section of the nation in open and growing rebellion, at the expense of the loyal people of the North?[1]

As Christmas Day dawned, prominent citizens of Pittsburgh worked to block the removal of the guns. At a meeting held in the county controller's office, a committee organized to call on Major Symington. A second committee formed to draft a message to President James Buchanan imploring him to have the order revoked. The second committee, led by Judge Wilkins, immediately telegraphed Buchanan: "An order issued by the War

Department to transfer the effective munitions of war from the arsenal in this city to Southern military posts has created great excitement in the public mind. We would advise that the order be immediately countermanded. We speak at the insistence of the people, and if not done, we cannot answer for the consequences." Secretary of State Jeremiah Black and Attorney General Edwin M. Stanton, two of Buchanan's closest advisers and both strongly opposed to Southern secession, received copies of the telegram. Their message drafted and sent, the committee members adjourned with the intention of reconvening in two days.[2]

As the community leaders waited for a response from Washington, local newspapers voiced the outrage of the people. The *Dispatch* portrayed the removal of the guns as an insult to the laboring class of the city. The guns were to be sent, the paper claimed, "not to defend the stars and stripes, for which our skillful mechanics made them, but to batter it down under the pirate flag of some Lone Star or Rattlesnake government." The *Gazette* asked whether the people of the city would "tamely stand by and see the treason consummated before their eyes."[3]

On December 27, while the steamer *Silver Wave* sat at the Monongahela wharf awaiting its controversial cargo, tensions in the city grew. That afternoon a large gathering formed outside the county courthouse on Fifth Street in the Third Ward. By 2 p.m., the appointed time for the committee to reconvene, the crowd had grown so large that the proceedings moved from the supreme court room to the open air. The courthouse steps and the sidewalks of Fifth Street were crowded with excited citizens described by the *Post* as a "tremendous gathering of people . . . a sea of upturned faces, numbering thousands." Congressman James K. Moorhead delivered the opening speech. He commended the citizens for their spirit but also cautioned them not to take any action that could be construed as illegal and thereby strengthen the case of secessionists. "Let the guns go," advised Moorhead, so Pittsburghers can "preserve their reputation of union-loving, law abiding citizens." The resolutions subsequently passed likewise lauded the people's passion while warning against rash acts.[4]

In the succeeding days, Pittsburghers continued to await word from Washington as they anxiously watched local events unfold. Major Symington's response to the committee on the twenty-fifth had been that, in the absence of a countermanding order, the guns would move as instructed. Meanwhile, a local militia company had placed artillery on Brunot Island, at the confluence of the Monongahela and the Allegheny, and vowed to fire on the steamer should an attempt be made to remove the guns from the city.[5]

The controversy in Pittsburgh seized the attention of the whole North. Republican newspapers across the country reported daily on the situation there. The *Chicago Tribune* characterized the order to send the cannons south as further evidence of treason within the federal government. The *New York Daily Tribune* applauded the people of Pittsburgh for resisting.[6]

The crisis finally defused on January 2, 1861. With U.S. soldiers and guns standing by at the wharf and hostile parties vowing not to let the guns go, the countermanding order was received and the guns returned to the arsenal.[7]

Although the controversy surrounding the Allegheny Arsenal ended, the sentiment it stirred in the people of Pittsburgh remained alive. Nearly four months before the firing on Fort Sumter that would trigger civil war, the people of the city were aroused by what they perceived as the treasonous acts of Southern rebels and their abettors. Republican and Democratic newspapers of Pittsburgh emphasized the bipartisan nature of the committees that addressed the crisis and of the crowds that attended. Three Democratic judges were among the signers of a resolution on December 27 proclaiming

FIG. 1. William Wilkins, 1860. Library of Congress.

FIG. 2. James K. Moorhead.
Library of Congress.

that "We, the law abiding citizens of Allegheny County, are ready to aid in preserving the Union and the Constitution from the hands of traitors."[8]

During the secession crisis, Northerners did not need to wait for the direction of community leaders and politicians. No self-interested group of elites leading the people along and inciting their passions orchestrated the resistance of Pittsburgh to the removal of the guns. Rather, the community leaders who stepped forward during the crisis reflected and responded to the widespread indignation of the community. Their speeches and resolutions were not mere political rhetoric; these community leaders genuinely believed in the cause they voiced. However, they recognized the potential for disaster should they fail to temper the peoples' excitement. While commending the loyalty of the citizens, leaders also cautioned restraint lest they "manifest the same want of respect for the laws that [was] then being manifested in the southern states."[9]

The gun removal controversy was a big event in strengthening the community's resolve against secession. Though a shot had yet to be fired in the sectional crisis, the nefarious acts of Southerners and their allies in Washington had threatened to make Pittsburgh complicit in the dissolution of the United States. Iron cannon cast in the city's foundries would be used against the federal government; the product of the city's laborers and a symbol of its strength would become an implement of treason. From that point forward—many in Pittsburgh believed—the nation was already at war. In his closing comments to the assembly at the courthouse, Congressman Moorhead stated that "when the tug of war does come—if it must—and Heaven forbid that it should—I know my constituents will show the same alacrity which they now exhibit in maintaining the integrity of the Union, not only by expressions of sentiment, but by the exercise of physical force."[10]

That same afternoon, one group of men within the community began to prepare for the conflict they were now convinced would come. Following the public meeting at the courthouse, the marshals of the Republican Wide Awake clubs gathered at a militia armory to discuss the state of affairs. They decided that each club should reorganize itself into a military unit. This being accomplished by the individual clubs, delegates from each would then meet again "to perfect a military organization" of the twenty clubs in the city and county. Two days later, in response to the resolutions of the Pittsburgh meeting, the Wide Awake clubs of Allegheny met across the river to denounce the removal of the guns and pledge their service in the country's defense.[11]

The resolutions passed by the Wide Awakes offer valuable insight into the sentiments and actions of Northerners during the secession crisis. They called for unity in opposing secession "without distinction of party"; Pittsburghers must pledge themselves "to each other as American citizens." Although local elections were only three days away, the Wide Awakes declined to associate Democrats with treason and disunion, but rather emphasized their common responsibility to defend the nation from "traitors at home." This setting aside of party rivalry was undoubtedly thought through for its political soundness, yet was also grounded elsewhere. The Wide Awake resolutions celebrated the "triumphant vindication of the capacity of the people" to resist the rebellion. After all, the federal government had not prevented the subversion of Northern military readiness in the gun removal crisis, but rather a loyal community determined to strike a blow against secession. The lesson that many in Pittsburgh took from this was that the will of a unified people was the best hope of sustaining the Union. Community leaders in Pittsburgh struck a chord of local pride and commitment that, as the war loomed nearer, echoed in cities and villages across the North.[12]

The Wide Awakes already had a plan for channeling that pride and commitment in Pittsburgh: community-wide mobilization for military action.

Just days after South Carolina seceded, they called on the people of Pittsburgh to come together "as citizen soldiers" in defense of the country. The community's representatives in the state legislature, Wide Awakes argued, should take immediate steps to arm and provision a people's military force. Existing volunteer militia companies, they urged, should take action to fill their ranks. Compromise with secessionists was not even entertained as a possibility.[13]

The Wide Awake clubs calling for mobilization were thoroughly primed for a transition from political activism to military service. Comprised mostly of young men, rigidly structured, and energetic, the clubs employed martial symbolism and activities that gave them a sense of identity and purpose in the growing sectional conflict. Wide Awakes marched in formation, wore uniforms, and even recognized a rank structure. As quasi-military organizations, the clubs provided a formative experience for men who would soon join the army and go into battle. John Donaghy, who enlisted in Pittsburgh in the spring of 1861, later remembered his "first military experience" not as a soldier in camp or on the march but "as a member of a company of 'wide awakes' in the presidential election of 1860." Captain William Easton characterized his Pittsburgh Wide Awake club as a "kindergarten for the volunteer soldiers of the early sixties."[14]

The mobilization advocated by Wide Awakes proposed, for now, only a "precautionary movement—looking only to the perpetuation of our government and to the integrity of the Union." Their resolutions contained no antislavery language and no attacks on the "slave power" that had become such a common target in the growing sectional conflict. Whatever their true sentiments at this point, Republican leaders at the local level were not yet ready to link their actions to the debate on slavery. Those most determined to organize militarily recognized that treason against the United States was the threat that would most effectively mobilize the community.[15]

The resolutions of the Wide Awake meeting appeared in the local papers on election day. Voters that morning—already agitated by the yet unresolved gun removal order—were further excited when they read the Wide Awakes' assertion that "[t]he government is now in a state of anarchy and *traitors* occupy the high places of power." Back in November, when Pittsburgh gave its overwhelming support to Lincoln in the presidential election, people had voted Republican for a variety of reasons. While the slavery issue primarily motivated many, others responded to concerns with a more direct local impact such as tariffs and railroad taxes. However, the threat of treason now energized voters. The municipal elections of 1861 were a referendum on the community's position on secession and, if voters in other Northern cities were reconsidering the wisdom of electing a Republican president, Pittsburghers showed no wavering in their conviction. While Republicans had enjoyed a majority in Pittsburgh government for some years, in the 1861 election, they virtually swept the municipal offices. Of the nine wards in the city, Republicans ran unopposed in three, defeated all opposition in two others, and won a large majority in three more. Only in the Third Ward did Democrats win a majority of the contested offices. Whatever the dangers of a forceful stand against secession, they were not enough to cow the citizens of Pittsburgh into backing down in the face of treason. The result at the polls demonstrated the peoples' endorsement of the Wide Awakes' call to arms.[16]

In the following months promoters of military readiness continued to stoke the passions of the people against secession. On the evening of January 3, citizens met in Wilkins's Hall over the mayor's office to discuss the county's preparedness. Building on the example of the Wide Awakes, they passed resolutions urging every ward and the surrounding boroughs to begin thorough military preparations. The principal means by which the community should ready itself, the resolutions urged, would be the creation of a new regiment. Not all in Pittsburgh, however, were ready to embrace such vigorous mobilization.[17]

In the weeks after the resolution of the gun removal crisis, Alabama, Mississippi, Florida, Georgia, Louisiana, and Texas left the United States. To these exciting national events was added the drama of Major Robert Anderson and his small garrison's defense of Fort Sumter in Charleston harbor. Through the winter, Anderson and his men became a symbol of defiance against secession and the people of Pittsburgh anxiously awaited news of the beleaguered heroes.

As they watched the United States dissolve, communities across the North pledged themselves to preserve the nation but were divided over how best to accomplish that. Many Northerners advocated compromise with the South. While the majority of Pittsburghers took a militant stand, a Democratic minority in the city urged caution. Throughout the secession winter, the *Daily Post* joined with Democrats and conservative Republicans across the North in calling for a compromise to avert war. Democrats in Pittsburgh were keenly aware, however, that theirs was the minority sentiment in the city. On January 23, Russell Errett wrote to Simon Cameron in response to his expression of readiness to entertain a compromise solution to the secession crisis. Errett cautioned him that "[t]hose who are familiar only with the public sentiment at Harrisburg, Philadelphia, New York and Washington can have no idea of the fierceness of the sentiment here in opposition to anything that looks like compromise. It amounts almost to a fury." Compromise-minded Democrats in the city thus had to take care in how they defined their position. While they opposed the use of arms to hold the United States together, they had to craft their argument in a manner that conveyed concern for the North rather than sympathy for the Rebel states. The *Daily Post* chastised the local Republican journals for their calls to arms, accusing them of being "utterly careless of the interests of the manufacturing community by which they are surrounded, and the workingmen, who are the main stay of our prosperity." Promoters of mobilization countered this position with their own economic arguments. Compromise, they said, was the real threat, citing foreign investors' lack of confidence in the perpetuation of the Union as a major cause of falling stocks. "It is easy to conceive that foreign capitalists could have no confidence in a country which must buy off traitors."[18]

Soon, however, Democratic Party leaders in Pittsburgh began to join the mobilization effort and further cement the support of the community. On February 18, Democrats from across the county met at the courthouse in Pittsburgh to elect delegates to the state convention to be held in Harrisburg later that month. There, they would consider possible measures to preserve the Union and determine the state party's position on secession. Among the delegates was former county judge Peter C. Shannon. Born in neighboring Westmoreland County in 1821, he later settled in Pittsburgh and studied law. He was admitted to the bar there in 1846 and immediately established himself as a staunch Democrat. Over the next six years, he was twice selected as the Democratic candidate for Congress. In 1852, the governor named him a district court judge as a reward for his party loyalty.[19]

Appointed chairman of the February 18 meeting, Shannon addressed the assembled Democrats. The audience undoubtedly expected a stout condemnation of the recent calls for mobilization, but, after briefly admonishing the Republican Party for its dangerous sectional views, Shannon shifted the blame for the current political situation to his own party. He claimed that the Democrats' self-induced fracturing over the presidential election had placed the Republicans in power. Shannon then surprised the crowd by vehemently defending local Republicans and their calls for military preparedness. "It had been said," he declared, "that the Republican party has thus far failed to meet in a proper spirit of conciliation and compromise the overtures made for the settlement of national difficulties. But what then? Do not seven staunch Democratic states equally fail to accept those overtures. . . . Have not those six or seven states trampled the Union and the Constitution in the dust?"

Shannon went on to recall all the insults the seceded states had inflicted on the nation before he proclaimed the futility of compromise: "Talk, indeed, of your overtures for concession and compromise, when treason stalks with unblushing front through the Cotton States, and grim visaged war knocks at your very doors! They boldly tell you that they laugh at your overtures; that reconstruction is impossible. Before chiding too severely the Republican party of the North, go and try to repel the surging waves in the far-off South. Idle and fanciful would it be as childhood's fairy dream. In all the mobs that are recorded . . . there has been a rallying cry; the last touch is secession, whilst from the extreme North comes the echo of 'NO COMPROMISE!'"[20]

Despite the enthusiastic cheers that followed, Judge Shannon's remarks were not yet enough to completely turn his fellow Democrats from the course of compromise. The resolutions that passed condemned any coercion of the seceded states and implored Northerners to find a peaceful course to preserve the Union. Shannon's surprise departure from the party line of conciliation did, however, have an effect on the convention, for a handful of delegates were inspired to denounce the resolutions. Thus, while Republicans in Pittsburgh were strongly united in favor of mobilization, Democrats were now dividing. Samuel Harper criticized the resolutions as proposed and urged that a call "for their Southern brethren [to] surrender now and for all time the right of secession" be included. The resolutions were finally passed, but, for Judge Shannon, the way ahead was now clear. From that day forward, he would be a loyal ally of the Republican administration and the Union war effort. The defection of such a prominent and respected Democrat cast doubt on the arguments for compromise.[21]

Early in the afternoon on February 22, masses of citizens gathered in the principal streets of the city, eager for the day's festivities. The occasion was George Washington's birthday and this year's observance came with particular excitement and promise. Around 2:30 p.m., a large crowd at the Monongahela wharf watched as vessels carrying the local militia companies steamed down the river and docked at the wharf. The companies singly debarked and fell into ranks. Once assembled, they marched toward their designated gathering point. As they paraded through the city, citizens followed along the sidewalks flanking their route. Onlookers leaned out of second- and third-story windows amid dozens of flags fluttering from public and private buildings. Of particular interest were the Pennsylvania Zouaves, whose new, flamboyant uniforms evoked loud cheers. The procession crossed the river into Allegheny and, after marching through that city, assembled in the open field of the West Common. There, the troops entertained the crowd with a brief demonstration of drill before marching off the field past the senior officers in the reviewing stand.[22]

While ceremonies honoring important national events and figures were not new in Pittsburgh, those on this particular day took on a different tone. For weeks now, a rush of events had excited the people of Pittsburgh. In addition to the gun removal crisis and the rousing demonstrations by the Wide Awakes, an immense patriotic meeting of workingmen was held on January 11 at city hall. When the meeting adjourned following a series of fervent speeches denouncing secession, the attendees spilled out into the street with a chorus of "cheers for the Union, national flag, and Major Anderson." Eleven days later, the city's pride in its industrial might again linked with mobilization when the workers of the local Fort Pitt Foundry cast the largest cannon the world had yet seen. This new columbiad-style gun had a fifteen-inch bore, was nearly sixteen feet long, and weighed forty-nine thousand pounds. Pittsburgh's Knapp, Rudd, and Company, which operated the foundry, fittingly dubbed the cannon "Union." As Pittsburghers intently followed these events, as well as the intensifying pace of secession, military organizations in the city redoubled their recruiting efforts. By mid-February, seven new companies had raised and would proceed to form the core of the 61st and 103rd Pennsylvania Volunteer Infantry Regiments the following summer. Finally, just days before the celebration of Washington's birthday, three Southern students attending the Western Theological Seminary dropped out, citing their reason as "the want of conservative sentiment in Allegheny County."[23]

Although the people gathered in Pittsburgh on February 22 undoubtedly had a deep affection for George Washington, on this occasion, they were drawn to the streets by something more. The national news and the local military preparations had brought them to a fever pitch of excitement. One observer remarked that "anyone in the city, whether a stranger or not, must have felt aware that something unusual was on hand. . . . The patriotism of Pittsburgh was aroused, and long before one o'clock the anxiety to see the military was very great." The *Daily Gazette* reported that, hours before the parade commenced, the streets filled with spectators, "anxious to witness the soldiery of Allegheny, and at the same time to honor the memory of the great and good Washington." The official object of the parade had become almost an afterthought amid the people's anticipation of the military pageantry.[24]

This mood was not lost on the organizers of the day's ceremonies. The soldiers' spectacular arrival by boat on the banks of the Monongahela mimicked an amphibious assault on enemy shores. The companies' exercises on the West Common grounds represented bold tactical maneuvers in the face of an opposing force. While local civic and military leaders employed traditional ceremonies that day, they did so to an extent and in a manner that drew the community closer to its military.[25]

That night some four hundred of Pittsburgh's prominent citizens gathered at city hall for a banquet. The militaristic tone that characterized the day's events manifested here as well. Washington's portrait was suspended over the stage, flanked by battle scenes from the Napoleonic wars. Pyramids of cannon balls stood next to miniature artillery pieces and the stacked rifles of the Washington Infantry and Jackson Blues lined the sides of the hall. Placed close to the national colors were pictures of Major Robert Anderson and Fort Sumter. However, not all present were won over by the patriotic icons and stirring images of fighting men.[26]

Dinner completed, master of ceremonies Thomas J. Bingham called the assembly to order. He then offered the customary toasts, each one answered by a brief musical piece from the Washington Cornet Band and an enthusiastic response from a designated guest. After toasting the day, the president, the governor, the judiciary, and the army and navy, Bingham raised his glass and emphatically offered "to the Union!" As the band's abridgment of the "Star Spangled Banner" ended, Judge Charles Shaler rose for the response. He opened by affirming the importance of the Union. However, he continued, it was necessary to recognize that the true cause of the peril that now faced the Union was that, after fifty years of Democratic administrations that protected the interests of the nation, power was about to transfer to enemies of democracy who scorned the Constitution. Secession was illegal, he said, but the seceding states could not rightfully be brought back into the Union by armed force. The only way to save the Union was through the "restoration of the principles of Madison, Monroe, Jefferson, Jackson, and the Democracy of old."[27]

Shaler's words provoked an immediate response. Thomas Bingham rushed across the stage and grabbed the national flag. Waving it back and forth, he stated that, in little more than a week, "they intended to inaugurate an administration which would be the legitimate successor of that of Jefferson, Madison, and Monroe." Still flourishing the flag, he asked the band to again play the "Star Spangled Banner."[28]

Through the winter of 1860–61, events transpired on both the national and local level that moved the people of Pittsburgh closer to endorsing war with the South. Though a small group of conservatives continued to promote compromise with the South, the overwhelming popular sentiment in Pittsburgh, by the end of the secession winter, was strong antipathy to treason and a readiness to embrace military action if necessary.

On the evening of Friday, April 12, a packed house at the Pittsburgh Theater enjoyed H. T. Craven's domestic drama, *The Chimney Corner*, fresh from its debut in London. Suddenly, a theater employee rushed onto the stage, a telegram in hand, and excitedly delivered the news: the Confederate forces surrounding Fort Sumter had commenced a bombardment and Anderson's brave soldiers had returned fire. The audience reacted with thunderous applause, galvanized by the outbreak of military action however uncertain the outcome. After considerable difficulty, the staff managed to reestablish order and resume the play.[29]

The sun rose over Pittsburgh on Saturday morning casting its rays on crowds gathering in the streets eager for news. Nineteenth-century Americans were not content with waiting for the next edition of their newspaper when important events were unfolding; they actively sought out information from as close to the source as they could find. At an early hour, masses of people flocked to the telegraph offices, anxious to learn the fate of their gallant soldiers in Charleston harbor. Others huddled on street corners, where copies of the newspapers' extra editions were posted. Workers and shopkeepers neglected their duties in order to come together and discuss this shocking news. Over the next forty-eight hours, while the beleaguered U.S. garrison sustained the barrage of shot and shell, the people of Pittsburgh endured their own barrage from the press. A stream of conflicting and sometimes outlandish reports poured into the city. Eventually, there came reports of the garrison's surrender on April 14. Pittsburghers were reluctant to credit these reports until they could no longer be denied.[30]

The Confederate attack did not stir the people so much as the defense waged by Anderson and his men. The bombardment just confirmed the treason that had already been consummated in many other ways, but now the Unionist spirit of Northern society was for the first time embodied in military action. After months of unchecked rebellion, answered only by political rhetoric and military pageantry, U.S. soldiers resisted treason by the force of arms. The advocates of mobilization were now vindicated and any further endorsement of compromise would reek of treason.

April 15 was a turning point for community mobilization in Pittsburgh. Once the surrender of Fort Sumter was confirmed, events moved swiftly. Having received the news officially, President Lincoln issued a proclamation on the fifteenth calling on the loyal states for seventy-five thousand volunteer militiamen to put down the Southern rebellion. Once again, the community leaders in Pittsburgh acted to organize the city's response. Following the common pattern of community activism, one hundred prominent citizens signed a petition to the mayor calling for a public meeting on the fifteenth to determine how the city would support the federal government. And once again, the people of Pittsburgh assembled in the streets to take part. William Johnston later recalled that "City Hall was densely crowded with people who were determined that the Rebellion should be crushed at whatever cost." William Wilkins, selected to address the assemblage, gave a rousing speech. "In the present crisis of affairs," he demanded of his listeners, "are you prepared to sustain the general government? Are you willing to aid the Executive in putting down treason and preserving the Constitution?" A thunderous response affirmed the crowd's acceptance of this challenge. Wilkins then called on Pittsburghers to abandon party loyalties and rally around the president. Lincoln, he declared, needed every loyal citizen's aid to eradicate treason. "It is purely a question of preserving the country that is now before you," and this "was the only question pervading the Union now!" In the crowd that evening was James McClelland, who later recalled in his diary the large gathering outside of city hall and the "great excitement" throughout the city. John Donaghy remembered that, while attending the meeting, he "was affected to tears at the prospect of a dissolution of the Union."[31]

The public meeting on April 15 produced more than just patriotic speeches. Resolutions passed and decisions were made that set the city on a course that would continue, in one form or another, for the entirety of the war, but any action taken had first to be infused with a purpose. The public meeting was declared by resolution to be "a fit occasion to renew our obligations of untiring fealty to that government and that Union which we have been taught to regard and revere as the palladium of our liberties at home and our honor abroad; and in their defense and support, by whomsoever assailed, we will endeavor to prove ourselves worthy sons of patriotic sires."[32]

The language of this resolution illuminates the ideology that motivated Pittsburgh's citizens to support the Northern war effort. In referring to the federal government as the safeguard "of our liberties," the authors expressed the profound conviction of nineteenth-century Americans that theirs was the world's best system of governance and the worthiest model for the rest of the world to emulate. For Americans of this period, the preservation of the Union was anything but a shallow objective; for many, it was the loftiest purpose possibly conjured to justify war.[33]

Yet, from the outset of the war, some in Pittsburgh recognized that, to preserve the United States, they needed to go a step further and recognize the source of the threat now facing the nation. On April 16, the *Daily Gazette* declared that "[t]he long accumulating power of slavery—a power which has kept us in turmoil and confusion for many years—has at length had the audacity to put on the livery of treason, and strike its fangs into the bosom which had, with mistaken leniency, nourished its life and strength. Few, until this treason manifested itself, suspected its malignity; but now all see it in its true character and are inclined to deal with it accordingly." The *Gazette* was, of course, thereby endorsing the Republican Party platform to a predominantly Republican readership, but, while this editorial linked the war with slavery, it did so in a manner that drew on the powerful symbol of the Union and distanced Pittsburghers from abolitionism, while simultaneously absolving them of any guilt in permitting slavery's existence thus far. According to the *Gazette*, the inherent evil of slavery had not warranted Northern mobilization but rather the treason of self-interested slaveholders, which threatened the survival of the United States.[34]

That summer, Senator Edgar Cowan of Pennsylvania addressed the same topic at a Union meeting outside Pittsburgh. He began by dismissing the argument of Southerners that the federal government under Lincoln was poised to attack slavery. The government had no such design, he insisted, and was, if anything, far too accommodating to slavery. This point established, he then issued a warning to the secessionists: "[T]his cannot long continue, and, if the war lasts, the rebels may find themselves bringing upon themselves one of the very evils [abolition] they pretended to avoid by their treason." Thus Cowan, too, at an early stage, steered the Northern war effort toward an acceptance of abolition as a just and necessary measure. "Would it not be a singular retribution," Cowan asked, "if they were made the ministers of their own punishment for this lie, by having it made good by their own act?"[35]

In exploring why Northern civilians chose to support the war, scholars must make a careful distinction. Just as the question of why Southern men and women chose to support the Confederate war effort is a completely different issue from why Southern political leaders chose to secede from the United States, so too are the factors motivating Northern civilians to support the war distinct from those that motivated Republican leaders to prosecute it. The people of Pittsburgh embraced the war and their role in it for a variety of reasons that would continue to evolve with the course of the war and that will be examined in later chapters herein. However, from the beginning of the war, Republican advocates of mobilization in Pittsburgh, in contrast to party leaders in most Northern communities, recognized the centrality of slavery to the war and worked to move the people to accept abolition as a necessary war aim.[36]

Community mobilization and the intimations of radical war objectives were fostered by the bipartisan spirit that swept the city in the wake of Sumter. The appeals from Judge Wilkins and other community leaders proved more than just hopeful rhetoric. With the outbreak of hostilities, the Democratic minority in Pittsburgh rallied around the banner of Unionism. The voices that had only days before cautioned restraint and chastised the destructive radicalism of Republicans now joined them in condemning secessionists. James P. Barr, editor and proprietor of the Democratic *Daily Post*—thus far the lone organ of compromise in the city—made an abrupt about-face. Sumter convinced him that compromise had never really existed as a possibility. On April 17, the *Daily Post* proclaimed that "the Southern oligarchy has always intended to initiate hostilities. . . . The war which has been consummated by the attack and capture of Fort Sumter, was in effect, commenced months ago." Barr now viewed the seizure of forts and arsenals in the South and the transfer of military arms—such as those ordered sent south from Pittsburgh in December—as "acts of war" and "usurpation and resistance to constituted authority." Prior to Sumter, Democrats had warned of the cataclysmic effect of war on the city's economy. Now, the *Daily Post* assured Pittsburghers that, although they were "suffering under a perfect stagnation of business here, owing to the war excitement," the policy of the Lincoln administration would soon bring about a "revival of business in this city." Barr would, before long, further demonstrate his new-found zeal through participation in community efforts to support the Northern war effort.[37]

The way forward for the city had to be established by more than just declarations of loyalty and denunciations of the enemy. Measures to establish an army were now being put into motion; plans were needed to mobilize citizens to aid that army. In Pittsburgh, this began soon after the April 15 meeting with the establishment of the Committee of Public Safety, an organization composed of one hundred citizens independent of municipal government. It declared its mission to be "to see that the Patriot Cause receives no detriment in this region." Its members came from various social strata and from every ward. John Hanna, a propertyless Irish bricklayer from the Seventh Ward, sat on a subcommittee with the wealthy iron manufacturer George Black of the Fourth Ward, who had three servants and owned property worth $78,500.[38]

The Committee of Public Safety incorporated a complex network of subcommittees with diverse functions and its far-reaching activities made it a subject of debate. Its members were charged with collecting funds to support local regiments, organizing the citizens of Pittsburgh into military units for home-front defense, and suppressing subversive activities. Although the committee enjoyed strong bipartisan support, this last role made it a subject of some uneasiness. Democrats sought to make it clear that this body was not a "vigilance committee designed to initiate a system of terrorism over individual opinion." Although firmly committed to the war effort, Democrats feared that the rapidly growing war fever in the city might pose a threat to individual liberties.[39]

Others in Pittsburgh, however, seemed skeptical of upholding citizens' liberties if it meant tolerating "traitors" in their city. On April 16, the *Daily Gazette* declared that "[i]n this time of peril . . . there must be no coldness or lukewarmness among us. He who is not with the government is against it. . . . We cannot afford to have one traitor in the community." Two days later, Lewis Hays, a newly-minted member of the Washington Infantry, was spending the evening at the company's armory with his fellow soldiers when an Irish-American riverboat crewman by the name of Murta came by. Without warning, Hays attacked Murta, throwing him to the ground. Other soldiers restrained Hays, allowing Murta to get away. Hays then explained that some weeks earlier he had been in New Orleans, where a crowd threatened him with violence unless he left the city immediately; Murta, he claimed, was among that secessionist mob. By the morning following Hay's assault on Murta, word of the alleged secessionist in Pittsburgh had spread and a group of angry citizens had taken to the streets in search of the Irishman. Nabbing him at the corner of Fourth and Smithfield streets, they attempted to suspend him from a light post as a testament to the city's loyalty to the Union. Murta escaped, however, and later denied any part in the New Orleans incident. He then publicly proclaimed his desire to join the war effort as a volunteer soldier.[40]

After the Murta incident, community leaders and the local press stepped up their efforts to dissuade the public from acts of mob violence. This does not mean, however, that Pittsburghers were encouraged to tolerate disloyalty, nor were they advised to rely on the municipal authorities to deal with such concerns. Citizens were instead encouraged to turn to the Committee of Public Safety as the city's safeguard against subversion. In the early weeks of the war, this body of citizens operated with a conviction that reflected the mood of Northern society in general. They met in session multiple times a day, determined to exhaust every effort in managing the community's response to rebellion, but, during the earliest months of the war, the committee remained highly active in what some believed its most important function: weeding out subversive activities within the city.[41]

On the afternoon of April 21, 1861, a young man passing through the Pennsylvania Railroad depot in the Ninth Ward came across a load of cargo marked for shipment to Charleston, South Carolina. His suspicions aroused, he set out to find Dr. George McCook, a respected community leader and a member of the Committee of Public Safety. After hearing the man's story, McCook headed for the depot. As word of the suspicious cargo spread, other citizens joined him. Word also quickly reached Mayor Wilson, who, with Police Chief J. G. Patterson, set out to meet McCook. When Wilson saw the size of the crowd accompanying McCook, he was sufficiently concerned to call on the Washington Infantry under Captain John Rowley to assemble at the depot to protect the property of the Pennsylvania Railroad.[42]

The crowd was not disappointed. On inspecting the cargo, McCook and his party discovered material clearly intended for equipping an army. The crowd cheered as boxes full of uniform fabric, blankets, and leather muzzle guards for cannons were pulled from the rail car and loaded into carts. They had been shipped from New York. A second procession now moved back through the city with more excitement and pageantry than the first. The carts were paraded with military escort to the mayor's office, the people surrounding them and waving the national flag over them along the way. The next day, the *Gazette* used the event to showcase the proper attitude Pittsburghers were expected to display, proudly declaring that "[t]he rebels may find traitors in New York to supply them with such articles as those, but they may depend upon it that our citizens will not let a dollar's worth pass this point. . . . We anxiously await the next shipment for the South!"[43]

The Committee of Public Safety responded to the excitement over the seized contraband by intensifying its efforts to root out treason. On April 28, it announced a series of resolutions aimed at Pittsburgh merchants. These required that all shipments from the city bound for the South be held until they could be searched by representatives of the committee. Through the spring and summer, inspectors regularly boarded steamboats and freight cars, opening containers in search of items that could support the Confederate war effort. The Committee of Public Safety seized and stored any cargo deemed contraband.[44]

During the first months of the war, Republican papers publicized other incidents to stoke the people's apprehension about subversive activity in the city. On April 28, while inspecting a rail car, members of the Committee of

Public Safety came across crates loaded with friction primers for firing artillery. One crate exploded, severely wounding several of the men. While the cause of the explosion was never determined, the local press suggested the possibility of sabotage by Southern sympathizers.[45]

Perhaps the most public of the committee's actions was its role in a case of fraud involving two local clothing manufacturers. At the beginning of the war, the War Department was unprepared to equip the massive number of volunteers called into service. In the rush to expand the federal army from a strength of sixteen thousand in the spring of 1861 to more than five hundred thousand a year later, civilian contractors were heavily relied on and their products were not rigidly inspected before being sent to the front. Some regiments were supplied with shoddy clothing and equipment that did not hold up to the demands of camp and battlefield.[46]

On May 21, 1861, a story appeared in the *Philadelphia Inquirer* alleging that Frowenfeld and Bros. and Morganstern and Bros. of Pittsburgh had defrauded the state by knowingly supplying Pennsylvania regiments with clothing of such poor quality that the soldiers actually suffered. Subsequently, the Committee of Public Safety in Pittsburgh sought to have the owners of the two firms indicted. Though ultimately never tried, the local press publicized the case through the summer and fall of 1861. The significance was not the case's outcome but the arguments presented in the proceedings. The county judge directed the grand jury to regard the alleged fraud by the Frowenfelds and Morgansterns as providing aid and comfort to the enemy. The public temper in the city seemingly had by that point become so heated that a simple case of unscrupulous business practices was construed as treason. The attorney for the defense recognized this and petitioned to have the case removed to the Pennsylvania supreme court, arguing that the defendants could never receive a fair trial there due to the community's bias(es).[47]

The Committee of Public Safety continued to guard Pittsburgh against potential treason through the summer of 1861, but, by September, things changed. The Union defeat at the Battle of Manassas in late July made it apparent to the people of the North that the war would not be the quick affair they had anticipated. In May, Lincoln had called for forty-two thousand more volunteers, this time for three years of service, and Pittsburgh, like other communities across the North, intensified its efforts to recruit and equip troops. As Pittsburghers focused their attention on recruitment, anxiety about subversion waned. On September 16, the Committee of Public Safety suspended activities.[48]

The mobilization of Northern communities during the Civil War was deeply connected with that of military forces. The unpreparedness of the Union army at the beginning of the war left a void in every aspect of organization and support that invited the participation of civilians and private businesses. This was not a new phenomenon for the American home front. From the Revolutionary War to the war with Mexico, volunteer companies and regiments typically originated in a specific community and were accustomed to relying on that community at least as much as on the federal government for initial support. However, the Civil War demanded an expansion of this tradition of community mobilization to an extent never before experienced. The vast scale of the conflict, the proximity of the armies to the home front, the modernization of transportation and communication, and the ideology of the national cause all combined to draw local communities into the conflict more intensely than ever. This began in the first months of the war as communities reacted to rebellion and the army struggled to satisfy the communities' demands.[49]

After the fall of Fort Sumter, support for armed action became so pervasive in Pittsburgh that the dissenters either fell silent or announced their conversion. The mood of unity and militancy was apparent in the rush to volunteer for military service and in the resounding endorsement of the Republican Party in the local elections. Whether motivated by a determination to suppress treason or a fear of threats to their own liberties, the overwhelming majority of the people of Pittsburgh demanded a strong and immediate military response to the Rebels' challenge to the sovereignty of the Union.

The United States Army in 1861 was unprepared to provide such a response. Its sixteen thousand officers and enlisted men were mostly scattered across the Western frontier in small garrisons. In the wake of the attack on Fort Sumter and Lincoln's subsequent call for volunteers, many soldiers deserted or resigned their commission and subsequently entered Confederate service. Few of the officers who remained and who were fit to take the field had ever commanded anything larger than a regiment. Moreover, inept management and a lack of cooperation between senior civilians and the military plagued the War Department.[50]

This is not to say that the federal government was negligent or that Northern communities only reluctantly assumed a central role in mobilizing military forces. The United States Army was organized and deployed to deal with the threat that most preoccupied the country at the time: Native American resistance on the Western frontier. Military leaders did not anticipate conventional warfare against a modern army. Once the Civil War began, most Northerners in and out of the army believed the war would be a short affair and even those who foresaw a long struggle did not place their chief reliance on the regular army to wage it. Americans had always tended to put their faith in the citizen-soldier, who, at least in the popular narrative of military history, had acquitted himself well in past wars. Therefore, when the call to raise an army went forth in 1861, the people of Pittsburgh turned to the organization that best exemplified that tradition: the militia.

In the spring of 1861, there existed ten militia companies in Pittsburgh and Allegheny city. Several had organized in the wake of the exciting visit of Colonel Ellsworth and his Chicago Zouaves in 1860; others had existed for decades. The Jackson Independent Blues, the Duquesne Greys, and the Washington Infantry traced their history back to the Mexican War or even the War of 1812. Several companies boasted veterans of the former war whose service under General Zachary Taylor was celebrated in local street names such as Palo Alto, Resaca, Buena Vista, and Monterey.[51]

The state of martial readiness among nineteenth-century militia companies varied greatly, not only across the country but within communities as well. Some companies took their role as the defenders of the home front seriously, drilling regularly and earnestly and maintaining their discipline and tactical proficiency. Others took a more relaxed approach, turning their musters into social events that focused more on camaraderie and revelry than military training.

Whatever their weaknesses, the local militia companies played a central role in the mobilization of volunteers. These quasi-military organizations were significant not so much for providing trained and disciplined fighting units but rather for providing a mechanism by which Northern citizens could indulge their fervent desire to actively participate in the defense of the Union. Local militia companies were deeply enmeshed in the fabric of the community. They served as living symbols in public ceremonies that connected Pittsburghers to their cherished national heritage, they showcased the virtues associated with manliness in nineteenth-century American culture, and, when the call for volunteers came after the attack on Sumter, they offered a place for young men who longed to step forward from the cheering crowds and into the parading ranks.[52]

With no federal recruiting system in place, the ten militia companies in Pittsburgh and the surrounding area served as the nucleus of the more than forty companies that would comprise the city's initial ninety-day volunteers. They began recruiting immediately in response to the president's call and their ranks quickly swelled. The Washington Infantry grew to 232, enough to divide into three companies that would be mustered in as A, D, and F of the 13th Pennsylvania Volunteer Infantry Regiment. Some companies did not even wait to be organized into regiments before departing for the front. On April 17, an advance party from the predominantly German-born Turner Rifles, under Captain Henry Amlung, left for Harrisburg to tender its services. Less celebrated militia organizations also moved swiftly to join the war. The Hannibal Guards, a company of Pittsburgh blacks, likewise offered itself to Governor Andrew Curtin just two days after the president's call. However, this unit was turned away and their volunteerism not reported by local papers. In the first months of mobilization, an estimated eighty-five hundred black men organized several military organizations in cities across the North. The War Department or local authorities rejected all.[53]

The exodus of citizen-soldiers, the public advertisements for recruiting, and the daily demonstrations by militia companies were infectious. Many young men who had not been moved enough by the attack on Sumter to volunteer soon found themselves unable to resist the allure of mobilization. In April 1861, John Donaghy had just started into business for himself in a small art studio on Fifth Avenue and was planning a summer sketching trip in the Allegheny Mountains with some fellow artists. Joining the war was far from his mind. However, as the excitement and activity in the city increased, he found himself unable to focus on his work. "The martial music on the street would draw me out to look at the enthusiastic volunteers who were marching about," he recalled. "Work lost its charm for me, and though the prospect for business was good . . . the patriotic war fever proved stronger than all else, and I resolved to enlist."[54]

Pittsburghers responded to the growing military spirit in other ways than taking up arms and joining the ranks. On April 22, a group of eighty-four women signed a letter, addressed to the Committee of Public Safety, in which they offered their services in support of the soldiers going forward from Pittsburgh. "We are willing to go where and when called upon," they wrote. "Our neighbors, relatives and friends are in the ranks, and we are anxious to be useful as far as we can to serve the cause of our country and humanity." At Lafayette Hall, on the corner of Wood and Fourth Streets, these women and many more gathered daily to help equip the new volunteers, making bandages, shirts, socks, and other articles.[55]

On several occasions, these women demonstrated their support by making the flags that the companies would carry into battle. Some flags were presented in public ceremonies designed to further encourage the active participation of civilians in the war effort. On April 23, Captain John S. Kennedy, commander of the Duquesne Greys, stood on the same balcony of the Monongahela House from which President-Elect Abraham Lincoln had addressed the people back in February. A group of women had made a flag for the Greys and the Committee of Public Safety had decided to oversee its presentation. A. W. Loomis of the committee stood by Kennedy on the balcony and addressed the crowd gathered on Smithfield Street. The women of the city, he said, had made a worthy symbol, around which the company would bravely rally. Linking the efforts of the home front with those of the soldiers, Loomis proclaimed that through the flag "woman's heart and woman's influence will be there. The American female never was, and this testimonial assures you that she is not now, indifferent to the calls of patriotism."[56]

The community needed to provide more than flags, however. Even the well-established militia companies were short of equipment and there was concern for the families that the volunteers left behind. Newspapers published calls from community leaders for cash donations to help the soldiers and their families. To channel these funds, the Committee of Public Safety created a subcommittee of relief, comprising two collectors for each ward, that solicited contributions from businesses and individuals. Newspapers periodically published the totals collected and the names of donors. At times, the committee issued direct requests, such as a call on the local banks requesting twenty-five thousand dollars to arm the city's volunteers and help defend the home front. In addition to the funds secured by the ward collectors, money was donated directly to the military units. One such contribution was from S. M. Lane, who had moved from nearby Butler County to Pittsburgh shortly before the war; he authorized John Purviance, commander of the Butler County Blues, to draw on him for a hundred dollars to arm and equip his men.[57]

Through the winter and spring of 1860–61, Pittsburgh evolved into a bastion of support for the war effort. This did not happen solely in response to the Confederate attack on Fort Sumter nor did it represent any widespread desire to end slavery. Rather, this mass movement stemmed from a pervasive belief in the sanctity of the Union and a firm local identity shaped by a combination of regional distinctiveness and national issues. The strong base of Republican support and the manufacturing character of the community served as accelerants for the conflagration sparked by the gun removal crisis. Secession was already ill-received by the city, but, when this episode threatened to hijack the products of Pittsburgh's laborers, the result was a powerful and growing determination to quash treason endorsed by every social class in the city.

The initial mobilization of the community was neither a purely bottom-up nor a purely top-down movement. While many Pittsburghers required no more inspiration to support the war than that provided by the treasonous acts of secessionists, others were swept up in the rituals of militarism or the rhetoric of local and national loyalty. In calling for mobilization, community leaders drew on familiar symbols, actors, and objects of veneration as they responded to, and channeled, the people's energy. While turning points such as the gun removal crisis, the attack on Fort Sumter, and Lincoln's call for troops were important in galvanizing the community in support of war, so too was the continuing campaign of public ceremony employed by the advocates of mobilization. In a matter of months, Pittsburghers of every sort came together, eager to preserve the Union and destroy treason. Over the next four years, thousands of them would help do just that in myriad ways.

By April 24, 1861, only nine days after the president's call for volunteers— and largely due to the efforts of the community—the majority of the soldiers from Pittsburgh and the surrounding area were organized into the 12th and 13th Pennsylvania Volunteer Infantry Regiments and made their way to the front. On that day, the last elements of the two regiments were set to leave the city. Early that morning, the soldiers mustered on the East Common in Allegheny. Brigadier General John S. Negley, commander of all Allegheny County military forces, had planned a grand review to mark the occasion. However, as the soldiers formed on the field, the sun disappeared behind dark clouds and a heavy shower commenced, subduing the joyous mood and compelling Negley to call off the ceremony.[58]

It seemed a bad omen, but, once the drenched soldiers made their way down the muddy streets to the Pennsylvania Railroad depot, they again were sustained by the labors of the people. An abundance of food was laid out on long tables in Kier's Warehouse adjacent to the depot and, in the thirty-three cars waiting to receive the soldiers, a full day's ration and a tin of coffee were placed on every seat. As the trains pulled away from the station, the soldiers and the people of Pittsburgh cheered one another for their shared commitment to the momentous task that lay ahead.[59]

3

★ ★ ★ ★ ★

EVERY PROMINENT POINT WILL BRISTLE WITH CANNON AND BAYONETS

Soldiers and Soldiering in the City

Beat! Beat! Drums!—Blow! Bugles! Blow!
Over the traffic of cities—over the rumble of wheels in the streets;
Are beds prepared for sleepers at night in the houses?
No sleepers must sleep in those beds,
No bargainers' bargains by day—no brokers or speculators—
would they continue?

-WALT WHITMAN-
"Beat! Beat! Drums!" in *Drum-Taps* (1865)

hen the first regiments from Pittsburgh departed, they left in their wake no fewer than forty companies of volunteers that could not be mustered into federal service. The initial wave of enthusiasm for the war effort was so great that the Pittsburgh area far exceeded its quota and was now faced with an abundance of volunteers with no army in which to serve. This unforeseen consequence of such effective mobilization created a problem for community leaders. Expecting a brief war, the War Department decided within weeks of Lincoln's first call for volunteers that it possessed all the men necessary. Secretary of War Simon Cameron implored governors not to send additional regiments to Washington. In Pittsburgh, however, community leaders were reluctant to dismiss companies already organized. For one thing, they were fairly certain that more regiments would soon be needed and, should another call come, their city must not be outdone in the timeliness of its response. Furthermore, they were apprehensive about the effect of turning away volunteers on the morale of the community. If community leaders now marginalized the sacrifices of the volunteer, how could they later call on the people to take up arms?[1]

The dilemma facing community leaders was how to keep these companies mobilized when the War Department had no need for them at the front. Their solution established a camp in Pittsburgh that would hold the companies as a reserve force. Mayor Wilson and the newly-minted Committee on Quartering Troops and Furnishing Provisions petitioned Governor Andrew Curtin to authorize such a camp. This was essential, they argued, not only to retain the excess companies from Pittsburgh but to accommodate those from across western Pennsylvania still pouring into the city. Curtin replied that he lacked the authority to approve the camp or the reserve force but promised to bring the matter before the state legislature when it convened in a few days. Not willing to wait for word from Harrisburg, Pittsburghers took it upon themselves to establish the local fairground in the Ninth Ward between Penn Street and the Pennsylvania Railroad line as the assembly point for the unaccepted companies. Organizers quickly began to convert the site into a military camp, naming it Camp Wilkins after Judge William Wilkins, who had been so active in energizing the community during the secession crisis.[2]

The recent riots in Baltimore stoked the sense of urgency about preserving these excess companies. On April 18, four companies of Pennsylvania militia, the first troops to pass through Baltimore en route to defend Washington, were met by a crowd of secession sympathizers who hurled bricks at them, injuring several soldiers. The next day, a mob again impeded the movement of federal troops on their way to Washington. As the soldiers pressed on through an onslaught of insults, clubbings, stabbings, and gunfire, they suffered thirty-six wounded and four dead. Responding to these incidents, the Democratic *Post* declared that: "[Our] State government is too dilatory. The people are in advance of it. It is the imperative duty of Pennsylvania and every Northern State to send on all available troops, regardless of expense."[3]

Pittsburghers' insistence on moving forward with a camp was, however, motivated by more than just strategic concerns. On April 26, the *Gazette* carried a report from the *Philadelphia Bulletin* that the state government had appropriated funds to establish four camps for the purpose of consolidating troops for the defense of the state. Of the four locations designated—Harrisburg, York, Chambersburg, and Lancaster—none was west of the Alleghenies. Pittsburgh, like its unaccepted companies, was to be left behind in the undeclared contest for community mobilization.[4]

On April 27, Governor Curtin authorized Pittsburghers to move forward with their plans for Camp Wilkins. The committee immediately instructed all the companies gathered around Pittsburgh to rendezvous at the fairground. However, that same day, Governor Curtin ordered the admittance of only companies arriving from outside Allegheny County to the new camp. The cost of supporting those from Pittsburgh and the county, he declared, was unwarranted since the federal government already had more troops than it had requested. Mayor Wilson then hastened to Harrisburg with local manufacturer and chairman of the committee on troops and provisions Samuel McKelvy to convince the governor to rescind this order.[5]

The honor of these "unaccepted companies," as they came to be known, was at stake. They already felt insulted by being left behind while the rest of the local volunteers went off to preserve the Union. Now, they were to be denied even the most basic martial identity offered by encampment: the ability to live and function together as a unit and the opportunity to be celebrated for their patriotism as were the units gone to the front. These Pittsburghers had volunteered for what they saw as the most extraordinary event of their lives, and—not foreseeing the ample opportunity they would have to serve in the years ahead—wanted to enjoy at least a modicum of the glory they had signed up for. For the citizens of Pittsburgh, Camp Wilkins was not just a military installation but a symbol of the city's support of the war effort. Wilson and McKelvy had the task of persuading the governor that sustaining the morale of the people outweighed concerns about exceeding military necessities.

On April 28, Mayor Wilson wrote from Harrisburg to advise the various war committees in Pittsburgh that Governor Curtin had dispatched an officer to assume command of Camp Wilkins. The final say on who would occupy the camp was left to him. No companies, instructed Wilson, should be admitted until after his arrival. The following day, Colonel Phaon Jarrett arrived and immediately inspected the fairground. His assessment severely disappointed Pittsburghers. Jarrett, a West Point graduate, had just been appointed colonel of the 11th Pennsylvania Volunteer Infantry and, eager to accomplish the task that distracted him from his command, he was all business. With dozens of companies anxiously awaiting what they believed their last chance to serve, Jarrett announced his conclusion that the site could hold no more than six companies; that quickly, the promise of Camp Wilkins as the center of wartime Pittsburgh ended.[6]

On May 1, Colonel Jarrett selected the six companies—the Iron City Guards, Chartiers Valley Guards, Pittsburgh Rifles, Duncan Guard, Garibaldi

Guard, and Anderson Guards—and they went into camp, leaving more than forty companies from Pittsburgh and the surrounding area again without a place in the army. The camp that was intended to unite the volunteers and the people of Pittsburgh now became a source of divisiveness. The *Post* expressed concern that many of the unaccepted companies would now disband and implored them to hold out, assuring them that their service would yet be needed.[7]

The captains of these companies met daily over the next three weeks to determine a way by which they could still serve. At the first meeting, in the Common Council chamber, twenty-eight captains briefly debated disbanding then adopted resolutions that were merely symbolic. The represented companies were organized into regiments; that accomplished, the regimental officers would "submit plans for future actions." The next day the captains met again and designated three representatives to appeal to the Committee of Public Safety for aid in sustaining their units. If there was no place for them at the front or in camp as reserves, perhaps there was a need for the two independent regiments to protect the city. The captains proposed that the committee establish a new camp for them and provide equipment and food. The problem for many of the captains was that, in the initial wave of excitement at the onset of the war, they had organized and sustained their companies at their own expense. Though the Committee of Public Safety did ultimately get permission for four more companies to be admitted to Camp Wilkins, nothing more was done for the rest. The meetings of the captains of the "unaccepted companies" devolved into mere venues for venting frustrations. They held their final meeting on May 22. Many of them subsequently took their men to western Virginia or New York where their service was accepted. Others were soon vindicated by the president's call for forty-two thousand, three-year volunteers and entered the army through new Pennsylvania regiments.[8]

At its second meeting, the Committee of Public Safety created an alternative for men wanting to help defend the Union. P. C. Shannon proposed a resolution that every ward in Pittsburgh, as well as the surrounding boroughs and townships, organize a company of citizens for local defense. These "Home Guard" units would greatly differ from the volunteer regiments heading to the front. They would remain completely voluntary and not subject to any military regulations or to "any other authority than that of the Committee of Public Safety." Immediately following the publication of Shannon's proposal, citizens in every neighborhood held meetings to organize. Enthusiasm was exceptional. Within three weeks, sixty-five companies formed with an initial enrollment of 3,077 men.[9]

Home-front defense, however, was not the only inspiration behind the formation of the Home Guards. While there were some in Pittsburgh who saw their city as a likely target of Rebel invasion—a concern that not only spurred volunteering in the Home Guards but also enhanced the prestige of serving in the organization—the structure of the Home Guards rendered it ill-prepared to deal with such a threat. Organized into an excessive number of companies that lacked uniformity, it was far better suited to inspiring the citizenry than battling invaders. Many companies reflected their close ties to their neighborhoods through the names they chose. One hundred men from the Fifth Ward formed companies A and B of the Fifth Ward Guards. Others chose names as colorful as those of their federal counterparts, such as the Union Rifles and the Ellsworth Guards. Some companies were rooted not in a particular neighborhood but in the business that employed them. Thirty workers from the Allegheny Arsenal organized the Arsenal Rifles while another thirty-six from the Fort Pitt Foundry came together as the Fort Pitt Artillery. And like the soldiers who filled the ranks, the officers who led the Home Guards were far better suited to promoting support for the war than actually fighting said war.[10]

The most elite advocates of mobilization in Pittsburgh assumed roles as the senior "officers" of the Home Guards. "Major General" William Wilkins, at seventy-nine years of age, was named overall commander. In July 1861, he appeared before a review of the Home Guards in full-dress military uniform astride his horse. Mansfield Brown, a wealthy farmer from the nearby village of Upper St. Clair, served as one of his three aides. William Bagaley, head of one of the city's wholesale grocery firms and a member of the Allegheny Bank board of directors, became "commissary general." "Inspector general" Thomas M. Howe was arguably the most prominent and influential of Pittsburgh's citizens. A descendant of John Howe, who had settled in Massachusetts in 1638, Thomas Howe moved in 1829 to Pittsburgh, where he found employment as a clerk in a dry-goods wholesale firm. He soon worked his way up in the burgeoning manufacturing industries and political organizations of the city. By 1861, the extensive list of financial, manufacturing, political, religious, and benevolent boards and societies of which Howe held membership revealed that there was hardly any aspect of the community he was not involved in. William F. Johnston, former governor, prominent attorney, and chair of the Committee of Public Safety's executive subcommittee, was appointed a "brigadier general" in command of the Home Guard's First Brigade.[11]

Though these men had no military qualifications to lead the Home Guards, their positions were anything but ceremonial. As with the recruitment of volunteer regiments, the organization of the Home Guards demonstrated that civilian initiative was at the center of mobilization for the war effort. During the summer of 1861, John Harper was named chairman of the Committee of Home Defense and charged with overseeing the formation of the Home Guards. Harper had emigrated in 1820 from County Donegal, Ireland and settled in Washington, D.C. In 1832, he worked as a clerk in the Bank of Pittsburgh; by the time the war began, he was the bank's president. Harper, like many of his peers, was a member of several commercial and benevolent associations and the city's citizens highly respected him. His oldest son, Albert, attended college at the Rensselaer Polytechnic Institute of Troy, New York in 1861. In September 1862, Albert left school to enlist in the 139th Pennsylvania Volunteer Infantry, in which he served for the remainder of the war. John and Albert corresponded with each other almost daily and their letters provide a remarkable perspective on the war on the Pittsburgh home front.[12]

William Wilkins assisted John Harper's military preparations in Pittsburgh. On July 26, Wilkins wrote to Major Symington, still the only federal military official in the city, to clarify who was in charge: "Sir, you will deliver to the Hon. William F. Johnston and John Harper, Esquire, ten thousand ball and buckshot cartridges for smoothbore muskets and change the order of the Hon. Secretary of War in favor of the Committee of Home Defence [sic]." To make certain that Symington understood who was in charge, Harper added a postscript giving detailed instructions on where to have the order delivered. Over the coming weeks, Harper managed the disbursement of the munitions and arms acquired from the arsenal and through his committee's funds; the weapons were issued to company commanders on bond. Shortly after its formation, the committee reported that 2,088 smoothbores and 882 rifles had been turned over to the Home Guards. John Harper remained deeply engaged in the city's military defense throughout the war. While retaining his position as president of the Bank of Pittsburgh, he frequently spent up to four hours a day in his committee office attending to the management of the Home Guards, coordinating with businesses and municipal authorities, and mobilizing reserve units to defend other parts of the state.[13]

Like their neighbors who volunteered for the army, the men of Pittsburgh who formed the Home Guards struggled early on to achieve competence to match their enthusiasm. The Home Guards immediately became a highly visible symbol of the war on the home front, but its martial prowess, in the public's view, was mediocre at best. The various companies drilled clumsily in an assortment of cheap uniforms, or in civilian clothes, and became the object of ridicule among the people, who derided them as "stay-at-home soldiers." It would take time before the Home Guards came to mean something more to the people of Pittsburgh.[14]

The exigencies of war had a way of transforming, over time, the focus and practices of soldiers and civilians alike. At the battlefront, egalitarian aspects of nineteenth-century American culture that impeded military discipline gradually gave way as enlistees learned the importance of strict obedience. On the Pittsburgh home front, more meaningful efforts to sustain the army and defend the city replaced martial pageantry and posturing. On September 16, 1862, as Robert E. Lee's Army of Northern Virginia threatened to invade Pennsylvania, John Harper wrote:

> We are all excitement here. The city looks like a camp, business being almost suspended. Companies are going off to Harrisburg by every train at the call of the Governor. Allegheny County is preparing for war if it should come upon us. Home Guards have ceased to be a mockery. A company is nearly formed of the clerks of banks who will go to any part of the state if needed. . . . We are constantly hearing startling rumors, sometimes favorable, sometimes otherwise. War is a dreadful business, probably as terrible in its shadow in the distance, as in the brightness of its fields of operation. The life of a soldier is action; the experience of his friends at home is silent anxiety.

By the summer of 1862, business in Pittsburgh was suspended three afternoons each week to allow the Home Guards to drill. P. C. Shannon, in his initial proposal for the organization, had predicted that it would serve as "the nucleus for future recruits for the public service of the country." This proved true. As more companies of volunteers went forward from the city, their ranks were in many cases filled from the membership of the Home Guards. Thus, the new volunteer regiments had the benefit of incorporating some recruits at least moderately familiar with military maneuvers and conditioned to some degree to respect order and discipline. Moreover, many of the company and regimental officers who came from Pittsburgh had first served with the Home Guards.[15]

However, the Home Guards also contributed to the war in less tangible ways. It offered a chance, for men who were unwilling or unable to enlist, to participate in the war in a manner that—while lacking the glory and romance of marching off to meet the enemy—still satisfied and showcased their patriotic yearnings. In addition to their usual drills and parades, Home Guard companies routinely lined the streets and assembled at gravesites to honor local fallen soldiers. This body of men in Pittsburgh was hardly necessary to keep the war in the consciousness of the people, for there was scarcely a man, woman, or child who did not know someone serving in the war; yet its continuous presence served to remind the people that there was more to do than wait for news from the front. The people of Pittsburgh were not merely an audience to the war, but active participants whose actions—or lack thereof—had a direct influence on the welfare of their soldiers and the fate of the nation.[16]

The Home Guards provoked a combination of envy and contempt among the soldiers of the reserve companies in Camp Wilkins, who often observed the guardsmen through the camp fence as they paraded up and down Penn Avenue. On the morning of June 17, 1861, Josiah Chambers, a volunteer from nearby Erie County in the Jefferson Light Guards, watched as four companies from the Fifth Ward marched past. Chambers was frustrated with his situation. Like all his comrades, he had enlisted with the hope of facing the Rebels. Now, after more than a month in camp, he was growing restless. Colonel Jarrett, attempting to establish order and discipline, had issued a series of orders on May 3 instituting in Camp Wilkins the same regimented schedule observed in camps at the front. Between the hours of drill and the various work details required each day, little leisure time was left for the soldiers. On May 10, Plymton A. White complained that "we are only allowed to leave the camp once a week and that only for the space of two hours." Their lack of uniforms and arms compounded the soldiers' frustration. Though willing enough to sacrifice their freedom in order to meet the enemy on the field of battle, the men balked at confinement to camp drilling with sticks in civilian clothing. The guardsmen who passed Camp Wilkins that June morning were already much better equipped than the reserve volunteers and the sight of them with their new uniforms and weapons infuriated Josiah Chambers and his comrades.[17]

That day, the citizens of the Fifth Ward presented a flag to Captain Francis Felix and his predominantly German Company B. Three other Home Guards companies joined Felix's for the ceremony and a subsequent picnic set to take place in Iron City Park, a short distance from Camp Wilkins. Around twelve o'clock, the soldiers in Camp Wilkins were released for the afternoon and fanned out to explore the city. Luther Furst and Al Akey had been friends at Jefferson College, just south of Pittsburgh, when the war began and, together, they had joined the Jefferson Light Guards. The pair enjoyed seeing the sights of Pittsburgh whenever they could get away from camp and on this occasion visited one of their favorite spots, the nearby Allegheny Arsenal. As they walked back to camp, they passed the park where the guardsmen were enjoying their picnic. A number of volunteers, mostly men of the Jefferson Light Guards, had already intruded on the festivities and partaken of the Home Guards' beer, among them Josiah Chambers. Soon, some of the volunteers moved through the crowd of guardsmen, insulting their hosts. Envious of the muskets of these "stay-at-home soldiers," Chambers tried to steal some. When a German officer attempted to stop him, Chambers drew a pistol. Furst and Akey ran back to Camp Wilkins for help. By the time their officers arrived with a squad, the disruptive volunteers had already been escorted to the park gate and the trouble seemed to have been defused. The soldiers, admonished by their officers, returned to camp, where they began to share the story of their little clash.[18]

Later in the afternoon, their picnic at an end, the guardsmen began their march home. As the column neared Camp Wilkins, dozens of volunteers massed along the fence line near the gate, jeering at the Home Guards. By the time the fourth company began to pass, the insults had turned to ethnic slurs. Several of the volunteers moved out into the street, following the guardsmen and threatening them with stones. The situation quickly deteriorated into a melee, the guardsmen breaking ranks under a hail of stones. Some loaded their weapons with pebbles and fired at the volunteers, who responded by throwing sticks, brickbats, and more stones. An unidentified volunteer approached guardsman George Eichenmiller, a baker and father of four. Eichenmiller fired his musket; the volunteer replied with a stone that struck Eichenmiller behind the ear. A few other guardsmen subdued the volunteer and carried the unconscious Eichenmiller from the fray. The sight of this casualty was enough to calm both sides, and the brawl quickly abated.[19]

Though the city reacted with outrage and the volunteers in Camp Wilkins prepared for an attack, no further violence occurred. But the following day, when Eichenmiller died of his wounds, the community demanded justice, particularly the German-Americans of the Fifth Ward. Local newspapers quickly criticized the volunteers. The *Gazette* reported that, when Captain Francis Felix of the Home Guards attempted to meet with the commandant following the incident, he was "treated in the shabbiest manner, and d——d out of camp." The *Gazette* continued, saying that "the outrage seems to have been altogether unprovoked. And if better order cannot be maintained at Camp Wilkins it should be broken up or placed in more competent hands."

Luther Furst recorded in his diary that Eichenmiller's death had made it unsafe for the volunteers to venture out of camp.[20]

The coroner held an inquest and concluded after two days of interviews that Eichenmiller had been killed by a stone thrown by an unknown person that hit his head. The coroner further opined that the violence resulted from "menacing" conduct of volunteers at Camp Wilkins and he charged five of them—a company commander and four privates—with inciting a riot. After a hearing before Mayor Wilson on June 20, the charges against the company commander were dropped and the four privates were ordered to post bail and await a hearing. However, the volunteers incurred no further punishment and, on July 1, they all marched out of Pittsburgh to join the war.[21]

Ethnic tension or conflicting views over the war or national politics did not cause the Camp Wilkins riot. The companies of Home Guards that were targeted by the volunteers in Camp Wilkins were indeed almost all German. Home Guard companies organized around neighborhoods and reflected their class and ethnic composition. It is also true that accounts included accusations of ethnic slurs against the Home Guards. Ethnic distinctiveness was typically more evident for Germans than other immigrant groups in the mid-nineteenth century and these differences gave the volunteer soldiers a target to direct their ire. And, undoubtedly, some or many of those volunteers harbored nativist tendencies in which the riot provided an outlet for. However, a different impulse than nativism or xenophobia triggered the attack on these German Home Guards. It was not the diversity of these Home Guards or how they challenged the idea of what an American should be that agitated the volunteers but rather their apparent superiority of mobilization.

These volunteers had come to base their self-worth, their sense of manliness, in their contribution to the war effort. They had volunteered to defend their country against its greatest threat heretofore. They told their mothers and fathers, their wives, their friends, and their neighbors that they were signing up for war and basked in the admiration and concern they received in response, only to be turned away, and then corralled into a dirty camp to languish, it seemed, as others marched off to war. Now, these "stay-at-home" soldiers, who were better equipped and enjoyed greater recognition than they, had chastised a handful of these volunteers. The volunteers' egos, now so interconnected with the Union war effort, required honor.

Pittsburghers soon grew disenchanted with the idea of a military camp inside their city. The fracas of June 17 was not the only source of friction between the people and the soldiers of Camp Wilkins. Luther Furst admitted that the volunteers "make free use of all the milk cows, ducks, chickens, etc.

that come into camp; and whatever of onions, lettuce and other vegetables they may meet with in their stroll through the neighborhood." And too, he noted, the volunteers' disregard for the Sabbath troubled the people of Pittsburgh. Throughout the war, citizen committees and newspapers waged a campaign against beer halls and other establishments that violated city ordinances by selling alcohol on Sunday. Though soldiers were rarely implicated in this type of blatant offense, any sign of irreverence toward the Sabbath deeply offended some Pittsburghers.[22]

The condition of the camp itself also helped cut short its existence. As early as May, officials had recognized that it could accommodate too few soldiers to justify the cost of maintaining it. Plans therefore eventually established a new camp farther from the city. This initiative was made all the more urgent by an act of the Pennsylvania legislature authorizing the raising of a Reserve Volunteer Corps to consist of fifteen new regiments, far more than Camp Wilkins could hold. By June 11, all regiments mustered from the region were directed to assemble just east of the city at Hulton Station, the site of the new and larger Camp Wright. Over the next few months, Camp Wilkins fell into disuse and, by the end of 1861, it ceased to exist as a garrison for volunteer soldiers.[23]

The most important factor behind the camp's obsolescence, however, was not its insufficient size but the advent of the Home Guards. Community leaders had pressed for a camp in Pittsburgh not because of military necessity but to sustain the people's connection to the war. While Camp Wilkins never made much sense strategically or logistically, it did mark Pittsburgh as a community loyal to the Union and the war effort. Furthermore, the presence of volunteers in the city kept the war tangible to the people, a focal point to encourage and direct their patriotic impulses. A local woman exemplified this public spirit in May 1861 when, wanting to do something for the soldiers, she came to Camp Wilkins and gave Plympton White a mattress, towels, and extra blankets to improve his comfort. However, the increasing prominence of the Home Guards provided a military presence less demanding to sustain and more closely connected to the city. The benefits of Camp Wilkins for community mobilization thus ceased to outweigh its drawbacks and Pittsburghers turned to other means to connect with the war and their soldiers.[24]

The removal of a military camp from within the city did not mean an end to the complications of soldiers' presence. The geographic and economic distinctiveness that made Pittsburgh the principal crossroads between Eastern and Western markets transformed it, during the war, into the gateway city for soldiers between the Eastern and Western theaters. Positioned at the head of navigation on the Ohio River and the junction of several railroads, Pittsburghers saw more troops pass through than did any other people in the North. Regiments that mustered in the East or West for service in the opposite theater traveled through Pittsburgh on their initial journey to the front. When Northern soldiers were wounded severely enough to return home, placed on furlough, mustered out of service, or paroled by the enemy, a voyage home crossing from one region to the other almost always meant a stop in Pittsburgh. As the case in other Northern cities such as Washington and Philadelphia, a large military presence in Pittsburgh did not come without its complications.[25]

In the first year of the war, soldiers in Pittsburgh became entangled in one of the city's largest social issues: temperance. As the threat of war loomed in the winter of 1861, Pittsburghers became concerned by the growing number of unregulated drinking establishments in the city. In February, the Pittsburgh Temperance Society called on the ministers of local churches to "revive the Temperance Cause" to stop this trend. In March 1861, the Select and Common Council passed an ordinance requiring that the proprietor of any establishment selling alcohol or exhibiting live entertainment must obtain a license from the mayor. However, poor enforcement of this measure had now led to the creation of a new type of establishment named "concert saloons." On March 9, 1861, the *Gazette* featured an exposé on these establishments, describing them as a combination of a gambling saloon, drinking house, and brothel that constituted the greatest "social threat" facing the city. Three days after the article ran, Mayor Wilson ordered the arrest of the owners and performers of the three most notorious concert saloons, all clustered in the Fourth Ward near the corner of Fifth Avenue and Smithfield Street: the Continental, the Melodean, and the Red, White, and Blue.[26]

Throughout the summer, as volunteer soldiers massed in the city, the concert saloon problem burgeoned. Newspapers reported frequent brawls outside the Smithfield Street establishments, prompting increased demands for public officials to suppress them. Sentencing for the arrests back in March was announced on June 9. The owner of the Melodean, Philip Klein, was fined fifty dollars and sentenced to five days in jail. The owner of the Red, White, and Blue, Julius Weisert, was fined a hundred dollars and confined for ten days, his violations deemed more flagrant.[27]

In September, the problem gained more notoriety when the salon and dance house of Philip Beilstein ejected a large group of soldiers, who then proceeded to pelt the establishment's doors and windows with brickbats and stones. The

Gazette, focused on inspiring support for the war, virtually exonerated the soldiers of any wrongdoing. "As they are all volunteers they will no doubt be released," it remarked, directing the blame instead to the citizens and community leaders of the Fourth Ward "for tolerating such an establishment."[28]

Public disturbances by intoxicated soldiers continued to beset the city. On August 26, 1862, a large group of soldiers was arrested for "heavy fighting" in front of the National Hotel during a night of drinking. By February 1864, such incidents were so routine that William Ross received the standard "disorderly soldier" treatment of arrest, a hearing before the mayor, a ten dollar fine, and the publication of his name in the paper all within twenty-four hours of downing his first drink. Even when soldiers were not directly engaged in the conflicts, they were often the focus of them. On February 22, 1862, a fight broke out in the beer hall of C. Geib at the corner of Second and Middle Streets near the National Hotel; the dispute reportedly began over which soldiers made the better fighters, the Irish or the Germans.[29]

As the war progressed, disorderly soldiers incurred harsher punishment from civilian authorities. In February 1862, several soldiers traveling through Pittsburgh on furlough were arrested for assaulting a railroad conductor. On Friday evening, April 1, 1864, David Gardiner was arrested for drunken and disorderly conduct. As he was escorted to the mayor's office to be held for a hearing, he kicked and injured the arresting officer. When unable to pay his twenty-dollar fine, the mayor confined him for thirty days. William Maxwell was arrested in Pittsburgh in the spring of 1864 for murdering a streetcar conductor in Washington. He had spent thirty days in Pittsburgh on furlough after the murder and then deserted to Louisville. When he returned to Pittsburgh, he was apprehended.[30]

The large presence of soldiers in Pittsburgh also engendered a problem of desertions. In 1863, Irwin Redpath was tried for aiding and abetting desertion of soldiers. Later that year, a Dr. King and his son were arrested for "enticing a soldier to desert." Disturbances also arose from attempts by military authorities to apprehend deserters. On July 14, 1863, a number of German civilians attempted to free a deserter from the custody of Captain H. K. Tyler in Allegheny City. They threw stones, wounding Tyler, who finally dispersed the crowd by firing his pistol. Three perpetrators were later arrested for the incident. At times, deserting soldiers themselves became the source of violent disturbances in the community. On Friday night, September 4, 1863, Edward Haskins—a soldier who had recently deserted from the Army of the Potomac after being wounded at Gettysburg—was arrested for the highway robbery of two Pittsburghers near the rail depot on Liberty Street.[31]

The public disturbance involving soldiers that provoked the greatest reaction in Pittsburgh was John Cooley shooting Thomas Farley. The case gained notoriety not only because of soldier involvement but also because of raised questions about the authority and responsibility of local government to regulate the conduct of soldiers in the city. Farley, discharged following three years of service, enlisted again as a substitute for a draftee. On December 10, 1864, he lodged at the provost marshal's office in the Girard House, as was the standard practice. That evening, he requested of one of his guards that he be allowed to walk around the city once more before heading back to the front. The sergeant of the guard, John Cooley, decided to escort Farley after receiving permission from his commanding officer, a Lieutenant Graham, to grant a half-hour pass. Accounts vary about what led to the ensuing tragedy. What is certain is that, sometime around nine in the evening, the pair's stroll ended on St. Clair Street in front of Elliot's Shirt Store with an altercation that resulted in the death of Farley, the end of Cooley's military service, and diminished public confidence in the military's ability to manage the conduct of soldiers in Pittsburgh.[32]

After the shooting, witnesses carried Farley into the shirt store and sent for a physician. A Dr. Gallagher arrived soon after, examined Farley, and pronounced the wound mortal. Farley was then taken to the Girard House and, at noon the next day, was brought to the General Military Hospital in the Ninth Ward. Three hours later, he died of his wound. Meanwhile, Alderman James Donaldson had been summoned to the scene of the crime. Technically in the army, having been drafted the previous summer, but continuing to hold his public office, Donaldson arrived in his officer's uniform to enforce his civilian authority. Summoning a police officer nearby, he took Cooley into custody.[33]

A jury began hearing the case on the thirteenth. The witness testimonies were contradictory. According to Cooley, as the time for their return drew near, Farley started to show signs of wanting to desert. He offered Cooley twenty dollars to take him across the river to Allegheny. Cooley refused, leading Farley to resist him and knock him to the ground twice. It was only then, said Cooley, that he shot Farley. Nearly all the bystanders claimed that Cooley was intoxicated. Several stated that the shooting was "willful, malicious, and unnecessary." William C. Elliot testified that he was returning home from a walk with his wife and a friend of hers, when their party observed the pair of soldiers walking arm-in-arm, swaying, and "talking to themselves as drunk men do." When his wife made a remark about their disruptive conduct, Elliot told her that "they were soldiers and had the right to get drunk." Samuel

Siegfried testified that he was passing the Red Lion Inn on St. Clair when he saw the two soldiers on the opposite side of the street. He stated that one soldier was urging the other along until they came in front of Elliot's store. Siegfried commented to the bartender of the Red Lion that the two soldiers were "on a drunk." A Mr. Gaffney observed Cooley dragging Farley by the collar. Cooley finally got him to his feet and made him walk ahead for a short distance before the scuffle began. Gaffney also claimed that the two soldiers were obviously intoxicated. Alderman Donaldson testified that Cooley hesitated to relinquish his pistol and that he was "very much excited and considerably under the influence of liquor."[34]

Lieutenant N. G. Cushing, the post commandant, filed a petition for Cooley's release from civil custody so he could be tried by court martial. District Attorney R. B. Carnahan, representing Sergeant Cooley, argued that as both the accused and the victim were soldiers, under an 1863 act of Congress, the military had jurisdiction. Judge Wilson McCandless denied the motion, claiming that since the accused was first arrested by state authorities, the court retained jurisdiction and Cooley must remain in the sheriff's custody.[35]

As the case dragged on, public sentiment against Cooley continued to grow. This soldier became the symbol of all that some Pittsburghers loathed about the military presence in their city: his drunkenness demonstrated immorality, his unruly conduct offended the sensibilities of respectable citizens, and his rough handling of Farley exacerbated resistance to military occupation. In defiance of those aligned against Cooley, the soldiers of his company organized a public display of support for him. On February 27, Lieutenant Graham assembled his soldiers to present R. B. Carnahan with a gold-headed cane in recognition of his patriotic service in defense of their comrade.[36]

On December 27, 1865, after more than a year of delays and legal maneuverings, the Allegheny County Court of Oyer and Terminer finally resolved the case against Cooley, ordering that he be released and the charges dismissed. By then, however, interest in the case had waned as the war moved into memory.[37]

The Cooley homicide case demonstrates the complexities of the military presence in Northern cities. While many Pittsburghers valued this presence as an outlet for their support of the war effort, the misconduct of soldiers often belied their status as heroes. Support for the soldiers fighting for the causes of Union, and later emancipation, could at times be more complicated than support for those causes themselves. As a result, Pittsburghers became largely opposed to any standing force of Union soldiers occupying the city, preferring instead to leave that role to the Home Guards and militia—a sentiment already manifested half a year before Cooley's arrest, when the city mounted a stout defense without the aid of federal soldiers.

As early as April 24, 1861, the *Post* had predicted that Pittsburgh would become a target of the Rebel army because of its importance for the Northern war effort. As a connecting point between East and West and as a "manufacturing city," the article claimed, Pittsburgh would be essential for Union military supply. "In every point of view it is important that our city should be prepared to defend itself." Furthermore, warned the *Post*, "In defending our city we must to a great extent act for ourselves and make our preparations."[38]

Through the first two years of the war, the threat of a Confederate attack preyed on the minds of Pittsburghers. On September 8, 1862, the *Gazette* reprinted an article from the *New York Times* that speculated about a Rebel strategy of "severing the Western from the Eastern States, by the occupation of the Ohio and Pennsylvania frontier." According to the *Times*, this was a "favorite idea with leading Southern papers. . . . The Alleghenies would furnish a safe basis of operations; the exuberant granaries of the two great States would feed the starved [Rebel] army." The article warned specifically about the catastrophe that would result if Pittsburgh fell to the enemy: the city, "with its shops and foundries would replenish their stock of cannon, arms and munitions, and send mailed iron boats and rams to recover the Ohio and Mississippi." The *Gazette's* editor added his own words of advice: "Let our citizens organize and drill."[39]

Lee's invasion of Maryland that fall exacerbated these fears, until his army was defeated at Antietam on September 17 and subsequently retreated into Virginia. On September 20, John Harper, chairman of the Committee for Home Defense, wrote to his son Albert in the Army of the Potomac, noting that Pittsburgh was now apparently safe from capture by Lee but that the threat of a destructive cavalry raid could not be dismissed. Harper was, however, confident in Pittsburghers' ability to repel such a raid. "Our people . . . are warlike. Three afternoons a week business is suspended for the people to drill." However, others were not so sanguine. The *Pennsylvania Daily Telegraph* reprinted a story from the Washington *Star* cautioning that despite the retreat from Maryland the Confederates were poised to strike the Ohio River Valley: "It is generally believed here that Jeff Davis is about to send fifty thousand of his best troops on a forced march over the mountains . . . and destroy the government arsenal and such, near Pittsburgh. . . . They also calculate on seizing sufficient steamers to transport an army of 50,000 whither they choose on the Ohio."[40]

By the first week of June 1863, fear of a Rebel attack on Pittsburgh had reached new heights. John Nevin wrote in his diary that "Western Pennsylvania is the most tempting and most vulnerable point . . . and the Monongahela a ready groove to slide down in. Look out Pittsburgh for your workshops!" Newspapers fanned the flames of anxiety by publishing travel accounts, real or fabricated, that professed to have inside information on Confederate strategy. On June 5 the *Gazette* carried an account of a Northern man just returned from Confederate territory who warned "that it had long been the intention of the rebels to destroy Pittsburgh" and "wished our citizens to be on their guard." One Pittsburgher claimed to have heard from a Confederate officer that the Rebels planned to destroy the Fort Pitt Foundry at the first opportunity.[41]

Whether such reports were accurate or not, the War Department did take the threat to Pittsburgh seriously. On June 10, Secretary of War Stanton established two new military departments, dividing the defense of Pennsylvania between them. The Department of the Susquehanna encompassed all of the state east of Johnstown and the Laurel Hill Mountains. The Department of the Monongahela, under the command of the newly promoted major general William T. H. Brooks, comprised the western half of Pennsylvania, as well as counties in southeastern Ohio and northwestern Virginia.

For the rest of the war, Pittsburghers came to view Brooks as the central authority for nearly all things related to the war. Family members pleaded with Brooks on behalf of their loved ones in uniform for such favors as transfers to the invalid corps or special staff assignments, but mainly Pittsburghers looked to Brooks to secure their city from secessionist threats. Brooks supervised the confinement of Rebel prisoners of war in a state penitentiary in Allegheny City, leading many to see him as the one responsible for dealing with those in the city found to be disloyal to the United States. Pittsburghers asked Brooks's department to arrest civilians for "disloyal statements" and hunt down "bands of deserters" hiding in the mountain ranges on the edge of the city. On April 18, 1865, G. P. Davis of the Pennsylvania Reserves in Pittsburgh reported to Brooks that he had rescued a P. Miller in South Pittsburgh from a noose-wielding lynch mob aiming to exact their own justice for his disloyal statements in the aftermath of Lincoln's assassination. Before all of this, however, Brooks began his involvement in protecting the city from rebellion in June 1863, when Pittsburghers were convinced that an attack by Lee was imminent.[42]

Prior to the establishment of the Department of the Monongahela, General Henry Halleck in Washington had sent some engineer officers to Pittsburgh to see to the city's defenses. On June 7, he dispatched Captain Cyrus B.

Comstock, a West Point graduate who had worked on the defenses around Washington. "The main objective of your mission," instructed Halleck, "is to assist the municipal authorities and the people in preparing for their own defense. They are capable, and, it is presumed, ready to defend their town against any efforts the rebels may make to capture or destroy it. You will assist and animate them in the performance of this patriotic duty." The next day Halleck sent Brigadier General John G. Barnard, chief engineer of the Department of Washington, to Pittsburgh to further ensure the city's readiness. Again, Halleck emphasized that the responsibility of defending Pittsburgh rested with the people and the municipal authorities.[43]

In his initial instructions to Brooks on June 10, Stanton expressed his belief that an attack on Pittsburgh was a real possibility: "Intelligence received this evening of the enemy's designs makes it certain that you cannot be too early or too busily at work, as Pittsburgh will certainly be the point aimed at by [Confederate cavalry commander J. E. B.] Stuart's raid, which may be daily expected." As would become clear in the succeeding days, this northward movement of Lee's cavalry was the precursor of a full-scale invasion of Pennsylvania by his army. That same day, Stanton wrote Thomas Howe in Pittsburgh, informing him that Brooks had departed Washington and was traveling to assume command there. "He is an able and resolute officer," wrote Stanton, "but will need all the assistance you and your people can give."[44]

Despite the urgency of the situation, however, Brooks met with resistance in his efforts to organize a military force of Pittsburgh citizens. It was not the people's unwillingness to take up arms but rather the people's uncertainty about the nature and duration of their service. In fact, Brooks reported that, within two days of arriving in the city, he had found a regiment of militia "nearly full, ready to turn out at a moment's call under my order, armed and partially uniformed." The men of Pittsburgh were more than eager to defend their city but were somewhat unnerved by the presence of a U.S. Army officer assuming command of their militia and other citizens under arms. To assuage such concerns, Governor Curtin issued a proclamation on June 12 assuring the men of Pennsylvania that their duties would be "mainly the defense of their own homes, firesides, and property from devastation." He went on to urge them to "respond to the call of the General Government, and promptly fill the ranks of these corps." Brooks added to this clarification in his General Order No. 2 of June 16, confirming that "under no circumstances" would the citizens volunteering to defend Pittsburgh "be transferred to any other department."[45]

Apprehension over the fate of Pittsburgh increased over the coming weeks.

On June 13, newspapers began alerting Pittsburghers of the threat: "The government is now fully aroused in reference to the importance of this city as a 'vital Union Point'; the enemy so look upon it, and we are assured that they are determined to sack our city." The War Department repeatedly warned of an imminent attack. General in Chief Halleck told Brooks on June 14 that "Lee's army is in motion toward the Shenandoah Valley. Pittsburgh and Wheeling should be put in defensible condition as rapidly as possible." Charles Knapp of the Fort Pitt Foundry, having traveled to Washington to meet with War Department officials, learned that Pittsburgh was "considered a most important strategical point." On June 15, Governor Curtin wrote Thomas Howe to warn him of three Rebel columns advancing north through Pennsylvania. "Make it public and arouse the people," said Curtin.[46]

Pittsburghers became consumed with the possibility of a Confederate attack. James McClelland wrote in his diary of the "great excitement on account of expected rebel invasion—works suspended and men set to digging intrenchments [sic]." John Harper noted on June 16 that "for three days past, our city has been the theater of intense excitement. From the telegrams, we were led to believe that a rebel raid was imminent." On that same day, Frances Bruce wrote that "Sunday night the Pittsburghers at last become alarmed and early Monday morning began to fortify the heights. . . . This afternoon we hear a large force is marching toward the Cumberland. . . . I truly think the rebels will come here if they can, perhaps by some back road that no one will think of." The next day, Thomas Howe announced "that a force of the enemy, at eleven o'clock this morning, had advanced twelve miles westward from Cumberland giving unmistakable indications of their purposes to invade this neighborhood." On June 18, the *Post* gave the most ominous warning yet: "If ever there was a time for the people of Western Pennsylvania to awaken in earnest, before the horrors of Civil War are thrust upon their homes and firesides, now is that time. Throw off all apathy—bring your ruined households and murdered families before your minds."[47]

Harper, chairman of the Committee for Home Defense, met frequently with municipal and business leaders, military officers, and workers to coordinate the defense of Pittsburgh. His letters described the citizens' enthusiastic mobilizing in defense of their city. "The ardor of the people is as hot as the weather, and will not come down. 'Pennsylvania must not be invaded' they say. If the rebels enter our mountains, they will find that they contain men that will defend them." On June 19, he reported that five thousand men worked at constructing fortifications on the heights around Pittsburgh. Every shop and factory in the city, he claimed, had closed its doors and sent

FIG. 3. John Harper, Cushing,
*History of Allegheny County
Pennsylvania*, 187.

employees to work on the rifle pits or to drill with the militia. The people of Pittsburgh "wait this great turning point of events with a firm reliance on the justness of our cause and its triumphant issue in the restoration of our glorious Union."[48]

On June 22, the newly established Committee on Fortifications met and resolved that "loyal and patriotic persons able to bear arms in defense of their homes and firesides, who have not already done so [should] form themselves into companies and elect their officers." These companies, instructed the committee, should be organized by neighborhood or by "professional, manufacturing, mining, commercial, agricultural, mechanical and other pursuits." In fact, Pittsburghers had by that time already begun to do so. Some 480 employees of Brown and Company (an iron and nail manufacturer) had enrolled, and 120 of the Soho Iron Works. Trade organizations such as the Draymen and Carters' Society and the "clerks from Market and 5th Street" mobilized to dig entrenchments and 116 citizens of the Liberty and Wood streets neighborhood signed up for the work. The Pittsburgh Coal Company kept a time book detailing the labor of employees on the

FIG. 4. "Reception committee for General Lee—citizens of all classes labor on entrenchments as Confederates threaten Pittsburgh and other Pennsylvania towns," in "'A Vigorous Defense': Pittsburgh's Forgotten Civil War Fortifications," Pennsylvania in the Civil War blog, accessed October 13, 2022, https://www.penncivilwar.com/post/a-vigorous-defense.

fortifications on Coal Hill in South Pittsburgh. The company paid $1.25 a day to workers who volunteered to help construct "Fort Mechanic." Boys who carried water to the workers were paid seventy-five cents. From June 15 to 22, the company employed 120 of its hands on the fort, paying out $699.20. Jones and Laughlin (iron merchants) requested guidance from the committee about fortifying the heights above their works and then funded construction using their employees as laborers. John Harper told his son that during a committee meeting one evening "a draymen came as a committee from his fellows to ask leave to name a fort built entirely by draymen 'Fort Draymen,' which was granted." The initial tally of the committee listed 9,289 civilian workers engaged in constructing defensive works on four hills surrounding Pittsburgh.[49]

The black community in Pittsburgh also rallied to ward off the threat of a Rebel invasion. While black volunteers had been dismissed two years prior, the government now accepted them into the new United States Colored Troops (USCT) regiments for service in combat. Those on the home front, therefore, did not hesitate to take action as the rest of the community prepared to defend their city. On June 18, black Pittsburghers held a large meeting at the A.M.E. Church on Wylie and Elm Streets to organize into militia companies for home defense. The organizers of the meeting recalled the treatment of blacks in Chambersburg at the hands of Confederate forces the previous October. The meeting was led by a handful of prominent black men from the community including George B. Vashon, principal of the black school, George W. Massey, and Rufus Jones, a wigmaker who would go on to enlist in the 8thth USCT the next month. On June 27, the *Gazette* called on all black men of Pittsburgh and Allegheny to gather in two days at the corner of Fifth and Grant streets. The committee to mobilize blacks was successful in procuring the task of erecting fortifications on Maguire Hill. Black businessmen were encouraged to close their shops. Hotels and other establishments employing large numbers of blacks were encouraged to release them for this task. Pastors of black churches were encouraged to promote this mobilization from their pulpits.[50]

The committee also endeavored to eliminate hindrances to mobilization, appointing a subcommittee on "closing stores" to maximize the available work force. The subcommittee specifically targeted the city's drinking establishments. It called on citizens to report the names of all such places that refused to close while the danger of invasion remained and threatened to keep a record of violators that the city authorities could use when considering future requests for liquor licenses. This apparently had some effect: a "Committee of Tavern Keepers" reported a force of 180 men ready to work, who were then assigned to the heights north of Allegheny City.[51]

Throughout June and into early July, until news came of the Union victory at Gettysburg and Lee's subsequent retreat to Virginia, the pace of work on the fortifications around Pittsburgh steadily increased. John Harper reported a week before the battle that as many as twelve thousand men were laboring on the city's defenses. Many other men took up arms in defense of their homes. Harper proudly told Albert that his younger brother had joined the militia: "Jack is in the ranks and makes, they say, a good soldier. He has only been two hours at home since he enlisted." The youngest brother, Charley, marched around the Harper home with two muskets and a cartridge box proclaiming that he would "defend the house if the rebels come." John Harper lauded the community's spirit in a letter on June 24:

> Our city is thus far safe, and presumably will continue to be so, as we are now pretty well prepared for defense. You would be surprised to see what has been done by our strong arm'd workmen. Thousands are every day on the trenches

and fortifications. . . . Think of the work that our whole population can do in a day, for nearly all the able bodied men are at work. It is a grand frolic. . . . Every prominent point will bristle with cannon and bayonets. . . . If the rebels visit us they will find that Pittsburgh has coal enough to warm its friends and iron enough to cool its enemies.[52]

Though the Rebels never arrived, the threat of invasion in the summer of 1863 enabled thousands of Pittsburghers to become active participants in the Union war effort. While they never put on a uniform, held rank, or witnessed combat, the experience of these ordinary citizens did not much differ from that of the thousands of soldiers who garrisoned Washington throughout the war. For one month in 1863, the war, and the pursuit of its objectives, was not the distant undertaking of the government or of neighbors and loved ones far away in uniform, but the lived experience of the people of Pittsburgh.

Joining the war effort and the community together remained a priority for Pittsburghers throughout the war. Through a variety of means and across diverse groups within the city, private citizens immersed themselves in the war effort and community leaders collaborated with government officials to make Pittsburgh instrumental to the war.

4

★ ★ ★ ★ ★

THE COUNTRY HAS A RIGHT TO THE SERVICES OF HER CITIZENS

The Draft, Emancipation, and Sustaining Local Volunteerism

> You have called us, and we're coming by Richmond's bloody tide,
> To lay us down for freedom's sake, our brothers' bones beside;
> Or from foul treason's savage grip, to wrench the murderous blade;
> And in the face of foreign foes its fragments to parade.
> Six hundred thousand loyal men and true have gone before,
> We are coming, Father Abra'am, three hundred thousand more!
>
> **–JAMES S. GIBBONS–**
> "We are Coming Father Abra'am" (1862)

By the summer of 1862, providing the army with the men needed to sustain the war effort had become a challenge for the Lincoln administration. In contrast to the excess of volunteers in the spring and summer of the year prior, men on the Northern home front now required considerable convincing to volunteer. This was as true for Pittsburgh as anywhere else in the North. The prospective recruit in Pittsburgh in 1862 faced a different situation from that of his neighbor who had rushed off to war a year earlier: he did not have the illusion of a short, romantic, and bloodless war to prevail over his fears. He had read the extensive casualty lists from the Seven Days, he had walked along the Monongahela waterfront watching the wounded be carried off steamboats from Shiloh, and he had attended church services where neighbors consoled the families of the local fallen. In short, he now knew for what he was volunteering.

On July 1, 1862, Lincoln issued a call for three hundred thousand additional volunteers to bolster the ranks of the army and navy. This call-up would be the first in a series that over the next thirty months would summon more than one and a half million men from across the North to fill the void left by the staggering casualties produced in one campaign after another. In Pittsburgh, this call for troops sparked a campaign by community leaders and newspaper editors to sustain volunteerism and the local pride that came with it.

Another challenge to that pride emerged in the second year of the war. That same month, Congress passed the Enrollment Act of 1862 that empowered the federal government to implement a draft on states who failed to meet their quota of volunteers. Pittsburghers quickly began to speculate that such a drastic measure would be necessary to acquire the troops needed to preserve the Union. "The subject of drafting has become one of considerable interest within a few days past, gaining currency that a draft from each state will be made to fill out thinned regiments in the field," warned the *Gazette*. In this first local printed mention of the possibility of a draft, the *Gazette* captured the revulsion of community leaders at the idea of conscription and implored the city's men to prevent it through their volunteering: "The country has a right to the services of her citizens, as none will dispute; and to avoid the disagreeable necessity of a forced exaction of such service, the thinned ranks of our shattered army should be filled at once by the voluntary tender of every man who can by any means leave home." Fears about a potential draft were confirmed on August 4, when Lincoln announced an additional call-up of three hundred thousand troops. This time, the president added a provision mandating that any deficiencies of quotas as of August 15 would be made up for by a draft conducted by the various states of all men enrolled under the militia law.[1]

Advertisements for recruitment employed various tactics to attract volunteers to fill the city's quota of troops. A common one in 1862 appealed to virtues such as "manliness" and "courage" in an attempt to shame those who failed to do their part in the war. Some advertisements attempted to strike a chord of ethnic pride among the large foreign-born population of the city. On September 24, Pittsburghers held a meeting to establish an Irish regiment from the city for service under Brigadier General Michael "Mick" Corcoran, who had recently returned from Confederate captivity and had become a celebrity among Irish-Americans in the North. The assembled citizens passed resolutions extolling the tradition of Irish-Americans' service to the nation dating back to the Revolution and lauding their commitment to preserving the Union: "The Irish population of this city are, like their fellow countrymen throughout the states, unalterably attached to the Constitution and

Government of the United States, and will at all times give all they possess, even their very lives, if necessary, in defense of the same."[2]

Many recruitment appeals portrayed volunteering for particular units as a great opportunity that should not be missed. Some units being formed enhanced their attractiveness by adopting the name of a prominent Pittsburgher. The J. K. Moorhead Infantry advertised in papers as a "crack company" and Pittsburghers were warned that the chance to serve with such a fine unit would soon pass, for its ranks were "sure to fill quickly." By this point in the war, the advantages of serving in the artillery as opposed to the infantry were well known to men on the home front; a position in that more appealing service thus became more difficult to secure. An advertisement in August announced that "[a] few more men will be accepted for Hampton's Light Battery," which was leaving for the front that same day. This was the "last chance for men wishing to go into the artillery, as no more will be accepted from Pennsylvania." That same day, an announcement appeared ordering members of the Keystone Infantry to meet on Smithfield Street for medical examination before their 8 p.m. departure for Harrisburg. However, those on the fence about volunteering still had a chance: the ad closed with the encouraging note that "ten or fifteen good men will be accepted to fill up the ranks."[3]

Efforts to promote enlistment met with another challenge in 1862. Speculation about the Lincoln administration's intent to emancipate those enslaved prompted outrage from the Democratic press in Pittsburgh over the supposed perversion of the war's objectives and the threat of those freed dominating the Northern labor market. Concerned about the effect such incendiary claims would have on recruitment, the Republican *Gazette* claimed that Lincoln "was not elected to preserve slavery, nor to abolish slavery; but he was elected to emancipate the administration and the republic itself from the domination of slavery interest." Democratic editorials, however, continued to incite racial tensions, warning white Pittsburghers that blacks would threaten their economic wellbeing. "This is a question which is seriously agitating the minds of the working class in our midst," said the *Post*. "The great influx of contrabands [i.e., persons freed from slavery] has only commenced, but loud are complaints against them. While the white laborer commands but poor requital for his toil, that of the negro comes in and in some instances takes his place." Making emancipation an aim of the Union war effort, the *Post* lectured its readers, was a dangerous development: "Our people have not reached fanaticism to such an extent as to believe that a darky is just as good as a white man, if not a little better. There can never be an equality of the races—like oil and water, they are incompatible."[4]

Throughout 1862, the newspapers of the Republican and Democratic parties engaged in a continual debate over emancipation and its meaning for the war. The *Post* based its opposition on two ideas: an appeal to white supremacy and the original goals of the war for which Northern society signed on. Emancipation, warned the *Post*, would threaten the economic prosperity of white Pittsburghers by unleashing on the city throngs of unskilled black laborers who would accept far lower wages undercutting and driving white workers from the labor market. Republicans, claimed the *Post*, were hypocrites for championing white labor in their campaign platforms and then risking it through the reckless pursuit of emancipation, all while opposing immigrant labor. The *Gazette* countered that free blacks would also become consumers and would therefore create more than enough demand for an increase in workers.[5]

The more prevalent theme in the Democratic challenges in Pittsburgh to emancipation was the distortion of the intended, or at least professed, aim of the Union war effort. Emancipation, they argued, threatened the critical objective of preserving the United States for the frivolous and inconsequential vision of radical ideologues. "If at the expense of a thousand millions of treasure and rivers of blood, we fail to crush the rebellion, reestablish the authority of the Government, and incidentally work out emancipation," warned the *Post*, "it will be because the wickedness and blindness of slavery is surpassed by the fanaticism of ABOLITION." The *Post* claimed that Northern abolitionists should be held responsible for this precipitous manipulation of the Union war effort. Lincoln, Barr argued in an editorial, had acquiesced to political pressure only after he was "bullied into it by radicals." The nation should concentrate its efforts not on emancipating four million slaves from their masters, he proclaimed, but on emancipating the president from the "thraldom of Abolitionist traitors."[6]

The *Post* also encouraged Pittsburghers not to deflect on the blacks of the community the disdain that should be leveled against abolitionists for the unrest that emancipation would surely bring. "It is not the negro who has thrust himself upon you," urged the *Post*. "He is the principal cause of your present and fast increasing trouble, but he is the helpless, if not innocent cause. . . . Respect the law always and leave it to punish even the beastly licentiousness of the ignorant black, newly turned loose upon Northern society by the fanatic sympathy of crazy destructives [*sic*]." Such messages of white supremacy and the existential threat emancipation posed to Northern society appeared in papers across the North.[7]

The Allegheny County Democratic Committee of Correspondence issued its official response to the prospect of emancipation in its annual resolutions of 1862. The declaration conveyed these two central themes of preserving the war's original objective and protecting white laborers from competition with free blacks. The chairman, Thomas Farley, reaffirmed the party's absolute commitment to sustaining the administration in the prosecution of the war "in every legal effort" that pursued the goal of reestablishing the authority of the Constitution over the entire nation. The resolutions closed with a stern denouncement of plans for gradual emancipation in the border states as it would "damage the Northern laborer by subjecting him to new and unpleasant competition."[8]

However, while emancipation and its place in the Northern war effort divided Pittsburghers, the more present and immediate threat of conscription brought community leaders together like few other causes did during the war. City wards and the surrounding boroughs and townships began holding public meetings to raise troops for the July call-up. The War Department assigned quotas to each state; governors, in turn, imposed quotas on each county. These public meetings and demonstrations all manifested the same central theme: the importance of demonstrating the community's continued commitment to the war effort by producing the requisite number of volunteers. Troop quotas became the only metric that truly mattered in measuring a community's loyalty to the Union. All other forms of support, including Pittsburgh's vast production of war material, palled in comparison to this singular benchmark of allegiance, and community leaders would exhaust themselves to achieve it. On the morning of July 24, a large open-air meeting was held in the West Common of Allegheny City. In promoting it, the *Post* urged "all who love their Country, her Laws, and Constitution, who value the blessings of Liberty, and desire victory to crown our Army, [to] come to the rescue. The Constitution and the Union must be preserved, and treason put to the sword." Attendees heard speeches encouraging volunteering and strolled among the numerous recruitment stands while a brass band played patriotic music. The following day the *Post* celebrated the event in language reminiscent of the large military review of the city's first volunteers in response to Sumter: "Never was the pre-eminent patriotism and deep-seated love of our national institutions . . . more strikingly manifested than yesterday." This Democratic paper praised the city for "taking the necessary measure for putting in the field the quota of men required from the Old Keystone [Pennsylvania] under the new call for troops."[9]

Newspapers vocalized not just their support of efforts to meet the quota but also in their denouncement of those who failed to do their part.

Publications frequently compared the volunteerism of other cities and states to that of Pittsburgh in an effort to spur enlistments. Throughout August, the *Gazette* printed reports of the progress of Ohio, Indiana, and Iowa in meeting their quotas. In July, the *Post* attacked other communities for being "insensible to the demands of the country's necessitys [*sic*]." It pointed to the "lamentable failure" of Philadelphia's recent public meeting to "sustain the government," but the *Post* also quickly criticized Pittsburghers. The lack of zeal evident in Philadelphia, said the *Post*, was just as apparent at home.[10]

As soon as community leaders in Pittsburgh began their campaign to encourage recruitment, the key to volunteerism became apparent: money. While Northerners were now aware of the risks of death and maiming that military service entailed, they were also keenly aware of the financial risks. The thirteen dollars per month paid to Union army privates through most of the war failed to keep pace with wartime inflation. Moreover, the pay system was unreliable and it was common for soldiers to go months—sometimes as many as six—without pay. Communities therefore attempted to attract volunteers with local bounty payments that augmented service pay. The federal and state governments also paid bounties but, as those were the same for all volunteers from a given state, the generosity—or lack thereof—of a particular community greatly impacted on its ability to meet its quota.[11]

During the summer of 1862, the Republican *Gazette* and Democratic *Post* attempted to outdo one another in their criticism of wealthy Pittsburghers who failed to contribute to these local bounty funds. The *Post* began the exchange when taking aim at merchants and manufacturers in the city who were doing well from wartime contracts: "There are hundreds of individuals [in the city], to whose capacious pockets the country's troubles have conveyed very large profits. . . . In the profits arising from what has beggared others, Pittsburgh has enjoyed a very large portion. . . . Now that the Government has again called upon her children for support, let us not be behind in furnishing our full portion. What say our brother of the *Gazette* to this: has it time to devote a little of its attention to the pressing necessities of the Government?" Two weeks later the *Gazette* responded by attacking those "immensely wealthy, whose welfare depends altogether on the permanence of the Government, and who have made their fortunes in Pittsburgh" but who "have given but little compared to their means, or have not given anything at all. . . . There are men who are now coining money from Government contracts whose subscriptions are a disgrace to them." Not to be outdone, the *Post* blasted the same class as "the most contemptible men of all. . . . They are for the war, and for it indefinitely, so long as they are piling up fortunes made off Government contracts."[12]

Thus, from the summer of 1862 until the war's end, community leaders in every ward of Pittsburgh and Allegheny, as well as those in the surrounding areas, engaged in a ceaseless campaign to solicit subscriptions—payments from individuals, banks, and businesses—to the several bounty funds of each neighborhood. The primary motivation was preventing the need for a draft that would tarnish the patriotic reputation of a community. On August 18, Thomas Howe, chairman of Pittsburgh's Executive Committee for all matters related to the war, called on every Pittsburgher to "contribute to the extent of his ability to aid in placing in the field, in the shortest possible time, the quota of volunteers required of this county." In July, the Pennsylvania Railroad Company responded to the call for bounty subscriptions with a commitment of fifty thousand dollars. Each ward established a committee for soliciting and collecting subscriptions to its bounty fund. To promote these local funds, newspapers regularly printed lists of donors along with the amount they contributed, arranged from greatest to least. By August 9, with the deadline for quotas less than a week away, the committee of the county bounty fund reported a balance of seventy-five thousand dollars, enough to pay fifty dollars to each of the fifteen hundred volunteers under the July 1 quota. There was not, however, enough to pay volunteers under the August 4 call-up. With time running out, the committee recommended selling 6 percent of bonds in the amount of $200,000.[13]

With five days remaining until the deadline for volunteers, the official tally of men from Allegheny County newly enrolled in Pennsylvania regiments was 8,414, some 2,179 short of the county's quota. District provost marshal officers distributed handbills in the city giving notice that a draft, ordered by the state, would be conducted on the fifteenth, but confusion over how the draft would be conducted led to delays and the deadline passed with no action. City newspapers expressed indignation at being subjected to a draft and cited figures contradicting those of the provost marshal. George Thurston traveled with Thomas Howe to Harrisburg with figures disputing the count and asked to examine the official records. Their real concern was not that the city's men would be unjustly impressed into military service. Nor did they and other community leaders express fears about potential resistance and riots, as experienced in other cities across the North. Rather they were set on protecting Pittsburgh's reputation of patriotism: "No where [sic] in the state have men been more freely tendered; no where [sic] has money been more liberally expended . . . and it would not only be unfair to tax us with a draft, but it would be virtually stigmatizing us as lacking in liberality and patriotism."[14]

Newspapers stoked the people's excitement about the impending draft. The *Post* warned that time was running out for the city to meet its quota before the draft, "looked upon with so much repugnance, will begin." On August 25, the *Post* conceded that "it would now seem that there is no means of escaping the draft in Allegheny County," blaming the community's shortfall of recruits on the War Department's policies. Instead of allowing volunteers to form their own companies and regiments—as normalized in the first year of the war—recruits under the new call-ups were to be used to strengthen existing regiments depleted by casualties. The efforts of recruiting officers, claimed the *Post*, could not compete with those of ambitious local citizens raising companies to secure their own commissions. With the draft seemingly inevitable, newspapers encouraged Pittsburghers to decide how they would support the war: serve if called on, provide a substitute if unwilling, or contribute to the bounty funds if exempt.[15]

By late September, the draft had still not been enforced. On the twenty-third, an order arrived from Harrisburg postponing the draft until October 16. Earlier in the month, Governor Curtin, along with Governors Edwin Morgan of New York and Charles Smith Olden of New Jersey, had petitioned Stanton for a delay, citing a lack of readiness, and had underscored their desire to fill their states' quotas entirely with volunteers. On October 8, the deficiencies stood at 655 for Pittsburgh and eighty-three for Allegheny City and it seemed that the draft was at hand. Certain other Northern cities had also come up short and their drafts had already commenced. To motivate men to volunteer, Pittsburgh newspapers carried stories of the turmoil the draft caused in those communities. The *Gazette* reported armed resistance to the draft in Indiana, where citizens destroyed ballot boxes and enrolling papers and drove off the commissioners and provosts. The following day, Pittsburghers read an account of the draft in Cleveland's Fifth Ward featuring the story of a laboring man with seven children who, though visibly shaken, appeared to "choke down his grief" when his name was called. However, six days later, the *Gazette* triumphantly declared "No Draft in Allegheny County!," thanks to a recount based not on official muster rolls but on the Pittsburgh Executive Committee's records of bounty payments made to volunteers, many of whom had yet to actually be enrolled but were still credited toward the county's quota. "We have all along contended," claimed the *Gazette*, "that our noble and patriotic county had sent more than her full quota into the field."[16]

Pittsburghers thus managed to prevent the dishonor of the first draft. By

March 1863, however, all signs pointed to another call-up and, with the recently passed federal Enrollment Act and the large number of soldiers whose enlistments were about to expire, another draft (this one federal, not state) seemed imminent. To remind Pittsburghers that supporting the war was their patriotic duty—even in the event of a draft—the *Gazette* condemned protestors in other cities, among them Daniel Tuttle, who challenged his fellow Ohioans to "have a bullet ready for the bastards who order one drafted man to leave his home." The *Gazette* pointed out that the Enrollment Act made it a crime to resist the draft or incite others to do so.[17]

With the Emancipation Proclamation now in effect, the Democratic *Post* resumed its tirades against the administration's distortion of the original justification for going to war. Now that they had gotten what they wanted, said the *Post*, abolitionists should cease condemning the draft and should, in fact, themselves be ushered to the front lines to relieve the brave men who had fought so valiantly, not for emancipation but for the Union. Just prior to the March call-up, the *Post* called on the government to "repeal all the nonsensical legislation by Congress in relation to Confiscation and Emancipation . . . and return to the old idea of a prosecution of hostilities for the restoration of the Union." Thus, Democrats argued, political objections to military service would be defused and erstwhile objectors would become "enthusiastic volunteers."[18]

On July 8, an order conscripting twenty-seven hundred men from Allegheny for a period of three years surprised Pittsburghers. Unlike the call-ups of the previous year, with their protracted stages of recruitment and threats of drafts only if quotas were not met, this called for an immediate draft to fill the quota. "We were under the impression that this mode of raising troops would not be resorted to," said the *Post*, "but it appears that preparations have been quietly progressing, and our people must be prepared to face the music." The War Department had indeed coordinated plans for some time with the provost marshal general's office; the plans included positioning troops in Pittsburgh, Harrisburg, and Philadelphia in the event of riots. That same day, Pittsburgh's first draft commenced. The proceedings were open to the public but were held in a small room limiting the number of observers. Slips with the names of all in the first class—men ages eighteen to twenty-five and unmarried men twenty-six to thirty-five—were placed into a wheel. George W. Cyrus was selected to draw names. Blindfolded, Cyrus pulled a slip and handed it to provost marshal captain Heron Foster, who read the name aloud before passing it on to the local draft commissioner, William H. Campbell. Campbell verified the names and passed them to the clerks and reporters for recording. Wards one through six were completed that morning, seven and eight in the afternoon.[19]

Democratic and Republican messages deliberately encouraged and celebrated Pittsburghers peacefully accepting the draft. Among the names called was that of one of the clerks recording the results and commissioner Campbell, remarkably, even read his own name, leading the *Gazette* to remark that "[n]o one will be disposed, with these facts in view, to question the fairness of the drawing." Also drafted was Samuel Riddle, owner and editor of the *Gazette*. The *Post* lauded him, and "the honorable service he will render," as examples for all draftees. When three clergymen of St. Paul's Cathedral were drafted, Reverend Father E. McMahon, the church's pastor, stated that "the draft was conducted in a just and honorable manner" and it was the duty of the people to "give a willing support to the government both in men and money." Two days after the conclusion of the destructive draft riots in New York from July 13–16, the *Post* commented that "[w]e doubt if there is a city in the Union where the draft has been swallowed as good naturedly as here."[20]

The draft of July 1863 may have passed with quiet acquiescence in Pittsburgh, but soon tensions rose over the prospect of continued conscription. Just days after beseeching Pittsburghers to support the draft, the *Post* took a position against its continuance, although the editor declined to offer any "reason for opposing." The *Gazette* accused the *Post* of moving "in the direction of resistance, as the laws would permit, and the time and temper of this community were likely to tolerate." If the *Post* published in New York, claimed the *Gazette*, it "would have belched out treason without measure or disguise," but, in Pittsburgh, "it could not indulge that way."[21]

The main point of contention between the two publications was the commutation policy, permitting drafted men to pay a fee of three hundred dollars in lieu of serving. The *Post* argued that this allowed the wealthy to buy their way out of the army while the poor were forced to serve. The *Gazette* countered that this "poor man's clause" effectively capped the price of substitutes, thereby affording common laborers an alternative to serving. Though the commutation fee represented approximately one year's wages for a laborer, many draftees in Pittsburgh were able to use this provision to evade serving, due in part to the high wages and plentiful jobs that the city's wartime manufacturing created.[22]

In fact, the avoidance of service by draftees was epidemic in Pittsburgh. Between Pittsburgh and Allegheny City, more than one in four paid the commutation fee. Even more found some grounds for securing an exemption. Newspapers published the reports of the provost marshal detailing the names and reasons for exemptions. Some 178 conscripted Pittsburghers avoided the July draft: seventy-six paid the commutation fee, thirty-five hired a substitute, and sixty-seven were declared exempt for reasons that varied from caring for a widow or elderly parent to having two brothers already serving. In September, the *Gazette* raised the issue of Pittsburghers' inadequate response to the draft and encouraged "a re-kindling of the flame of patriotism which illuminated the states and inspired the people in 1861 and 1862." Some Pittsburgh draftees evaded service fraudulently, or at least tried to. In September, physician D. J. Scroggs and clothier Samuel Marshal were charged with conspiring to defraud Benjamin Powell and other drafted men from the county by promising that, for a fee, they would use their influence with the enrollment board to secure exemptions.[23]

Included in the draft that July were at least three black men from Pittsburgh and Allegheny City. While the Second Confiscation Act passed in July 1862 paved the way for the acceptance of black volunteers, it also made them subject to conscription. Ben Richards, a thirty-four-year-old farmer, served honorably in the 6th USCT until his discharge in July 1865. Thomas Scott, a twenty-six-year-old cook was also drafted into the 6th USCT where he served with distinction until he was killed in action at Chaffin's Farm in September 1864. Three more black Pittsburghers volunteered that July, contributing to the district's quota. Rufus Jones, who had led the efforts of the black community to mobilize during the Gettysburg campaign, served in the 8th USCT along with William Jones, a twenty-five-year-old barber who signed up as a substitute for William B. Reynolds, a white laborer with a wife and young child. William Jones survived the war participating in the Battle of Olustee, the Siege of Richmond and Petersburg, Chaffin's Farm, and the surrender of the Army of Northern Virginia at Appomattox Court House. One of the first black men from Pittsburgh to volunteer was an eighteen-year-old waiter named Samuel Carter. Carter volunteered to serve with the 1st USCT. That July, he traveled to Washington D. C. for muster, where he spent weeks drilling on Mason's Island in the Potomac River just five hundred yards from the White House. Carter was wounded in front of Richmond on 27 October 1864 and continued to serve honorably until his regiment was mustered out in September 1865. However, probably the first black Pittsburgher to volunteer was Toussanit L. O. Delany, son of Pittsburgh abolitionist Martin R. Delany. The senior Delany served as a recruiting agent for the 54th Massachusetts Infantry Regiment and his eighteen-year-old son left his studies and answered the call, volunteering in March 1863. Several other black volunteers from Pittsburgh marched to the front with USCT regiments mustered in

Ohio, New York, Connecticut, Maryland, Rhode Island, and Indiana. Black enlistment, once authorized, was not a foregone conclusion.[24]

In late September, newspapers again began to report indications of another draft, citing the failure of the most recent one to provide anywhere near the number of soldiers required by the army. The *Post* mocked the draft, pointing out that it had secured only about sixty conscripts in Pittsburgh while the bureaucracy of provost marshals, clerks, aides, and enrollment officers totaled seventy-five thousand men. "Better to draft that army, already under pay," said the *Post*, "and let the conscripts go." The draft in Allegheny County was far more effective at raising money than men. The provost marshal's office for Allegheny City and the Twenty-third District reported two months after the July draft a collection of over $200,000 in exemption fees, while nearly two hundred men had failed to report for the draft.[25]

The threat of another draft soon became a reality and Pittsburghers were again engrossed in the business of maximizing volunteers. A new call went out in October for three hundred thousand more troops and the War Department returned to imposing the draft for failure to meet assigned quotas. If required, this draft would commence on January 5, 1864; the quota for Pittsburgh and the Twenty-second District was 1,915. This time the city was slow to begin recruitment efforts. The *Daily Commercial* printed several articles calling for action to enroll men. In December, the *Gazette* began to print calls from Pittsburghers for ward meetings to organize recruiting. One petition proposed that the city secure a loan of $71,600 to fund bounties of two hundred dollars to each volunteer required under the latest call-up. In late December, community leaders of the Fifth Ward called a meeting of all men twenty and older at the ward schoolhouse. The purpose of the gathering was to motivate these men to volunteer, thereby preventing a draft. The *Post* encouraged all wards to take similar initiatives. The *Post* also emphasized the importance of black volunteers being credited against the city's quota.[26]

Despite campaigns to stimulate volunteerism, many Pittsburghers continued to search for ways to avoid serving. In the weeks leading up to the January 5 deadline, more than two thousand men filed for exemptions with the enrollment board, which heard a hundred cases per day to meet the demand. The hearings between December 7 and 31 alone resulted in the exemption of 1,261 men. This immense demand for draft avoidance encouraged an entirely new stream of business for private agents. W. J. and Hall Patterson and J. B. Jones and Company ran advertisements in Pittsburgh newspapers offering their services in obtaining exemptions and finding substitutes. Men committed to seeing that Pittsburgh met its quota were concerned about the ever-decreasing pool of prospective recruits. In addition to the growing number of exemptions, advocates for volunteering worried about losing men willing to volunteer to other districts paying higher bounties. They formed a committee to encourage the county council to enact a property tax to enhance local bounties. That December though, eleven black men volunteered in response to the recent call up. All went on to serve in the 22nd USCT, one of the first regiments to enter Richmond. The 22nd also served as an escort for Lincoln's funeral and participated in the pursuit of John Wilkes Booth and his conspirators.[27]

On January 27, 1864, John Harper and other community leaders hosted a large public meeting at the Monongahela House. The guest of honor was Major General Winfield Scott Hancock, hero of the Union defense of Cemetery Ridge on the third day of Gettysburg. Hancock was on a tour of Pennsylvania to rally volunteers for his II Corps of the Army of the Potomac. He encouraged Pittsburghers to offer generous bounties as Philadelphia and other areas of the state had done. With two artillery batteries in the II Corps, said Hancock, Allegheny County had a great interest in supporting the corps. Pennsylvania, however, was more in arrears than any other state in the Union after the last draft. Volunteering there, he went on, seemed less animated than in any other state. The solution, Hancock told the crowd, was for citizens to generously fund local bounties. Unlike commutations, which took the money out of the community, bounties remained in the hands of the volunteers' families. John Harper, who so energetically mobilized Pittsburgh's homefront defenses, offered a resolution that Allegheny County be organized into subdistricts with a three-man committee for each to coordinate the raising of money for bounties.[28]

Some Pittsburghers took Hancock's words to heart. By mid-February, Allegheny City's Fourth Ward, under the direction of Thomas Howe, raised funds sufficient to pay a bounty of $150 in addition to the federal bounty. The First Ward of Pittsburgh also strove to enroll volunteers to meet its quota. After organizing block committees, leaders held recruiting events while committee members and volunteers went door to door soliciting subscriptions for a bounty fund. The Sixth Ward committee reported collections totaling twenty-one thousand dollars in February but committed to continue canvassing the neighborhood daily. In order to pay a bounty of two hundred dollars each to the 185 volunteers needed, the ward had to raise another sixteen thousand dollars. Some in Pittsburgh were concerned about the alternative if these efforts to secure voluntary contributions failed. On February 15, a group of property holders met at the county courthouse and passed resolutions challenging the city to "redouble efforts to raise funds from private sources" rather than impose a new property tax. Again, the press in Pittsburgh also stressed the importance of capitalizing on the black community to help stave off the draft, citing the Enrollment Act passed the previous Spring declared that all able-bodied black men ages twenty to forty-five would be enlisted.[29]

The uncertainty surrounding the draft grew as the days progressed. On March 7, the draft was postponed until further orders. However, nine days later, Lincoln ordered that it commence on April 15. Furthermore, he increased the call for troops by two hundred thousand, raising Allegheny County's quota from 3,361 to 4,390. After months of delays and wrangling to prevent a draft, it finally commenced in Allegheny City for the Twenty-third District on June 2. Soon thereafter, Pittsburgh's draft began. Many local people were surprised and disappointed, having assumed that the wards had raised sufficient funds and men to escape the draft. The initial quota for Pittsburgh was 2,382, but, by draft day, credits and adjustments had reduced that number to 1,201 and three of the nine wards had escaped the draft altogether.[30]

Frustration grew as the threat of the draft seemed to loom unceasingly over Pittsburgh. Just before the June draft, the *Gazette* reprimanded Pittsburghers for contributing through their apathy to Pennsylvania's shameful status as "the most backward [state] of all in filling her quota": "Are we less loyal than our neighbors? Or are we more indolent and indifferent than they? . . .The reply is with the people . . . [u]nless they bestir themselves with greater vigor than they have yet displayed, they will not only be caught yet by the draft, but they will achieve the disgraceful preeminence of being citizens of the only state in which a draft was rendered necessary." The *Daily Commercial* acknowledged a similar accusation by the Chicago press criticizing Pennsylvanians for their failure to respond to troop call-ups with the same vigor as Midwestern states.[31]

On July 20, Pittsburgh received the news of yet another call-up, this time for five hundred thousand more troops, with a draft set for September 5. This came just weeks after Congress abolished commutation, leaving fewer options for conscripted men wanting to avoid serving. Rumors already circulated of a mass exodus of men attempting to flee the draft. Provost Marshal Foster called on the citizens of Pittsburgh to "take prompt measures" to prevent this. The *Post* noted that, to move after enrollment in the face of a pending draft, violated the law. Why then, it asked, did the provost marshal not stop it himself?: "If he has not bayonets enough, more can be procured for the asking."[32]

Pittsburghers became more energized in response to this call-up than any previously. Every ward appeared to come alive with initiatives to raise money and recruit men. The failure in the last call-up seemingly spurred the city to swift and decisive action. On August 27, the *Daily Commercial* reported on Pittsburgh's notably inactive markets: "the business of filling up our quota in order to avoid the coming draft seems to occupy the attention of our people to the exclusion of everything else." The Third Ward recruiting committee announced that it would be available in its office "at reasonable hours" and would pay "a cash bounty to all volunteers." Still, many local men made their best effort to avoid serving. Only three weeks after the call-up, news spread that the Fourth Ward had already met its quota. In response, several men from other wards and the surrounding area informed Provost Marshal Foster of their intention to move to the Fourth Ward. Captain Foster became suspicious and shared his concerns with community leaders. A committee was established to investigate these applicants. At least one—Thomas Woods of Lawrenceville—was charged with perjury on the recommendation of the committee. The case was handed over to the U.S. district attorney "in order to deter others from a like effort to evade their duty."[33]

The call for eight hundred thousand men between October 1863 and July 1864 spurred the greatest response of the war from the black men of Pittsburgh. Forty black volunteers joined the ranks of the 41st, 42nd, 43rd, and 45th USCT regiments in which they experienced the dramatic final chapters of the war in the eastern theater. Joseph A. Douglas was a twenty-nine-year-old laborer from Ross Township on the outskirts of the city. His service in the 45th USCT carried him from guard duty in Arlington, to Lee's surrender at Appomattox, to patrolling the Rio Grande in Texas before being mustered out on 4 November 1865 and returning to Allegheny County. In all, of the approximately 550 military-age black males in Allegheny County, at least 146, or 27 percent, answered the call between the spring of 1863 and the end of the war. Ninety-two volunteered or were drafted within Pittsburgh and were credited to the city's quota of soldiers. Another fifty-four volunteered for regiments that were organized in other states.[34]

To forestall a draft this time, community leaders enacted innovative measures to secure sufficient bounty funds to induce volunteering. On August 19, 1864, the recruiting committees from several Pittsburgh wards and surrounding boroughs and townships met in convention to establish a uniform policy on bounties. Some of these subdistrict committeemen resented the generous bounties being paid by a handful of their neighbors, which, they claimed, "foster[ed] a purely mercenary feeling among the volunteers." The committees agreed to adopt a standard bounty of three hundred dollars per volunteer regardless of the length of service and they formed a vigilance committee to monitor payments made by all recruiting committees in the district. On August 30, the First Ward, Allegheny City, held a public meeting. The organizers adopted a radical policy to encourage volunteering and subscriptions. The names of all enrolled men in the ward were read aloud along with the amount they had contributed to the bounty fund. From that point forward, the certificates that would normally be submitted to establish a credit against the draft for each volunteer would be withheld. The draft in the First Ward would be allowed to go on. Any man drafted who had contributed his proportionate share to the bounty fund would be credited as a prior volunteer and paid his bounty. Any man who had not would be required to serve without a bounty or find a substitute. A week later, the Sixth Ward followed suit. A meeting was held for all enrolled men in which they were called on to donate to the bounty fund "in portion to their means." All who were delinquent in their subscriptions would find their names published. Ward leaders further threatened legal action to collect what they deemed was owed.[35]

The extreme measures to increase volunteerism quickly paid off. On the evening of September 13, the Second Ward in Pittsburgh celebrated reaching its quota and forestalling another draft. A procession marched from the mayor's office with the Great Western Band at its head. William Phillips was presented with a gold-headed cane for his energetic work on the ward recruitment committee and his personal subscription of three thousand dollars to the ward bounty fund. The procession made its way to the houses of other prominent contributors, presenting gifts and lauding their service to the war effort. After two weeks of delays, the draft finally commenced on September 20. All of the nine wards of Pittsburgh as well as those of Allegheny City met their quota. A handful of the surrounding neighborhoods, however, had less success and were subjected to a draft. Draftee Charles Robinson of Birmingham, just south of Pittsburgh, attempted to escape to Canada; he was chased from his saloon through the streets before being apprehended by provost detectives. Reports indicated that several other draftees managed to flee. Of the fifty Birmingham men drafted, only fifteen reported for duty.[36]

Despite the strain to the community's support of the war caused by conscription and emancipation, the majority of Pittsburghers continued to endorse the administration's handling of the war effort. In the midst of the call ups and drafts in the fall of 1864, Pittsburghers voted in elections that presented a choice between sustaining Lincoln's policies for prosecuting the war or turning over its handling to the Democrats and General George B. McClellan, their candidate for president. The Democratic campaign promised an immediate cessation of hostilities. If Lincoln was elected again, warned the Democratic press, the war would last at least another four years as the Republicans sacrificed the lives of white men for the liberation of the ne-gro. Republicans countered that Lincoln came to office without the men or resources needed to quell the rebellion. Now, said the *Gazette*, "look at the shrunken Confederacy and its exhausted armies." When victory is within our grasp, asked Republicans, shall we concede and offer terms?[37]

In the Congressional election in October, Allegheny County reelected J. K. Moorhead 11,233 to 7,013. In all, Republicans won six of the seven contested Congressional districts in Western Pennsylvania. In the presidential election that November, Lincoln carried Pennsylvania aided greatly by his landslide victory in Allegheny County where he received 21,519 votes to McClellan's 12,414.[38]

The final call for troops was issued on December 19, 1864. Once again, a date was established—February 15—for a draft to make up any shortfall in volunteers. For weeks, the *Post* had railed at the prospect of another draft. The Republican papers, it claimed, had given Pittsburghers false assurances that if they reelected Lincoln there would be no need for another draft. The *Daily Commercial* countered that the recent presidential election vote had demonstrated the resolve of the people of Pittsburgh to support the war effort. This commitment would be essential if Pittsburgh was going to fend off yet another draft. "In the absence of any new legislation," said the *Commercial*, "the efforts of individuals and of communities, acting as organized bodies, must be depended on to stimulate volunteering." The *Post*, more concerned with preventing a draft in its community than with partisan quibbling, en-couraged every Pittsburgher to "put his shoulder to the wheel and push forward the general work. . . . [W]e will have to arouse ourselves again and unite our efforts in raising the necessary number of men."[39]

Recruitment for this last call-up proved difficult. The *Daily Commercial* pointed to the scarcity of remaining civilian men of military age as the cause. The hiring of substitutes however, thrived. With the commutation ended, men received between seven hundred and a thousand dollars in Pittsburgh for just one year of service. On February 6, President Lincoln delayed the draft with an executive order to establish a board to examine and correct the quotas of the states and districts. Provost Marshal General James Barnett Fry ordered his district deputies to begin drafting if recruiting came up short. Newspapers continued to keep the threat of a draft in the minds of Pittsbur-ghers. When the draft commenced in New York on March 7 due to a lull in volunteering, the *Gazette* warned that it would be the same for Pittsburgh if recruiting did not increase. The *Daily Commercial* cautioned that to believe there would be no draft was delusional. The *Post* likewise claimed that the "draft was positively coming." Pittsburghers had "only one week left to decide" if they would volunteer or be drafted. On April 12, following General Robert E. Lee's surrender to General Ulysses S. Grant, the *Gazette* asked, "now that the war appears to be over . . . will the draft be made?" Many men still had not contributed their service to the war, the *Gazette* charged, and it seemed unfair for them to escape fighting while so many others had sacrificed so much. But if the war was ending and men were no longer needed, why draft them? "If things have changed since the 19th of December from deep gloom to bright sunshine, from storm to calm, from peril to safety, why not change our policy?"[40]

From the summer of 1862 until nearly the end of the war, the draft dominated public discourse in Pittsburgh. There was scarcely a day that each newspaper in the city did not carry at least one article on the subject. Local pride continued to play a large role as Pittsburghers negotiated this aspect of mobilization. The Lincoln administration's use of the draft primarily in response to a community's failure at volunteerism prompted a purposeful campaign by community leaders. The goal was the preservation of local pride by preventing the ignominy of a draft. It was not enough to supply the men needed to crush the rebellion. They wanted Pittsburgh to do so in a manner that upheld the city's claim of being a pillar of support for the war.

The cause of emancipation and its transformation of the Northern war effort exacerbated the dissention of Democrats in Pittsburgh. Driven by a desire to preserve the supremacy of whites in Northern society, Democrats propagated threats that emancipation would undermine the economic prosperity of whites. These challenges were moderate however, compared to other Northern cities given the strong Republican majority in Pittsburgh. Attacks mostly focused on radical abolitionists rather than the administration. Ultimately, those opposed to emancipation came to accept it even if they did not embrace racial equality. Black soldiers came to be seen as a means to prevent conscription and preserve the community's pride by helping to meet volunteer quotas. Black men eligible for service navigated the same system as their white neighbors, serving as substitutes, receiving bounties, and reporting when drafted.

Through the turmoil of increasing calls for troops, threats of conscription, the emancipation of the enslaved in the rebellious states, and the opening of combat service to black men, community leaders and organizations continued as the driving force behind sustaining the volunteerism of the people. Even as the federal government became more directly involved in the mobilization of men, local committees and businesses continued to lead on initiatives to motivate potential volunteers. The radical changes to the Union war objectives and to the social order incited debate and illuminated tensions over race and the handling of the war. Parties in Pittsburgh differed over what the Northern war effort should look like, but they remained unified in their resolve that the city support that cause, however it evolved.

5

★ ★ ★ ★ ★

YOUR PATRIOTISM, AS WELL AS YOUR HONOR . . . IN THE PERFORMANCE OF YOUR DUTIES

Manufacturing a War Effort

In all history, no nation of mere agriculturists ever made
successful war against a nation of mechanics.

-WILLIAM TECUMSEH SHERMAN-

1860

From the very beginning, Pittsburgh's manufacturing identity shaped the ways its people connected with the war. On June 5, 1861, workers transported ten cannons and four mortars from the city's arsenals to a site on the north shore of the Allegheny, where the guns would be tested. A crowd of local iron manufacturers and investors gathered there, accompanied by several women and other onlookers. The assemblage enjoyed an al fresco banquet prepared by a local confectioner, which added a festive atmosphere to an otherwise militaristic event.[1]

Early demonstrations such as this encouraged the establishment of new manufactories in the city. In the first year of the war, the already crowded field of seventeen iron foundries increased by two, nail manufacturers increased from fourteen to seventeen, and the city's first rifle manufacturer, Brown and Tetley, opened on Wood Street. Moreover, many of the city's businessmen converted their operations in response to the growing demands of the Northern war effort. Mill operators, for example, turned from supplying flour to the public to producing it for a single consumer, the War Department.

Pittsburgh soon took on the feel of a military city, as its citizens would boast, "second only to Washington."[2]

On December 17, 1861, a group of prominent businessmen met at the Board of Trade office to draft a proposal. Now that it was clear that the war would go on for some time, a congressional committee reenergized a debate over the need for a national armory and foundry west of the Allegheny Mountains; these community leaders, with William Wilkins as their chairman, were determined that, if such a facility was built, it would be in Pittsburgh. The only national armory at that time was located in Springfield, Massachusetts, a fact that for decades had been objectionable to leaders of Western cities. The Pittsburgh committee criticized this "disposition of New England to retain a monopoly" on the production of arms for the military. Moreover, the committee said, when President Andrew Jackson had argued for the necessity of a Western armory, he did so in response to South Carolina's defiance of the government. As the United States now again faced a Southern rebellion, it badly needed a means of producing arms in the West: "Had there been a foundry at the head waters of the Ohio, we believe our troops today would have been occupying every city from Cairo to New Orleans."[3]

The chief competitor of Pittsburgh in this matter was Chicago. A committee from that city had already petitioned Congress and the Pittsburgh proposal focused on countering the Chicagoans' arguments, citing every aspect of Pittsburgh's economy to demonstrate that no city in the Union was better suited than "the Iron City [to meet] all the demands and requirements of a National Armory and Foundry."[4]

While their aspirations for this venture were never realized, the businessmen of Pittsburgh were nonetheless considerably engaged in the material support of the Union war effort. The first contract given to a Pittsburgh firm was on July 29, 1861, when the Sterling and Moore company agreed to supply one thousand uniform hats at eighty cents each. One week later, William, Dodd, and Company was selected to provide twice as many hats at ninety cents each. Another early enterprise for Pittsburgh firms was the transportation of soldiers by riverboat. D. G. Breikell contracted to carry fifty troops to Louisville on November 23, 1861; he was paid six dollars for each officer and two and a half for each enlisted man. In April 1863, Thomas Wood accepted a contract to haul ordnance of various sizes ranging from thirteen-inch mortars at eleven dollars each to ten-inch Columbiads at seven dollars. One of the principal goods manufactured in Pittsburgh for the War Department was the wagon. On June 6, 1862, Fred Aeschleman agreed to furnish the army with two hundred covered, six-mule wagons at $105 each. The wagons were constructed according to the specifications on file at the Pittsburgh quarter-master office, with thirty-five delivered by June 20 and thirty-five more each week thereafter. Two months later, Aeschleman secured a second contract, this time for three hundred wagons at $112 apiece. He did well throughout the war, earning $145 per wagon by June 1863.[5]

Several firms landed contracts to supply other essential items for the army. Eight different businesses signed with the War Department to deliver a total of 4,750 horses at an average cost of $127 each. Many companies benefited from the abundance of coal in the Pittsburgh area by catering to the army's expanding demand for that commodity. These contracts called for quantities of coal ranging from one hundred thousand to five hundred thousand bushels, typically delivered by riverboat to Cairo and Memphis, then later to Vicksburg and New Orleans. In 1862, the price per bushel was twenty-two cents, a year later thirty-three. By 1865, the firm of Thomas and Walton Fancett charged the War Department seventy cents for each of the five hundred thousand bushels delivered to New Orleans, for a total of $350,000. At times, businesses signed contracts to supplement the manufacturing of munitions when the normal suppliers could not meet the demand. The cotton mill of James Park Jr., Jacob Painter, and David E. Park shifted from the production of sheets, carpets, twine, and batting to assembling cannon rounds. In March 1862, the firm filled an order for more than four thousand.[6]

The boom in Pittsburgh business and industry ignited by the war went beyond the awarding of War Department contracts. By the fall of 1861, railroad earnings increased 32 percent. Hotels thrived, too. In September 1863, people seeking lodging were turned away from every hotel and boardinghouse in the city. Regular guests unable to secure a room were provided cots instead. The increase in manufacturing coupled with the exodus of men in uniform created a scarcity of labor. To combat this, community leaders implemented strategies that challenged existing labor structures. When coal companies faced a depleted and dissatisfied work force in 1864, they adopted machinery for cutting coal already in use in Europe. Newspapers advocated immigration to overcome the shortage of labor in Pittsburgh. The Allegheny Arsenal developed a procedure for obtaining temporary exemptions when workers were drafted into military service.[7]

In May 1864, the *Post* suggested the most drastic idea yet for dealing with the labor shortage. "The only solution of the difficulty," said the editor, "is to call young ladies into the manual departments thus left vacant. There are a thousand kinds of light employment which can be performed by ladies as well as gentlemen." Females could serve apprenticeships or receive other training to gain the necessary skills. In fact, in many areas of labor "the delicate fingers of a lady are much better adapted than the coarse rough muscles of the male sex." To see the merits of this case, the *Post* argued, Pittsburghers needed only to consider the field of education: females were once inconceivable as teachers but now were accepted as "true and worthy exemplars of morality and virtue." "[W]e doubt not that similar results will flow from the employment of ladies in any other branch of business. . . . [T]hey have brains, and hands, and tongues, as well as the 'lords of creation.'" Furthermore, women should retain these positions in skilled labor "at least until a generation of young men have grown to take the places in civil life of those who have fallen in the fearful struggles now transpiring in our beloved country."[8]

The procurement of government contracts and the expansion of businesses did not necessarily translate into support for the war. Although most businessmen were in fact ardent Unionists, they were also pragmatists and any new business venture needed to first be profitable, then patriotic. However, the commercial and manufacturing identity of Pittsburgh did have an important effect on the way its citizens were drawn into and experienced the war. Community leaders frequently evoked this identity to affirm the city's important role in the war and to reinforce the people's support and, through their role in Pittsburgh's industry and trade, many common people found a way to participate directly in the Northern war effort.

Two industries in Pittsburgh became especially ingrained in the city's wartime identity. Both were prominent before the war but were modified and took on new meaning once applied to supporting the Union war effort. One was the manufacturing of large ordnance for the army and navy. For two decades preceding the war, Charles Knap and his Fort Pitt Foundry had worked with the War Department's Ordnance Bureau to improve the design and manufacturing process of large artillery pieces. Knap worked closely with ordnance officers, including Major Thomas J. Rodman, to test new methods for casting these guns, frequently corresponding about the various trials, setbacks, and advancements along the way. In 1847, Rodman patented a new method of manufacturing cannons from iron. Using iron was not new and guns had a tendency to burst when fired when made from it. The cause, Rodman discovered, was the practice of casting solid iron cannons, boring them out, and cooling them with water from the outside; this created cracks in the gun. Rodman's process called for casting the cannons hollow and cooling them from the inside out; this resulted in a gun more structurally sound. Rodman then partnered with Knap, assigning him the patent in exchange for half a cent per pound on every gun the Fort Pitt Foundry manufactured using his process.[9]

When the war began, the majority of the cannons in the army's inventory were obsolete. To rectify this, the Ordnance Bureau quickly adopted a system of manufacturing cannons using the new process and contracting the work to civilian foundries. A key component of this system placed ordnance officers in every foundry to serve as inspectors. In the early months of the war, Knap worked with the chief of ordnance to define the roles and responsibilities of each party. By August 24, the Fort Pitt Foundry was in full operation casting cannon for the Union war effort: "We have cast six of the IX inch guns ordered," wrote Knap, and "are now casting daily 100 shells on your order and hope to increase that number considerably the coming week." Knap believed in the importance of this production to the war and worked hard to meet the War Department's needs both in the number of guns required and in their reliability. In September, he reported that "[o]ur lathes are running day and night. . . . We are doing all in our power to hasten the finishing of the IX inch guns. You are probably aware that there is an enormous amount of labor required to finish these guns and of a character which cannot be slighted." On December 19, 1861, Ordnance Officer A. B. Dyer wrote to General J. W. Ripley, chief of the Ordnance Bureau, about the importance of expediting the work of civilian foundries: "That the Columbiads now on hand cannot be relied on for service, has been established beyond question by the bursting of a large number of them. . . . To correct this evil, several modifications have been made within the last two or three years, in the mode of casting and in the models of those guns . . . with marked improvement in the quality." Dyer urged the speedy mass production of these new guns.[10]

Throughout the war, the Fort Pitt Foundry experienced challenges in meeting government demands. Cold weather, scarcity of water suitable for cooling guns, and conflicts with the Ordnance Bureau were a few issues that disrupted production. In January 1863, J. M. Berrien, Ordnance Bureau inspector at the Fort Pitt Foundry, wrote to the chief of ordnance to defend himself and the foundry after a naval officer reported receiving defective shells from Pittsburgh. Inspectors at foundries were meant to serve as a check on civilian manufacturers and were expected to take the side of the Ordnance Bureau in any disputes, but Berrien consistently aligned himself with the Fort Pitt Foundry in such conflicts. Inspectors like Berrien worked closely every day with their contractors in a common purpose to support the war, acting more as advocates of the civilian firm than of their military command.[11]

In January 1863, the partnership between the Fort Pitt Foundry and the Ordnance Bureau became strained. Officers in the field began to complain about the quality of some of the guns that they received from Pittsburgh. Specifically, they decried the inconsistency in the hardness of the iron. Knap argued that complete uniformity of iron was impossible to achieve, particularly because the huge demand for guns required the use of multiple furnaces to keep pace. In June, Captain A. Dahlgren, chief of the Ordnance Bureau, established a board to examine the guns cast at the Fort Pitt Foundry. In the first lot inspected by the board, four of eight guns were rejected.[12]

Despite these setbacks, the Fort Pitt Foundry played a vital role in sustaining the Union war effort. Knap hired scores of new workers and invested $240,000 in upgrading his operations. Throughout the war, his foundry sold approximately $3 million in guns and projectiles to the Ordnance Bureau, making it one of the leaders in this war industry. The Fort Pitt Foundry came second only to Robert P. Parrott's West Point Foundry in value of ordnance sold to the War Department and accounted for -15 percent of the artillery and projectiles procured by the Ordnance Bureau throughout the war. This firm did more than just produce guns. The staff tested guns produced by new processes, recommended modifications to the military's specifications to improve the durability of guns, and advised the Ordnance Bureau on revising field practices to reduce accidents and increase safety. In February 1864, the Fort Pitt Foundry reached its zenith of wartime gun manufacturing with the production of the twenty-inch Rodman, the only gun of its kind cast during the war. The undertaking was immense. Preparations had begun in May 1863 and required extensive new construction, including buildings, cranes, and furnaces. The finished guns were twenty feet long and weighed 116,497 pounds each. Pittsburghers celebrated the production in their city of "the greatest gun in Christendom" and praised the Fort Pitt Foundry for its role in putting "American artillerists in advance of the world" (see Figure 7).[13]

A second industry that transformed itself by going into business with the government was shipbuilding. In the spring and summer of 1862, the navy gave several contracts to firms in Cincinnati, Mound City, St. Louis, and Pittsburgh to construct ironclad riverboats. Tomlinson, Hartupee, and Company in Pittsburgh were contracted on May 16 to build two small vessels, the *Marietta* and the *Sandusky*, for $188,000. The largest contract awarded to a Pittsburgh firm went to Snowden and Mason on September 15 to build the *Manayunk* for $460,000 and deliver it to Cairo, Illinois six months from that date. The following April, however, the ship was not yet completed, prompting the navy to dictate stricter terms for the second vessel contracted to Snowden and Mason, the *Umpqua*. Instead of the fixed installments specified in the previous contract, payments totaling $395,000 would now be made only when satisfactory progress was verified. The Pittsburgh firm was again given six months to complete the job, with a deadline of September 9, 1863.[14]

Complications throughout the construction process plagued these shipbuilding firms, forcing delays and creating conflict with the Navy Department. After repeated inquiries regarding the delays, Tomlinson, Hartupee, and Company wrote to Commodore J. B. Hull, superintendent of Western gunboats, on May 5, 1863, saying they hoped to complete the boats within three to four months, but, they added, the "impossibility of getting as many workmen as we require renders it very difficult for us to fix a positive time. . . . [W]e delayed replying until this time with the hope of . . . increasing the number of workmen so as to give you a more satisfactory answer." Contractors were also irked by naval officials who encumbered them with additions and modifications to their plans. In August, several contractors wrote for clarification as to the "precise amount of deference" they were expected to pay these officers. The general inspector of ironclads, Alban Stimers, routinely sent circular letters to all contractors communicating errors in drawings, modifications from the fleet, and practices implemented by other contractors that he deemed necessary to be adopted by all. Snowden and Mason became increasingly concerned about incurring additional costs that could not be recouped from the navy. The navy superintendents assigned to the various projects were instructed to advise their builder of the proper procedures to follow when they believed their contract was being interfered with in a manner that would necessitate raising their fee.[15]

On August 31, Stimers responded directly to contractors' concerns, providing a revealing glimpse into the tumultuous world of wartime contracting with civilian industries: "The building of Ironclad Steamers is a novelty in this country as in every other. It is therefore impossible to make a complete general plan and write complete specifications at one date . . . especially as the fleet already in service is actually engaged with the enemy and developing rapidly all the weak points of the original structures." Vessels currently under construction, Stimers argued, should incorporate all lessons being learned in the field. "But the mode of effecting them in such a manner as to create no confusion in settling extra bills," he conceded, "has not heretofore been very clearly defined." War and industry rapidly evolved in real time, challenging leaders in the military and manufacturing to find the middle ground for their competing interests and shared goals. The procedure dictated by Stimers directed contractors to write his office whenever they received instructions they interpreted as a modification to the contract. The general inspector would then obtain authorization from the chief of the proper navy bureau for the extra payment required to complete the work. Furthermore, wrote Stimers, contractors were to disregard all correspondence that came from their local inspector rather than his office.

Stimers had determined that these inspectors, imbedded with their contractors, were known to write "unauthorized letters" favoring their contractor's interests over the navy's. If civilian contractors such as Snowden and Mason were frustrated with the frequent changes demanded by the navy and with the erosion of their profits, Stimers was equally dismayed with the inferior workmanship he perceived in the ships they built and he framed his indictments of incompetence in terms of loyalty to the Union and support for the war. In January 1864, he wrote John Snowden:

> Sir, the great damage which has been sustained by the Navy Department from the poor materials and bad workmanship used by some contractors in the manufacture of its steam machinery, requires that every possible precaution and vigilance on the part of its inspectors should be exercised to prevent their occurrence. . . . The loss to the Government . . . is immeasurably greater than financial cost. It may cause the vessel to be inoperable at a critical moment in battle or for our very national existence. . . . Your patriotism, as well as your honor, honesty, and professional reputation, is involved in the performance of your duties.[16]

On multiple occasions, Snowden and Mason requested payment for additional work ordered by Stimers. In December 1863, Stimers called for modifications to the *Manayunk*'s engine but the terms were ambiguous. Snowden and Mason were authorized to charge extra for this change, said Stimers, "provided the cost does not exceed a certain sum." The limit, however, was unspecified; more than a year later, the local inspector for Snowden and Mason was still petitioning for payment for this work, as well as for a $79,000 increase necessitated by an order to raise the height of the *Umpqua*'s deck. Demands for modification continued to come from Stimers's office, sometimes several in a single week and interspersed with impatient inquiries about the completion of the ships. On December 5, 1863, Tomlinson, Hartupee, and Company wrote to Commodore Hull: "It is very difficult to fix a time for the completion of the boats, as they are so entirely different from the boats we contracted for and labor scarce, we were in hopes that we would be able to have launched this fall but find it cannot be done." The firm hoped to be ready by early spring—if the navy could refrain from making further changes.[17]

By March 1864, naval officials reached the end of their patience with the Pittsburgh shipbuilders. The chief of the Bureau of Construction ordered Commodore Hull to respond to Tomlinson, Hartupee, and Company's stream of complaints and repeated delays: "Please inform these gentlemen that they are expected to comply with their contract." On October 20, Secretary of the Navy Gideon Welles dispatched Commodore Hull to investigate the work on ships in Pittsburgh and to pressure the contractors to complete their vessels. The partnership between the navy and Pittsburgh shipbuilders remained turbulent throughout the war. Neither the *Manayunk* or the *Umpqua* was completed before the war ended. The *Manayunk*, originally scheduled to be completed in March 1863, was not delivered until September 1865 and the contract price of $460,000 for that vessel was dwarfed by the final cost of $700,896. Despite the staggering price tag and the fact that the *Manayunk* missed the conflict for which it was constructed, the *Gazette* celebrated the boat and its maiden voyage as "a triumph of Western mechanism."[18]

The civilian shipbuilding snafus were, however, overshadowed by a more inspiring episode, in which Pittsburghers took part in the riverine war in a unique and unexpected manner. In the spring and summer of 1862, the river economy and culture of Pittsburgh attracted the attention of an engineer with an innovative mind who was determined to aid the Union war effort. Charles Ellet Jr., a Philadelphian, began his career as a rodman gathering data on the Chesapeake and Ohio Canal. In 1830, he went to Paris to complete his education at the École Nationale des Ponts et Chaussées. Over the next thirty years, he was instrumental in some of the most important American engineering accomplishments of the era. In 1842, he designed and supervised the construction of the country's first major wire suspension bridge. He also made important advances in river navigation by instituting the practice of using reservoirs to regulate water levels in wet and dry seasons. After extensive political wrangling, he designed and oversaw construction of the notable Wheeling Suspension Bridge. In 1850, the War Department commissioned him to conduct an extensive survey of the Mississippi and Ohio Rivers.[19]

Ellet became interested in the naval uses of steam power and, in 1855, he published a pamphlet that urged reintroducing the ancient tactic of ramming. Using steam engines, he argued, small, agile boats armed with rams could deliver devastating blows to larger vessels and could thus replace more expensive warships, but the proposal received little support in the Navy Department and the idea would be ignored until the war brought Ellet opportunities.[20]

Union strategy in the Western theater early in the war centered on the use of combined land and naval forces to seize control of principal rivers, especially the Mississippi. Compounding the urgency to control the Western rivers in 1862 was a growing fear of Confederate ironclads ascending the Mississippi and threatening Northern cities. In the wake of the Battle of Hampton Roads, Virginia during March 8–9, 1862, the War Department received reports that the Rebels were constructing river vessels at New Orleans "clad in railroad iron like the Merrimack [C.S.S. *Virginia*] to be used on the upper Mississippi and even on the Ohio." Ellet himself was passionate about the danger of Confederate ironclad riverboats and, even before the battle between the *Monitor* and the *Virginia*, he had published another pamphlet to promote his ideas on naval warfare. He also wrote letters to Assistant Secretary of the Navy Gustavus Fox, several of which Northern newspapers printed. By the time Secretary of War Edwin Stanton solicited proposals in March for how to combat the Rebel ironclad threat, Ellet's ram strategy had attracted so much attention that it finally received official sanction.[21]

On March 27, Stanton instructed Ellet to "proceed immediately to Pittsburgh, Cincinnati, and New Albany and take measures to provide steam rams for defense against iron clad vessels on the Western waters." Ellet wasted no time. He arrived in Pittsburgh the next day, set up in the Monongahela House, and began preparations to build his fleet. He would likely have read in the *Daily Dispatch* that day an editorial discussing the vulnerability of the navy's ironclad gunboats in their unprotected sterns. "Those who are familiar with the navigation of the Western rivers," said the author, "do not need an explanation" of the difficulty of keeping a boat's bow toward the enemy. It was almost as if he was speaking directly to Ellet. That same day, Ellet telegraphed General Henry Halleck, commander of Union forces in the West, informing him of his order from the secretary of war and suggesting that, if the Rebel threat was dire, he would immediately get a boat under way with mechanics and equipment to prepare her en route.[22]

Stanton was sensitive to the political and economic impact of Ellet's construction project. "Do not confine your work to one locality," he instructed. "Give a portion to Cincinnati, and to New Albany, so as to avoid the imputation of local favoritism." However, Ellet and his local advisors saw things differently. Motivated by reports of a Rebel ram at Memphis, the War Department sent James K. Moorhead to Pittsburgh to aid Ellet in his mission. Community leaders established a committee to facilitate Ellet's work and Moorhead was to make the introductions. No doubt influenced by the committee, Ellet resisted continued urgings to move on to Ohio and Illinois, arguing that the vessels he needed could be built only in Pittsburgh. With the introduction of steam power for river vessels, "towboats" became an es-

FIG. 5. Rodman Gun. The twenty-inch Rodman was heralded as "the greatest gun in Christendom." Here it is seen stopped in Harrisburg, PA, en route to Brooklyn, NY. Ken Turner Collection, SJHHC.

sential component of mid-nineteenth-century river transportation. Although these vessels took their name from the earlier practice of draft animals towing barges by walking alongside canals, by 1860, riverboat crews became masters at using specially designed steamboats (towboats) to push several barges lashed together to maximize their load. Ellet's plan was to take a half dozen of these powerful towboats, strengthen their hulls, and employ them as rams.[23]

From late March until mid-May, Ellet and his civilian crewmen prepared the fleet in relative secrecy. The War Department placed a gag order on the Pittsburgh press that proved effective for a while. It was not until the *Chicago Post* printed a story about the two ram vessels in St. Louis and the six on the stocks at Pittsburgh preparing to join the Western flotilla of Commodore Andrew Hull Foote that the *Gazette* began to report on them. For some weeks past, the *Gazette* ran articles about the threat of Rebel ironclad

MAKING GUNS FOR THE NEW MONITORS AT PITTSBURG, PENNSYLVANIA.—Sketched by Mr. Theodore R. Davis.—[See Page 535.]

FIG. 6. "Making Guns for the New Monitors at Pittsburgh," *Harpers Weekly*, 23 August 1862.

rams on the Mississippi. Now, with the silence broken, its editor was free to inform the people triumphantly that the instrument of naval salvation would be the product of Pittsburghers' labor. Pittsburgh firms were already active in manufacturing gunboats, but the news of Ellet's rams was sensational. These were heralded as "the best and strongest craft on the river. . . . The bows will be rendered almost a solid mass of timber and iron, provided with a projecting ram which will demolish anything with which it may come in contact."[24]

As significant as where and how they were constructed, though, was whom Ellet recruited to man his fleet. The Ellet rams were the last vessels of the United States military to be captained and crewed by civilians. While Ellet did hold the rank of colonel of engineers in the army, the pilots and engineers who operated the rams were neither enlisted nor commissioned in the army or navy; they were instead predominantly men who made their living in the bustling river commerce of the city. William Fish was forty in 1862 and a propertyless boatman living along the Ohio riverfront in Allegheny city's First Ward. When the war came, he supported his wife and four young sons by transporting cargo between Pittsburgh and New Orleans. Robert F. Ballard was born in New Hampshire. His father, Luther, brought the family to Allegheny County and, by 1841, operated a bucket factory in Pittsburgh's Fifth Ward. Robert, the second of six children, grew up working for his father as a machinist. When the war came, he was employed as a riverboat engineer in Pittsburgh and Allegheny city. Like Fish, Ballard was married with four young children.[25]

In late May, Ellet, with his brother Alfred and four rams, joined a flotilla commanded by Commodore C. H. Davis. Immediately, the two officers were at odds over Ellet's ambitious plan to promptly engage the enemy. Ellet argued that he was under direct orders from the War Department and therefore not subordinate to Davis. The commodore, wary of rushing to engage the enemy, believed Ellet under his command and ordered him to wait. Ellet won the argument and, on June 4, advanced on Fort Pillow (on the Mississippi River in west Tennessee) without Davis's gunboats. The next day, finding the fortifications abandoned, he sent his brother ashore with a small party to raise the U.S. flag over the fort.[26]

On June 6, Ellet's four rams and five of Davis's gunboats clashed near Memphis with the Confederate fleet of six gunboats and two rams. From all reports, the Pittsburgh riverboat men performed admirably. Charles Ellet took his flagship *Queen of the West* at thirteen knots into the side of the Confederate *Colonel Lovell*, sinking that vessel along with sixty-eight of her crew. Alfred Ellet steered the *Monarch* into the Rebel ram *Beauregard* and

FIG. 7. Colonel Ellet's Rams on the Duck River. From Warren D. Crandall and Isaac D. Newell, *History of the Ram Fleet and the Mississippi Marine Brigade in the War for the Union on the Mississippi and Its Tributaries* (St. Louis, 1907).

crippled her before a direct hit on her boilers from a Union gunboat finished her off. The Union flotilla then chased down and destroyed or captured four of the remaining five Confederate boats. In a matter of hours, Ellet and his civilian riverboat men had accomplished the mission that had begun in Pittsburgh two months earlier (see Figure 9).[27]

At the conclusion of the battle, which left Memphis undefended by Confederate forces, Colonel Ellet sent his son, Charles R. Ellet, a medical cadet, into the city to raise two flags, one over the custom house and a second over the courthouse, "as an evidence of the return of [the] city to the care and protection of the Constitution." The only casualty suffered by the ram fleet in the engagement was its commander. Ellet received a pistol shot in the leg, a wound initially thought minor but which developed complications and claimed his life two weeks later.[28]

In Pittsburgh, the victories of the rams were celebrated joyously. "It has been a glorious day," said the *Gazette*. The "ram fleet, offspring of the city of Pittsburgh, have done honor to the country." The Pittsburgh men who

FIG. 8. "The Total Annihilation of the Rebel Fleet by the Federal Fleet under Commodore Davis," Lithograph by Middleton, Strobridge, & Co, NH 42367. Courtesy of the Naval History and Heritage Command.

crewed Ellet's rams abstained from enlisting in the army or navy. Amid all the social pressure and the martial pageantry in the city, they chose to stay at home with their families and their work, but, when the events of the war intersected with their everyday lives, these civilians found themselves drawn to and immersed in the war in a way that paralleled the experiences of those in uniform: they faced combat with the enemy, suffered the loss of a respected leader, and returned home in triumph, lauded by their community. Their deeds served as an inspiration to the home front and their sacrifice for the preservation of the Union was honored as much as that of any volunteer regiment.[29]

For most, thoughts of Pittsburgh's experience in the Civil War conjure up images of bustling factories, sweltering foundries, and large riverboats laden with the materiel of war. Indeed, manufacturing was a central, and certainly the most tangible, aspect of Pittsburgh's support of the Union war effort. From the initiation of war in April 1861, the War Department called on Pittsburgh to supply every type of munition from musket cartridges to twenty-inch shells and every type of weapon that fired them, from small arms to the Massive Rodman guns and ironclad riverboats. Scores of small shops and manufacturers transformed their operations to assemble and provide the clothing, equipment, and accoutrements carried by soldiers. The city also played an integral role in the movement of all these goods, producing wagons that carried them, shoes and harness for the horses that pulled those wagons, and steam engines to power the boats that hauled them. Underlying all of this was a tremendous expansion of the coal industry that powered the factories, furnaces, ships, and trains to convert raw materials and labor on the home front into the tools of war employed at the front lines. Pittsburgh prospered greatly through this industrial and commercial support of the war. A clear indicator of this economic growth is seen in the internal revenue tax for the city which totaled $4.4 million in 1865, an increase of $1.9 million from the year prior. For the year ending 1 September 1863, the city produced cannon weighing a total of 7,173, 534 pounds as well as shot and shell totaling 2,972,916 pounds. Between 1863 and 1865, annual revenues rose 263% for coal, more than 300 percent for gun powder, and 900 percent for iron.[30]

However, despite the significance of manufacturing for the Union war effort, and the lasting growth it spurred for the city, industrial performance held a subordinate place in how Pittsburghers remembered the war. The busi-

TABLE 1
GROWTH OF PRINCIPAL WAR INDUSTRIES IN PITTSBURGH, 1860 1870

INDUSTRY	1860		1870	
	Number of Establishments	Value of Products	Number of Establishments	Value of Products
Iron Rolling Mills	13	$4,000,000	32	
Iron Foundries	17	$2,000,000	48	$29,000,000[a]
Coal[b]	16	$500,000	63	$12,000,000
Glass	8	$300,000	68	$7,000,000
Wagons[c]	—	—	12	$286,000

Notes: [a]The value of products from the iron industry were not specified by rolling mills and foundries in the 1870 records. [b]Summaries of the city's coal industry do not delineate between the proprietors of coal mines, coal merchants and distributors, and coal transporters when listing the value of bushels sold. The numbers in the above table indicate the merchants, dealers, and transporters listed in the city directories. [c]There are no firms in the 1860 Directory listed as manufacturers or dealers of wagons.

TABLE 2
ANNUAL REVENUES OF WAR INDUSTRIES IN PITTSBURGH, 1863-1865

INDUSTRY	1863	1864	1865
Coal	$318,425	$572,436	$835,994
Iron	$969,802	$2,891,062	$8,729,005
Gun Powder	$78,689	$155,302	$248,376

ness owners, workers, and their families who prospered from the economic boom certainly celebrated this avenue for supporting the war and its impact to achieving ultimate victory cannot be overstated. Furthermore, the city's identity as a mainspring of industry was frequently evoked in celebrating important wartime events such as the prevention of the gun removal, the testing of cannons in public gatherings, and the campaign of the Ram Fleet. Additionally, it is through such events that we see how manufacturing was integrated into the ideas and messages behind sustaining the war effort in Pittsburgh. Such messages far more frequently drew on how manufacturing connected people to the war than on the quantity of goods shipped to the front. Those munitions, guns, leather goods, wagons, and boats mattered, but for energizing the people, it was far more effective to underscore how manufacturing brought the war and their city together. Those who wrote the early histories of Pittsburgh during the Civil War and delivered the speeches commemorating the city's participation rarely emphasized how prolific local industry was in supplying the War Department. Far more prominent and heralded were the individual acts of service by Pittsburghers, not only those who fought in uniform but also the men and women who provided care to those soldiers at the front lines and on the home front.

6

* * * * *

THE VOLUNTARY AND SPONTANEOUS ACTION OF THE PEOPLE

Benevolent Mobilization on the Home Front and Front Line

With all loyal women of the land, I worked zealously in their
behalf; worked, because there was irresistible impulse to do, to act.
Anything but idleness, when our armies were preparing for the
combat, and we knew not who should be the first to fall,
who be called widow, or who fatherless.

–ANNA MORRIS HOLSTEIN–
Three Years in Field Hospitals of the Army of the Potomac (1867)

On October 15, 1913, Ellen R. Murdock Watson made the sixty-mile trip
by automobile from Pittsburgh to a small memorial park along the
old National Turnpike near Uniontown, Pennsylvania. A ceremony
was planned for that day to mark the unveiling of a new monument over the
gravesite of British General Edward Braddock who, in 1755, had been killed
in an ill-fated expedition to capture Fort Duquesne from the French. In 1862,
Watson followed the same route by carriage as she traveled to the front lines
of the Peninsula Campaign. Twice in that summer, she obtained from Union
military authorities "permission to visit the Army of the Potomac for the
purpose of rendering aid to the sick and wounded of the army." On several
occasions, under the auspices of the United States Christian Commission,
Watson served in field hospitals from Tennessee to Virginia, treating and
ministering to wounded soldiers. Traveling along the National Turnpike so
many years later, she undoubtedly reflected on her exciting times during

the war. Arriving at the Braddock memorial, she expected only to enjoy the ceremony, commemorating an important moment in western Pennsylvania history. However, when she began to move through the crowd, scores of Civil War veterans recognized her. By the end of the gathering, Ellen Murdock Watson, Pittsburgh veteran of benevolent wartime service, was among the most honored guests of the ceremony. Six weeks later, her life-long friend S. A. Bryant—in a letter read at Watson's funeral—called it one of the great moments of Watson's life. Bryant also wrote of Watson's two prized mementos from her service in the war: "The badge of the Christian Commission, a silver pin in the shape of an open Bible" and "a silk badge presented by the One Hundredth Pennsylvania Reserves, and bearing the inscription: 'the Soldiers' Friend, Ellen Robb Murdoch.'"[1]

Although Pittsburghers took great pride in the iron that John Harper boasted would smite the enemy, it was his "coal enough to warm its friends" metaphor that most aptly described their community's role in the war. The mobilization of civilians to provide aid to Union soldiers was the real heart of the city's wartime identity. The government's inability to fully provide for its soldiers spurred citizens to step in to help. The decentralization that characterized community efforts at the onset of the war was evident also in this benevolent mobilization, through which ordinary citizens worked for the benefit of soldiers on the home front and front lines alike. Soldiers' families became a new focus for those active before the war in aiding the less fortunate, but those who wanted to participate more directly in the war focused their energies on ministering to the soldiers.[2]

Civilian support for soldiers was one of the most highly organized aspects of the Northern war effort. In the first two years of the war, activists formed numerous benevolent organizations. While most were local and closely tied to individual communities in their origin and scope, the most famous centrally organized at the national level with direct connections to the federal government. However, even the national organizations depended on the local efforts of individual communities.

Preeminent among the national soldier aid societies was the United States Sanitary Commission (USSC). Headquartered in New York City and working in close partnership with the federal government, the USSC was commissioned on June 9, 1861 by order of Secretary of War Simon Cameron to promote the health and welfare of troops at the front. The recent European experience in the Crimean War provided a model: the British Sanitary Commission, which was established to reduce the staggering number of casualties resulting from disease and infection.[3]

The main strength of the USSC lay in its vast network of local chapters. Community soldier aid societies that formed independently in the wake of the firing on Fort Sumter came together to create the USSC and carried out the great majority of its benevolent work. After the war, the officers of the Commission reported that "[n]o complete and thorough organization throughout the country was ever effected, although it was approximated by some local committees, as for example by the one at Pittsburg [sic]. The work was too vast, the territory too large, and especially was the reliance, properly and necessarily, too much upon the voluntary and spontaneous action of the people, to admit of rigid and thoroughgoing organization."[4]

The Pittsburgh Sanitary Commission was established with the assistance of USSC agent Jacob Glosser in October 1861. Glosser and local leaders established a committee of women in each ward, township, and borough to gather and produce useful items for the soldiers at the front. Their efforts energized neighbors and warehouse and storerooms quickly filled with clothing, bandages, and Bibles. Pittsburgh was recognized by the national office as one of "the most important contributing depots under the control of the Commission during the war." The city's commercial transportation advantages enabled it to amass and ship large quantities of goods and publications to the front. Cash donations poured in as well. In 1864, the Pittsburgh chapter sent $92,705 to the central fund of the USSC. This was the largest contribution per capita of any Northern city, more than twice that of Philadelphia and Boston and more than ten times that of New York.[5]

Benevolent mobilization in Pittsburgh was for the most part steered by the same community leaders active in raising volunteers and defending the city. Directing the Pittsburgh Sanitary Commission was Thomas Bakewell, commissary general of the Home Guards. Others active in both the Sanitary Commission and military mobilization were Thomas M. Howe, William M. Edgar, and James Park. However, others came to leadership in the local commission as a natural extension of their antebellum leadership in reformist movements such as temperance, women's rights, and abolitionism.[6]

One of the most prominent members of the Pittsburgh Sanitary Commission was Felix R. Brunot. He was the youngest son of Dr. Felix Brunot, who had arrived in America during the Revolutionary War with his brother-in-law, General Lafayette, and had served on his medical staff. In 1797, the elder Brunot arrived in Pittsburgh and opened a practice on Liberty Street. He built a home on an island at the head of the Ohio River that still bears his name. The younger Brunot attended Western University in Allegheny City, then Jefferson College in Canonsburg, Pennsylvania. He cofounded the Singer,

Nimick, and Co. Steelworks and also served as director and later president of the Allegheny Valley Railway in the 1850s and 1860s. In the antebellum era, he established himself as one of the city's leading philanthropists, participating in several reform initiatives and helping to found the Young Men's Mercantile Library Association. When the Civil War began, Brunot took up the cause of improving the conditions of Union soldiers. Before the close of the war's first year, he witnessed firsthand the hardships faced by soldiers in combat and the experience reinforced his commitment to providing care for the sick and wounded at the front.[7]

In April 1862, the Pittsburgh Sanitary had its first real test in providing care for soldiers. On April 6 and 7, the Union armies under Ulysses S. Grant and Don Carlos Buell suffered more than thirteen thousand casualties at the Battle of Shiloh. Americans had never experienced such loss in a single engagement. When news of the awful bloodshed arrived in Pittsburgh, the Sanitary Commission rose to the challenge of providing assistance to the doctors and nurses in the field hospitals. Again, private citizens drew on their peacetime experience to guide their wartime support. The commission chartered two steamships, the *J. W. Hailman* and the *Marengo*, and loaded them with medical supplies and volunteers to aid the wounded of Shiloh. Brunot was chosen to lead the effort and under his supervision the Pittsburgh expedition evacuated four hundred wounded from the battlefield.[8]

The pair of floating field hospitals made its way back up the Tennessee and Ohio rivers as the citizen volunteers onboard moved from soldier to soldier providing care and comfort. The steamships delivered the wounded to river ports near their homes such as Paducah, Evansville, Louisville, and Cincinnati. There, they were met by local volunteers coordinated through telegrams from the Sanitary Commission in Pittsburgh. The *Hailman* and *Marengo* arrived in Pittsburgh on the twenty-sixth and twenty-seventh with sixty-eight wounded soldiers from Midwestern regiments who could not be carried to their own communities. Forty-eight were placed in the local marine hospital and the rest in Passavant's infirmary.[9]

A week later, the executive committee of the Pittsburgh Sanitary Commission met at the custom house to discuss the care and quartering of the wounded soldiers. Of particular concern was regulating visitors at the infirmaries. The committee resolved that only between the hours of one and six, two afternoons a week, would people be permitted to visit the casualties of Shiloh. Furthermore, visitors would have to obtain a pass signed by Brunot or one of the doctors serving in the Commission. The number of Pittsburghers thronging the hospitals to assist the wounded soldiers—or just catch a glimpse of the effects of the terrible battle—had become so overwhelming to the medical staff that the committee was compelled to intervene. These numerous visitors were not the families of these casualties, nearly all of whom were from Midwestern states; it is unlikely that in the span of a week any such families could have learned of their soldiers' fate and made the journey to Pittsburgh. Even if they had, the committee certainly would not have applied restrictions on visitation to them. The presence of these wounded Union soldiers in the city brought the war out of the newspapers and drew Pittsburghers who desired to experience the war in a tangible way. Several private citizens offered resources to the committee to assist with the casualties. William Phillips made the Girard Hotel available to convalescents and the Vigilant Engine Company partnered with others in the community to contribute horses and wagons.[10]

The experience with the Shiloh casualties spurred the Pittsburgh Sanitary Commission to take on even more ambitious endeavors. Following the example of the central office and capitalizing on its close relationship with the War Department, commission leaders in Pittsburgh began to coordinate their functions with military operations. While Brunot and his team were aiding the wounded of Shiloh, General George B. McClellan moved his massive Army of the Potomac toward the Confederate capital of Richmond. Since assuming command following the Union defeat at Manassas, McClellan transformed the army from the panicked mob that retreated from Bull Run into a disciplined fighting force. After landing on the Peninsula (between the James and York rivers), the army set out on April 4, 1862, moving northwestward up the Peninsula toward the capital.

As the Army of the Potomac besieged Richmond, Brunot again led a contingent from the Pittsburgh Sanitary Commission to ameliorate the hardships of soldiers at the front. On June 17, twenty-five civilian volunteers from Pittsburgh arrived with Brunot at Fort Monroe, on the tip of the Peninsula. A week after arriving, he left six nurses behind to work in the hospitals there and traveled with the rest to the front line at Savage's Station. When the Union army retreated, Brunot and his party remained behind at a field hospital. Confederate forces soon overran the hospital, capturing the Pittsburgh volunteers along with the wounded they tended. Brunot and his comrades were sent with the captured officers to Libby Prison in Richmond. When Secretary Stanton learned of their imprisonment, he issued special orders that any prisoner exchange that might be arranged include the release of Brunot and his party. When these civilian volunteers were freed, it was by the same system of parole that sent soldiers home, under a code of honor by which they pledged they would not return to active service until formally exchanged.[11]

Local chapters of the Sanitary Commission used expeditions such as Brunot's to educate their communities about the conditions of soldiers in the field and to excite in the people a desire for involvement. Pittsburghers could attend periodic meetings at the Merchants' Exchange on Saturday afternoons to listen to firsthand accounts from recently returned benevolent workers. A contingent from the Pittsburgh Sanitary returned from the Peninsula Campaign in June 1862 and shortly after participated in such a meeting. The report these workers presented dramatized the hardships endured by wounded soldiers. The city's civilians were compelled to action as they listened to descriptions of field hospitals that were "most miserable" and the vast number of soldiers "lying upon the ground . . . with inexpressible yearnings for something palatable and refreshing." Sympathy for suffering soldiers was a powerful motivator mobilizing civilians for benevolent work.[12]

The intensification of campaigning, rising casualty rates, and the swelling ranks of the armies through 1862 prompted the USSC to refocus its efforts. In January 1863, delegates from every region met with the wives of several congressmen to form a women's council to help decide the way ahead. Soon after, Thomas Bakewell declared that the Pittsburgh Sanitary needed to reorganize into "a more permanent form, with increased resources, and with more efficient means for the collection of the contributions of their benevolent fellow citizens and their subsequent distribution among the sick and wounded soldiers now in arms for the defense of their homes, firesides and families."[13]

Members of the Sanitary Commission in Pittsburgh believed, with good reason, that they were a part of the greatest enterprise of the war, providing the best care and comfort for their soldiers. In the universe of benevolent mobilization, the USSC boasted several points of superiority over other agencies: it was the only one formally sanctioned by the federal government; it had a highly-organized logistical and communications structure that kept it well informed of the condition of regiments, allowing it to respond promptly with the right supplies; its agents were more experienced than others and had connections in the War Department and within the army's command structure at the front; and it had the authority and the expertise to advise on sound practices of health and sanitation in Union army camps. These advantages seemingly made it likely that Northerners wanting to support the war effort would turn only to the USSC. However, community-based offices of the Sanitary Commission such as Pittsburgh's were forced to contend with powerful conflicting sentiments that the national office was too removed from to appreciate. In competition with the Sanitary for the support of the people was a constellation of local benevolent agencies, each appealing to its community's vision of how to care for soldiers.[14]

Pittsburghers who enlisted in the cause of benevolent mobilization generally wanted the fruits of their labor and sacrifice to be directed exclusively to their own soldiers. Moreover, they hoped to establish their community as an exemplar of benevolent mobilization in the North, which they feared could not be accomplished were their contributions lost in the mix of a national agency. When the mothers, wives, and sisters in Pittsburgh gathered in parlors to sew socks and shirts and scrape bandages, they did not intend for them to be lost in a sea of articles produced by any number of merchant suppliers and shipped indiscriminately to army camps and regiments. They wanted to know that they were providing comfort to their own loved ones. Thomas Bakewell recognized this sentiment of localism in Pittsburghers and understood the obstacle it posed to the Sanitary's effectiveness in his city: "In making this appeal to your patriotism and generosity, we disclaim all desire or intention to interfere with the resources of other organizations for similar purposes. . . . We are aware that the system adopted by the commission . . . of distributing the stores and supplies intrusted [sic] to their care . . . without regard to local affinities or individual preferences, involves in some degree the sacrifice of those laudable feelings which induce the mothers, wives and sisters of our land, while earnestly seeking to relieve the wants of those near and dear to them, to fondly believe that their gift would be more highly prized if the recipients of their bounty could recognize the source whence they were derived." Bakewell implored his fellow Pittsburghers to overcome these reservations and see that the USSC "from its extensive correspondence and systematic arrangements, presents the best agency for supplying the wants of the volunteers." By cooperating with the USSC, he argued, Pittsburghers would provide more effective aid to the Union cause than could be realized by any "exclusively local arrangement."[15]

If the Sanitary Commission could not wholly overcome this point of resistance, it could at least cater to the people's desire for national recognition of their community's outstanding effort. To better align its system with this spirit of local pride, the USSC began marking its shipments with their point of origin. Before arriving to the front, crates were stamped "Cincinnati Branch, U.S. San. Com.," or "Pittsburgh San. Com." The Commission also used its publication, *The Sanitary Commission Bulletin,* to ensure that local agencies and their supporters received proper credit. In November 1863, the bulletin corrected an inaccurate report giving sole credit to Chicago for thirty-nine wagon loads of stores collected by various Midwestern Sanitary Commissions lest the mistake be "discouraging to some of our home workers." The tremendous impulse of localism in benevolent mobilization remained the principal impediment for the USSC throughout the war. When Thomas Bakewell made his appeal for support in Pittsburgh, he made certain to praise the work of the local agency that Pittsburghers were the most proud of: "We gratefully acknowledge the labors of the Pittsburgh Subsistence Committee . . . and their successful arrangements for cheering the hearts and recruiting the frames of more than a hundred thousand volunteers, by providing comfortable meals on their passage through the city."[16]

In Pittsburgh, the Subsistence Committee was without equal among local efforts to aid soldiers. Every large city and many small towns across the North contributed to the war through similar agencies, but the Pittsburgh Subsistence Committee provides a remarkable example of how localism shaped benevolent mobilization at the community level.

The gateway role that Pittsburgh served in the Northern war effort made stops in the city by traveling regiments a regular occurrence. Regimental histories and soldiers' memoirs from across the North are filled with accounts of time spent in Pittsburgh. After describing the 79th New York Infantry's journey through Columbus and Steubenville, Ohio and the poor, or mediocre, accommodations provided by their citizens, the regimental historian recalled the unit's stop in the Gateway City: "At midnight we reached Pittsburgh, Pennsylvania, and enjoyed the hospitality of the . . . Subsistence Committee, and before leaving were supplied with three days' rations of biscuit, cheese and smoked beef! How we would have liked to spend the remainder of our time at Pittsburgh!" In March 1864, in the most famous trans-theater trip of the war, Ulysses Grant passed through Pittsburgh on his way to Washington for the reception honoring his promotion to lieutenant general and his arrival in the Eastern theater. Also traveling through the city that day was the 1st Company, Minnesota Sharpshooters. In December 1863, the majority of the company reenlisted and now the men were returning home on furlough. The excitement of a surprise meeting with General Grant was overshadowed by their memories of the city's hospitality.[17]

The formation of the Pittsburgh Subsistence Committee was born of a desire to fill an important need of soldiers and rectify an affront to the community's pride. When Union soldiers traveled through cities, they did so with enough rations for the anticipated number of days of the journey, but frequent delays of trains and steamboats extended travel time and left soldiers hungry and thirsty. Furthermore, wounded soldiers often needed interim care as delays protracted their trip home. In June 1861, a Western regiment made the journey east to join the war. Within days of the regiment's passage through Pittsburgh, rumors began to circulate in local newspapers about the regiment's dissatisfaction with the community's hospitality. According to these accounts, the soldiers complained in cities farther along their route about Pittsburghers' failure to provide any provisions. Whether or not the story was true, Pittsburgh newspapers responded with a mixture of shame and indignation and implored Pittsburghers to never again give cause for such a complaint, which reflected so poorly on their community and its dedication to the Union war effort. Many of the same community leaders overseeing the initial mobilization of volunteer soldiers already grappled with the problem of housing and feeding local bodies of soldiers before they departed the city. The earliest regiments were quartered in houses of entertainment and fed in restaurants and hotels, a practice that proved expensive and unsustainable. When the complication of provisioning regiments passing through the city was added to the problem, a committee chaired by Thomas Howe established a fund and arranged more efficient care for soldiers sojourning in the city.[18]

Just before midnight on July 28, 1861, the 24th Ohio Volunteer Infantry Regiment arrived at the Pennsylvania Railroad depot in Pittsburgh. The soldiers were no doubt surprised when a delegation of local citizens greeted them and escorted them to city hall. The troops arrived to find a large room prepared to quarter them for the night. In the morning, they were led back to the depot, where a committee served them a breakfast of ham, bread, and hot coffee as they waited for the train to carry them east. Overshadowed between the first departures of Pittsburgh regiments and the devastating result of the Battle of Bull Run, this benevolent act received little public notice. However, for those who participated, the experience was so inspiring that within weeks they formed the Subsistence Committee with the express purpose of caring for soldiers as they passed through their city.[19]

The Subsistence Committee was directed by the three members of its executive subcommittee. All were family members of entrepreneurs who helped establish Pittsburgh's manufacturing and commercial prominence. Harriet M. Atwood was the modestly wealthy widow of Moses Atwood. Moses had been born in 1801 in Haverhill, Massachusetts, into a family whose New England roots dated back to 1642. In 1831, he ended his business ventures in New Castle, Kentucky, married Harriet, the daughter of a well-known minister, moved to Pittsburgh, opened a warehouse on Water Street on the Monongahela riverfront, and thereafter became a successful commission merchant and a founding member of the Third Presbyterian Church. He died in 1848, leaving his estate on the outskirts of the city to his wife. In 1861, Harriet Atwood assumed her son Henry's position as secretary of the Monongahela Insurance Company. As the Subsistence Committee formed, she was certainly influenced by her two sons, Frederick and William, who had just enlisted in Hampton's Independent Artillery Battery.[20]

William P. Weyman, only twenty-four when the war began, worked as a clerk for his father, George, and still resided in his parents' home. George Weyman was a prominent member of the city's commercial elite and a lay organizer of the First English Lutheran Church of Pittsburgh. In 1823, he established a tobacco factory and distribution warehouse and, by 1861, amassed property worth thirty thousand dollars. The senior Weyman was a member of the committee formed in July 1861 to address the problem of caring for soldiers in the city. His young son William joined him in this endeavor and soon joined Harriet Atwood on the executive subcommittee.[21]

Joseph Albree was the son of George Albree. In 1829, George moved to Pittsburgh from Salem, Massachusetts and opened a wholesale shoe store. He rebuilt the store after it was destroyed in the fire of 1845 and reopened as George Albree, Son, and Company. Joseph was born in 1835. After attending Western University of Pennsylvania, he became highly active in civic organizations. During the 1850s, he served as the president of the Young Men's Mercantile Library Association and Mechanics' Institute, a philanthropic organization designed to advance the education and social standing of young men in Pittsburgh. In 1861, Joseph Albree worked with his father and lived on Cedar Street near the East Common in Allegheny City with his new wife Martha, ten-month-old son Chester, and a young Irish domestic servant.[22]

Like a great many others involved in American benevolent work, the twenty-eight permanent members of the Subsistence Committee were predominantly unmarried middle- and upper-class women. Eighteen-year-old Martha Dalzell was the daughter of James Dalzell, the wealthy owner of J. Dalzell and Sons wholesale groceries on Penn Street. Sabina Townsend was the daughter of Reese Townsend, wealthy wire and rivet manufacturer. Many members attracted other family members onto the committee. Just as volunteering soldiers often inspired brothers and cousins, sons and nephews, to join them, so too did participants in benevolent work for soldiers. Sidney Lemon was the daughter of a modestly successful cabinet maker. When she joined the Subsistence Committee, her younger brother came along and served throughout the war by her side. William Weyman's two brothers George Jr. and Frank joined, as did their sister Harriet. Mary Park's father, James Park, was one of the most active Pittsburghers in the advancement of soldiers' care and a driving force in the initial organization of the committee. Joseph Albree's wife was highly active on the committee, as was Henry Atwood's sister, Lizzie.[23]

With the help of local business and municipal leaders, the committee expanded quickly. After feeding their first regiment in the streets near the railroad depot, the committee members decided to secure better facilities. Albree, Atwood, and Weyman were initially named to chair a subcommittee responsible for providing meals. Within a week, they assumed control of a warehouse at the corner of Penn and Wayne streets in the Fourth Ward. The women volunteers furnished the place with dining tables and, on August 3, the subcommittee formally fed its first regiment, the 20th Indiana Infantry, at the new facility. Two weeks later, the entire management of the Subsistence Committee's operations was handed over to these three organizers.[24]

While employing this site was an improvement over feeding soldiers in the street, it proved inadequate to meet the needs of the great number of regiments now moving through the city. Over the coming weeks, Weyman and Albree worked with city officials to improve their accommodations; in early October, they were granted the use of city hall as a permanent central office for the committee and a dining facility for transiting regiments. The main floor was filled with ten long tables that could seat twelve hundred soldiers. They next turned their attention to opening a new site closer to the rail depot, for the building on Penn was far from where the soldiers were met. Albree acquired a warehouse on Liberty Street opposite the depot. This new facility, dubbed the Soldiers' Home, could provide lodging and meals to soldiers immediately on their arrival.[25]

The Subsistence Committee worked to ensure that every soldier passing through Pittsburgh knew about its available services. Young boys were charged with passing out handbills to soldiers as they stepped off the trains: "All wounded soldiers on this train are invited to come to the Soldiers' Home of the 'Subsistence Committee,' No. 347 Liberty Street, opposite the depot. Surgeons are in attendance, who will dress your wounds. Free meals and lodgings, are provided for all Union Soldiers. One of the Committee will meet you at the depot, to conduct you to the home" (see Figure 10). Local officials and businessmen also eagerly contributed where they could. Alderman William Shore, for one, frequently represented the committee at the rail depot, directing soldiers to the home. In January 1864, several of them brokered a deal with the Pennsylvania Railroad Company allowing the committee to utilize a large lot on Washington between Liberty and Penn.[26]

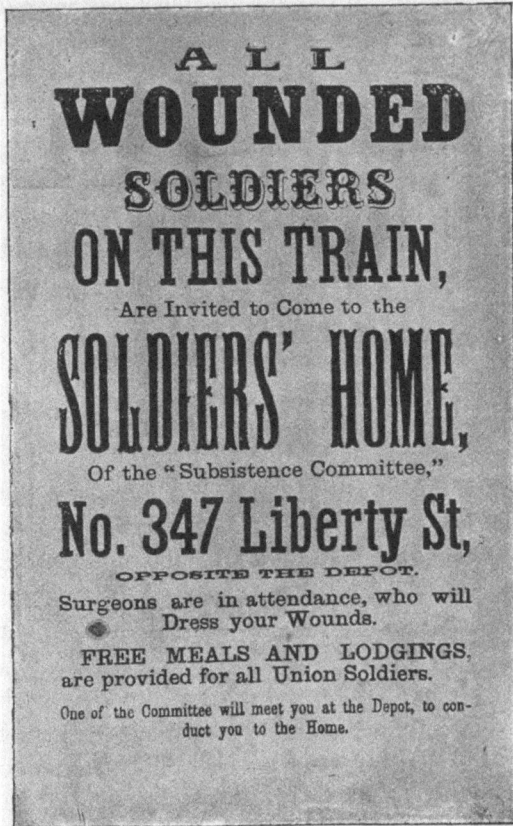

FIG. 9. Subsistence Committee Handbill. This handbill
from the Subsistence Committee was distributed by
young boys to soldiers arriving at Pittsburgh. In Grand
Army of the Republic, Department of Pennsylvania,
Proceedings of the 28th Annual Encampment, 38.

In November 1862, Weyman had a printer prepare one hundred thousand circulars for distribution in local churches. This not only increased support and volunteerism in the city, it also got the word out in camps at the front. Many soldiers heard of the Subsistence Committee through the letters of wives, siblings, and parents in Pittsburgh.[27]

In the fall of 1863, the 9th New Hampshire Volunteer Infantry Regiment stopped in Pittsburgh on its way to the Western theater. The passage in the regimental history describing this visit captured the welcome reprieve from the hardships of war that the Subsistence Committee provided: "The trip from Virginia to Kentucky was made pleasant by the Unionists along the route, but especially so at Pittsburgh, PA, where the brigade was given a collation." The soldiers were "waited on by ten of the handsomest ladies in the country, who filled their haversacks with cold meats, [and] bread . . . and their canteens with hot coffee." Before departing, the soldiers gave their hostesses "three cheers, and voted Pittsburgh, the 'banner city.'"[28]

Pittsburghers were proud of the Subsistence Committee's reputation among Union soldiers. Local pride was just as important in mobilizing benevolent work as it was for filling the ranks. Pittsburghers wanted to lead the North in caring for soldiers just as they did in putting soldiers in uniform. The Anderson Cavalry arrived in Pittsburgh on the evening of Saturday, October 8, 1862, and was treated by the Subsistence Committee. When Weyman wrote to Albree telling him of the hospitality shown the soldiers, he noted how "the Philadelphia companies in the regiment thought it far surpassed the Philadelphia rooms and especially the quantity and quality of eatibles [*sic*]. . . . They gave three cheers for the ladies, then for the committee, then for the city of Pittsburgh." Leaders of soldier aid organizations were always concerned with how their contribution to the care of Union regiments stacked up against that of other cities.[29]

The volunteers of the Subsistence Committee performed a variety of services for soldiers passing through. They gathered donations of medical supplies at their depots until the Pittsburgh Christian Commission, of which Weyman also principally organized, assumed that responsibility in April 1863. The Subsistence Committee also held prayer meetings for soldiers and distributed religious literature to them. By the end of 1863, praise for the committee from soldiers all across the North even reached President Lincoln's ear and piqued his interest. On January 27, 1864, Weyman responded to an inquiry from the president by sending him a picture of the large dining room where, he boasted, his volunteers could feed and entertain twelve hundred soldiers at one time. He also described their enormous coffee boiler that held 250 gallons, giving "each man as much coffee as he can drink, and then [allowing him to] fill his canteen." Weyman related furthermore how each regiment was greeted as it arrived in the city and how each regiment was subsequently served. As the soldiers made their way to city hall, volunteers set the massive tables; when the men arrived, they were each guided to a plate containing "two pieces of bread and butter, rolls, ham or beef, cheese, pickles, apples, cut cabbage, and such" (see Figure 11). Weyman also wrote

SOLDIERS' DINING-ROOM, PITTSBURG, PA.

FIG. 10. Soldiers Dining Hall. This room in Pittsburgh's city hall was used by the Subsistence Committee to feed soldiers passing through the city. In Moss, *Annals of the United States Christian Commission* (1868), following 346.

of the care provided to disabled men by the women of the committee: at the facility near the depot, "we have cared for 15,000 sick and wounded soldiers, giving them medical and all the care their conditions demanded. The ladies of this committee, besides this work, visit regularly the camps and hospitals around our city and provide the sick and destitute with any comforts their condition may demand."[30]

The work of the Subsistence Committee was central to Pittsburgh's wartime identity. The committee's reputation throughout the army and its uniquely local character were sources of great pride for Pittsburghers and many not directly connected with its operations were drawn to city hall to share in the experience. Civilians may not have been able to travel to the front to comfort their loved ones, but, thanks to the Subsistence Committee, they daily had large gatherings of other soldiers to lavish their kindness on.

The care of Union soldiers was ever-present in the mind of Pittsburgher Josiah Copely. The father of four sons who served in the Union army, he watched the efforts of local benevolent agencies with great interest. His oldest

FIG. 11. Winslow Homer's "Our Women and the War,"
Harper's Weekly, September 6, 1862.

son, John, was killed in September 1862 at the Battle of South Mountain. Less than four months later, his son Albert died of wounds received at the Battle of Stones River. With his two eldest sons gone and two more still serving, Copely was drawn to city hall to see firsthand the work of the Subsistence Committee. A few weeks after learning of Albert's death, Copely remembered, word reached him that a Midwestern regiment traveling to join the Army of the Potomac would arrive at city hall around midnight to be fed by the committee: "I lived in Allegheny City at that time, and had no active part in that good work. But still I felt that I must go over that night and see 'the boys.'"[31]

For a long while after entering the hall, Copely stood by a wall, taking in the scene of a thousand Union soldiers seated at the large tables enjoying themselves. The men appeared to be more than satisfied with the hospitality of the committee. Eventually, Copely struck up a conversation with a young soldier and asked if he had ever encountered any soldiers from the 78th Pennsylvania Reserves and specifically if he knew Albert. He was astonished when the Ohio soldier told him that indeed he knew Albert Copely; the two had been taken prisoner together at Stones River. They were placed in the same rail car and, over days of travel, the soldier tended to Albert's wounds. The captured Union soldiers were transported from Tennessee to Georgia and then north toward Richmond. At Knoxville, the two were removed with other wounded prisoners and placed in a hospital where, again, the soldier found himself in a position to care for Albert, now in the bed beside his own. Albert's wound did not appear mortal, but the strain of prolonged rail travel proved too much for him. After listening to the story, Copely took the soldier into a side room set up to treat the wounded and changed the dressing on his wounded ankle.[32]

The civilians who volunteered to work for the Subsistence Committee were daily in the presence of wounded and sick soldiers. When they arrived in Pittsburgh, rather than be forced to endure further travel, these soldiers were escorted to the Soldier's Home or local hospitals. Weyman and Albree spent as much time as they could directly caring for soldiers passing through Pittsburgh. Like their male and female volunteers, they became personally connected with the soldiers under their care and often went well beyond providing a meal or treating a wound. One evening in November 1862, Albree and Weyman greeted a large group of soldiers as they stepped off their train. While the volunteers greeted the soldiers and directed them to city hall, the two men were drawn to a particular young soldier named Morrison who was so gravely wounded that they decided to take him on to a hospital. Soon after, Albree departed Pittsburgh on business while Weyman continued to monitor the soldier's condition. On Tuesday evening, November 11, Weyman visited Morrison and found him to be rapidly fading. He wrote to Albree that he did not believe the young man would survive the night. The next evening, Morrison requested Weyman's presence and told him that he "thought he was sinking fast." However, Weyman observed, he appeared "willing to die" and regretted only that he could not see his mother again. His final request was that Weyman forward his letters and other papers, some to his mother and some to his sweetheart. That evening, after the young soldier died, Weyman telegraphed his mother and subsequently shipped Morrison's body home according to her instructions. Less than a week later, Weyman forwarded to Albree a letter from the mother thanking him for the kindness they rendered: "It perhaps seemed a small [deed] to some . . . but it has at least made the sorrow of one poor mother lighter, (and God only knows how soon my own dear brother [in the army] may need someone to sooth[e] his aching brow)."[33]

William Weyman, along with many others involved with the Subsistence Committee, was also active in the Pittsburgh chapter of another large wartime benevolent agency, Ellen Watson's beloved United States Christian Commission. On April 6, 1863, a meeting of citizens in Pittsburgh established the Army Committee of Western Pennsylvania, the Pittsburgh auxiliary of the USSC. Weyman served as the committee's receiving officer while Joseph Albree held the position of treasurer and later field secretary. The Christian Commission cooperated with the Subsistence Committee: the latter tended to the needs of soldiers in the city while the former cared for those at the front. Conflicts between the two were prevented not only by the cross-membership but by the division of responsibility between the home front and the front lines rather than between the services provided. In April 1863, the Subsistence Committee turned over to the Christian Commission its task of gathering medical supplies in depots for regiments at the front while continuing to hold prayer services—a primary function of the commission—for soldiers passing through Pittsburgh.[34]

The Christian Commission was organized in November 1861 at a convention of delegates of the Young Men's Christian Association from cities across the Northeast and Midwest. Like the leaders of the Sanitary Commission, those of the commission realized by late 1862 that the scope of the war was widening beyond their capacity to care for soldiers and thus a reorganization was necessary. They subsequently put into effect a five-point plan relying on decentralized, community-based benevolent work. According to the plan, "each auxiliary was to organize local societies in its own districts, collect funds, and secure delegates and commission them." Pittsburgh partnered with the auxiliaries of Cincinnati, Indianapolis, and Louisville to support regiments in the military departments of the Ohio and the Cumberland. Although "no complete and thorough organization throughout the country was ever effected," the Christian Commission experienced tremendous growth and provided extensive care at the front through "the voluntary and spontaneous action of the people" at the community level. In the commission's official records of its activities during the war, Pittsburgh was cited as essential in this respect. The final report of the their wartime accomplishments recorded that, while the cash receipts of Pittsburgh placed it behind the local auxiliaries of Boston and New York, the value of supplies the city sent to the front was second to none in the country. Its cash and material contributions together totaled $837,999.26. Overall, the Pittsburgh chapter was responsible for a fourth of all the USSC received from across the country for the entirety of the war.[35]

The mission of the USCC and its Pittsburgh auxiliary varied from that of other benevolent agencies: fundamentally it sought to mobilize volunteers and materials to promote the spiritual well-being of soldiers in the field. As the Reverend Herrick Johnson, delegate from Pittsburgh, said after the war, "the commission had in substance a three-fold office. It aimed to reach and link together the battlefield, home, heaven—the heart of the soldier, the parent's heart, and the heart of God."[36]

The *Presbyterian Banner* said of benevolent efforts like those of the Christian Commission that "[i]n every case [they were] accompanying these works of Christian charity with the word of Christian instruction and prayer . . . the combination of works of love with the Word of Truth—of practical with doctrinal religion." William Passavant, prominent Lutheran clergyman in Pittsburgh who served in field hospitals alongside his deaconesses, wrote that "Sickness, suffering and death are inseparable from war. However just and sacred a contest may be, these sad results are unavoidable. The duty of the Church and of the State is, therefore, apparent, and it is manifestly to relieve the sufferings and mitigate the sorrows of war by all the appliances of mercy within our reach."[37]

Volunteers from churches and organizations like the Christian Commission provided solace both for ˜the suffering soldier and for his family who could not be there in his hour of need. In November 1862, four sisters of the Pittsburgh order of the Sisters of Mercy arrived in Washington at the request of the War Department. They were charged with caring for the wounded at the recently established Stanton Military Hospital. They were joined by four others on December 8 and immediately began the task that they would sustain throughout the war. A local newspaper marked the sisters' departure from Pittsburgh with a poem that captured the meaning of their service to those on the home front:

> Raise the young soldier's head from the dark gory earth,
> He was cared for and loved in the land of his birth;
> No fond mother is near him oh! watch his last breath,
> And wipe from his pale brow the chill dews of death.[38]

While many officers in the field affirmed the value of religious services in camps, the government did not provide tents for chapels, nor would it transport those provided by a benevolent organization. Many chaplains relied on mess tents or barracks but these were not always available and their use depended on the cooperation of individual commanding officers. In a letter of May 18, 1861, from Camp Scott, Pennsylvania, Chaplain A. M. Stewart of the 13th Pennsylvania Infantry applauded the "liberality of friends in Pittsburgh" who furnished a chapel tent after learning that none was to be provided by the army.[39]

The most celebrated activity of the Christian Commission was ministering to wounded soldiers at the front. At the anniversary ceremony of the commission on February 11, 1866, Reverend Herrick Johnson recalled visiting the wounded after the Battle of the Wilderness and the efforts of his party to connect these soldiers with their families. According to Johnson, the Christian ministry of the Christian Commission agents penetrated the "roughness and the hardness through the reserve and the reticence, through the bolted and barred doors, down into the soldiers' hearts . . . and away went the messages of love from the sufferers to the loved ones at home, hundreds of them every day written by the delegates."[40]

The local press celebrated certain volunteers in the Pittsburgh auxiliary. Mary Moorhead, the daughter of popular local politician James K. Moorhead, made several trips to tend wounded soldiers at the front and the *Gazette* closely followed her travels and encounters. During the Peninsula Campaign, a reporter noted that among the passengers of a boat arriving in Washington from Fort Monroe was Mary Moorhead, who was returning home "after an absence of six weeks spent administering to the sick and wounded soldiers in the hospitals there. She went down the day before the Battle of Fair Oaks and has devoted herself ever since to the suffering brave." In the aftermath of Antietam, a *Gazette* correspondent in Washington followed her as she visited the casualties of that battle in the hospitals surrounding the city: "Miss Moorhead is here laboring most faithfully in the hospitals. One meets her wherever the misery and distress are the greatest, moving about like an angel of mercy. The worn and suffering soldier smiles at her approach. "[41]

Another correspondent traveling with Moorhead demonstrated how well-known Pittsburghers' participation in benevolent work was used as a model to inspire other potential volunteers. In his account for the *Gazette*, he told how Moorhead was caring for a wounded Midwestern soldier at Fort Monroe when the man suddenly exclaimed that he knew her. When Moorhead asked how he could possibly know her, he replied, "'I remember you gave me my supper at Pittsburgh,'" referring to her support of the Subsistence Committee on trips to Pittsburgh with her father. The reporter then challenged Pittsburghers not yet mobilized to take up benevolent work: "Is there not in this incident much to encourage our ladies to continue in welldoing?" The young Miss Moorhead, he wrote, should "not be the only person to enjoy personally the grateful remembrance of a wounded soldier." Pittsburgh newspapers also regularly featured articles celebrating the work of women on the home front and encouraged others to emulate them: "The following work has been cut out and made up by the Ladies' Christian Commission of Pittsburgh and Allegheny: 292 shirts; 184 prs. drawers; 570 arm slings; 370 handkerchiefs; 265 prs. of crutches, covered; 264 armslings; 10 bandages. The rooms of the Ladies' Christian Commission, at City Hall, are open every afternoon from 2–5 o'clock when all ladies (whether members or not) are invited to meet and assist in making up hospital clothing."[42]

On Thanksgiving Day, 1864, the Pittsburgh auxiliary of the Christian Commission and the Subsistence Committee crowned their achievements by simultaneously holding grand banquets for soldiers convalescing in and passing through the city. At the General Hospital, soldiers traveled from recovery rooms to a large dining hall specially prepared by the Christian Commission for the afternoon. As they entered, they gazed around the room to take in the array of patriotic decorations. The national colors hung on two sides, along the entire length of the hall. On the right was a banner inscribed "Sherman" and on the left one inscribed "Sheridan." Over the entryway hung a portrait of General Grant, flanked by busts of Henry Clay and Daniel Webster. Atop the portrait was an arch of evergreen and a banner that read "Lincoln, Grant, and the Union." With the men all gathered at their tables, a lieutenant asked them to rise for a blessing. When dinner was complete, one soldier remembered, "The Chaplain, Mr. Bear, moved that a vote of thanks be tendered to the ladies of the Christian Committee . . . for the good cheer provided us. This was done. The men all joined in singing the Christmas doxology, the benediction was pronounced, and we retired from the hall amid thrilling bursts of music from the band as it produced the 'Star Spangled Banner.' . . . None of us shall soon forget Thanksgiving in the Smokey City."[43]

Across town, the Subsistence Committee hosted another gathering of soldiers. One observer was taken aback by the fine tablecloths, silver, china, and glassware that adorned the soldiers' tables rather than the usual tin plates and cups. The food equally surprised him: turkeys, pies, cakes, and bread, rather than the bare essentials. After the soldiers took their seats and Joseph Albree's father, George, blessed the food, the ladies of the committee served the soldiers. When the meal was over, the observer remembered, "Captain Bates made a few impromptu remarks, thanking the committee for their kindness to him and his men. He paid a glowing tribute to the patriotism and liberality of the citizens of Pittsburgh, remarking that they were unequaled in these by any other city in the Union. He concluded by offering this sentiment: 'The ladies of Pittsburgh whose warm hearts and willing hands are ever ready to minister to the wants of our patriot soldiers.'"[44]

During the war, the efforts of benevolent volunteers mobilized to provide aid to Union soldiers became a great source of pride and inspiration to Pittsburghers just like the heroics of soldiers in battle. The care rendered in field hospitals and the comfort given on the home front by the men and women of the benevolent agencies were celebrated in Pittsburgh as much as the territory conquered and the enemies defeated by Union soldiers.

In the last year and a half of the war, benevolent mobilization took a new form that would showcase and amplify the participative spirit of the people. In October 1863, the Great Northwestern Soldiers' Fair, a public event to raise money for the Sanitary Commission, was held in Chicago. This event was made possible, almost entirely, by the efforts of women active in the Sanitary. The fair did not, however, garner much aid from the commission's central office and it became necessary for the ladies to travel to other Northern cities in search of support. Mary Livermore recalled that, when representatives reached Pittsburgh, the outpouring of donations overwhelmed them: "So successful were [the] appeals to the citizens of Pittsburgh, that it was necessary to fit up a booth for the reception of the articles contributed. Manufacturers, artisans, and merchants sent choice specimens of value, skill and taste from a huge sheet of iron, worthy of Vulcan, and a breech-loading steel cannon of terrible beauty." Ultimately, the fair was unsuccessful, failing to attract the attention of many Chicagoans, but, across the North, other people still believed in the potentiality of a grand public exhibition to raise money for the care of soldiers. The following February organizers in Cleveland and New York made their own attempts to hold a "Sanitary Fair." [45]

That winter, Rachel McFadden, secretary of the Pittsburgh auxiliary of the Sanitary Commission, shared with Charles W. Batchelor a number of letters from local hospitals pleading for medical supplies for sick and wounded soldiers. Batchelor was active in mobilizing Pittsburgh's home front since serving on the resolutions committee of the Union meeting on April 15, 1861. Now, he proposed to the leaders of the local Sanitary that the city should hold its own fair in order to supply the hospitals' needs. They agreed and named the popular and influential activist Felix Brunot to serve as president of the Fair Committee. Batchelor traveled with his brother to Cleveland to learn about the fair held there. After sharing their findings at a public meeting in Pittsburgh, the two returned to Cleveland and purchased the portable buildings, dining ware, and gas fixtures used in that city's fair, bonding themselves personally in the amount of $9,941.65.[46]

The Pittsburgh fair excited the people well before opening day. When the riverboats bearing the materials from Cleveland arrived, crowds of the same draymen and teamsters and others who had dug the fortifications around the city the previous summer now volunteered to unload the boats, transport the materials, and erect the fair buildings. On June 1, 1864, opening day, General Negley stepped into his familiar role as grand marshal of a parade heralding the fair. It was billed as a "Grand military and civic procession," echoing the events of three years prior.[47]

For weeks leading up to the fair, local newspapers stirred up excitement with columns promoting the exhibits and events to be offered. Promoters had high hopes for financial success and, after the committee received more than $100,000 in donations even before the fair opened, predictions for receipts from admission and sales soared as high as $250,000. When the time came, the fair did not disappoint. Pittsburghers marveled at the "Monitor Building," complete with a miniature lake and model iron-clad boats and enemy shore batteries. The boats and batteries were equipped with steam-powered guns and a mock battle was held between them. On the sixth day, patrons enjoyed a dramatization of *Uncle Tom's Cabin*; later events included demonstrations by local German gymnastics organizations and a concert by the German Band of Philadelphia, performing Felix Mendelssohn's Overture to *A Midsummer Night's Dream*.[48]

The success of the Pittsburgh Sanitary Fair surpassed all expectations. Felix Brunot's records show that receipts from the fair itself totaled $156,088.65. More than $14,000 was collected just on day one. He made special note of the "Ladies' Bazaar," which brought in $4,296.10, and admission tickets that accounted for another $5,730.66. Brunot praised the multitude of exhibits and the contributions "from 2,000 individuals, churches, societies, business firms, and institutions." One receipt in his records, a donation of $15, was contributed by "friends from Derry, Ireland." By the close of the fair on Saturday, June 18, Brunot's receipts totaled $361,516 to be used for the care of sick and wounded Union soldiers.[49]

The Sanitary Fair was Pittsburgh's most successful mobilization of private goods, resources, and services for the aid of soldiers. No other event brought so much of the city together for that cause. A popular pamphlet from the fair expressed the gratitude of the organizers to the people of Pittsburgh:

To the farmers, the merchants, mechanics, and banks,
To each and to all we would tender our thanks.
And the blessings of those whom their labors have cheered,
In whose memory their names will be ever endeared.
Oh think on the Soldier far distant who roams,
And when to his country restored through your care,
    will gratefully remember the Sanitary Fair.[50]

7

★ ★ ★ ★ ★

UNITE IN DOING HONOR TO THE DECEASED HERO

Managing Death on the Home Front

For lists of killed and wounded, see
The morrow's dispatch: to-day tis victory!
The man who read this to the crowd
Shouted as the end he gained;
And though the unflagging tempest rained,
They answered him aloud.
And hand grasped hand, and glances met
In happy triumph; eyes grew wet.

-HERMAN MELVILLE-
Battle-Pieces and Aspects of the War (1866)

On the morning of September 17, 1862, Joseph E. Bollman and his twelve-year-old daughter Mary made their customary morning commute along the twelve blocks from their home at 10 Milligan's Row, Ninth Ward, to their jobs at the Allegheny Arsenal. Entering the arsenal grounds, Mary made her way to the laboratory, where she worked in room number six making rifle cartridges, while Joseph went to the office of Alexander McBride, superintendent of the laboratory, where he was employed as a bookkeeper.[1]

Operations at the arsenal were at this time particularly intense. Workers were excited about recent newspaper accounts of the Rebel invasion of Maryland. Over the past couple of weeks, General Robert E. Lee led his Army of

Northern Virginia on a bold campaign to recruit soldiers, replenish supplies, and gain European recognition of the Confederacy by achieving a victory on United States soil.

Just before two o'clock, Joseph Frick, one of three workers charged with transporting materials within the arsenal, stopped his wagon by the laboratory. After placing several barrels of musket and mortar powder on the porches outside the laboratory rooms, he drove to a building about fifty feet away and began unloading powder for other workers. At that moment, Robert Smith, a twenty-four-year-old worker in room number one, stepped out onto the laboratory porch and called to Frick, asking him to return and haul away some of his empty boxes. As Frick approached, he saw a small flame on the ground just a few feet from where Smith stood next to the recently delivered barrels of powder. One of the workers had already opened one barrel on the porch rather than drag it into the room and, in an instant, the powder inside that barrel ignited. Smith was killed instantly. Part of his body was found more than three hundred yards away on top of the arsenal's magazine. Within minutes, two more explosions completed the destruction of the laboratory, collapsing the ceiling and walls and engulfing the structure in flames. Amid the chaos that ensued, Superintendent McBride attempted, unsuccessfully, to find his daughter, Kate. Joseph Bollman carried one young girl out of the flames then returned to search for his own daughter only to perish alongside her.[2]

The blasts were heard across the city and people from the neighborhood immediately rushed to the arsenal. There, they found a horrible scene. Witnesses reported young girls running and crawling, trying to escape the laboratory; many were on fire or in a state of bewilderment, wounded and bloody, their clothes burned from their bodies. The dead and dying were sprawled across the ground. Agonized cries from the injured filled the air. Ultimately, the tragedy claimed the lives of seventy-eight workers.[3]

Completed in 1814, the Allegheny Arsenal was at the time of the Civil War one of the oldest manufactories in the region. It produced munitions along with some leather goods and served also as a storage and distribution center for ammunition and arms to equip military units in both the Eastern and Western theaters. By the summer of 1862, Colonel Symington—promoted since the gun removal controversy of the winter of 1860–61—significantly expanded the staff and operations of the arsenal to meet the growing demand from the front lines. The number of workers increased from 308 in April 1861 to more than one thousand a year later. With the scarcity of adult male labor during the war years, Symington first turned to employing young boys as cartridge makers, but their carelessness and disinclination to follow safety regulations led Symington to dismiss them in ever-growing numbers until he finally decided to no longer rely on them at all. On October 2, 1861, he reported that he had "discharged all the boys at work in [one] portion of the laboratory, and will supply their places with females."[4]

At the time of the accident, there were 158 workers in the arsenal's laboratory, almost all of them girls and young women, preparing more than one hundred thousand cartridges a day. For many, work at the arsenal was a family matter. Like McBride and Bollman, many other male and female employees had children or other relatives who worked there. Phillip Miller left his job as a blacksmith and brought his nineteen-year-old daughter Sarah to work with him in the laboratory, where they packaged cartridges in room number three. Phillip was killed instantly when the roof collapsed; Sarah escaped but died of her wounds three days later. Sarah Maxwell was a seamstress before the war, helping her father, a laborer, support the family. When the arsenal began to hire women, she and her younger sister Elizabeth signed on, but, while the need to help a struggling family can explain why many chose to work in the arsenal, others were driven by the opportunity to support the war effort. Agnes Davidson, nineteen, and her fourteen-year-old sister May were the daughters of a prosperous carpenter. Edward Davidson emigrated from England and amassed by 1860 an estate valued at $27,000. The girls, who lived two blocks from the arsenal, were undoubtedly drawn less by the need for money than by the excitement of working outside the home and taking part in the war. Both lost their lives in the explosions.[5]

Less than two weeks after the tragedy, a coroner's jury released its findings. Testimony revealed multiple problems that contributed to the disaster, all related to the handling of gunpowder. Workers testified that the barrels used at the arsenal were inadequate for the storage and transportation of powder; they did not seal well and powder constantly spilled out as the barrels jostled around on the bumpy arsenal roads. Superintendent McBride testified that on several occasions he had complained about the poor quality of the barrels. Many other workers cited the careless practice of sweeping gunpowder from the laboratory rooms out into the streets. The jury found that the most probable cause of the immediate explosion was the metal rim of Frick's wagon wheel generating a spark that ignited powder lying in the street by the laboratory porch.[6]

The jurors unanimously declared the basic cause of the tragedy as "carelessness." As to who was responsible—Colonel Symington and his officers or the civilian supervisors such as Superintendent McBride—they were unable to come to a unanimous conclusion. This probably represented more an unwillingness than an inability to assign blame. McBride, well liked in the community, just lost his young daughter; and to vilify Union officers in Pittsburgh would seem unpatriotic. However, two jurors, foreman John W. Riddell and James B. Hill, issued a separate finding that blamed the civilian supervisors: "From so much as imputes negligence to Colonel Symington and Lieutenants Myers and Edie, we utterly and entirely dissent. The testimony, in our judgment, clearly discloses that this sad disaster is to be attributed solely to a disregard, by the Superintendents, of the wholesome and stringent orders of Colonel Symington; and we are unable to find anything in the evidence incriminating either of his lieutenants." On October 5, the War Department convened a court of inquiry to investigate the explosions. After examining the evidence for five weeks, the panel reported that "the cause of the explosion could not be satisfactorily ascertained," but added that Colonel Symington "took every care and precaution suggested by experience and prudence."[7]

On January 10, 1860, the Pemberton Mills in Lawrence, Massachusetts collapsed, killing 145 workers and injuring 166. The ensuing investigation concluded that substandard construction materials and design caused the disaster. In many ways, the tragedy at the Allegheny Arsenal paralleled that in Lawrence. Both were industrial accidents that killed or maimed many workers, most of the victims were girls or young women and, in both cases, there was evidence of negligence on the part of those entrusted with the lives of workers. Yet despite these similarities, the public reacted quite differently to the two events.[8]

The press blamed the Pemberton Mill collapse on the evils of industrialization. Greedy capitalists risked the safety of their employees to save a dollar. Poet Jacques Maurice branded the tragedy "The Slaughter of the Innocents." *Harper's Weekly* called it the "slaughter at Lawrence" and went on to say that "a responsibility at which all good men will shudder weighs on the proprietors of those mills; they are, in fact, before God and man, guilty of the deaths of some two hundred innocent creatures."[9]

The day following the arsenal tragedy, the *Post* did not characterize the accident as a senseless loss of life attributable to the greed or callousness of employers but instead portrayed the victims as "engaged in the service of their country." In a sermon ten days later, the Reverend R. Lea spoke of the loss of life in terms of sacrifice for the war and referred to the victims as "Noble Union girls." Rather than in terms of class conflict and the social evils of industrialization, Pittsburghers interpreted the arsenal disaster through the lens of patriotism.[10] Local papers described the scene of the explosions in a manner more reflective of the aftermath of a terrible battle than of a domestic accident:

> Bodies, charred and swollen, were scattered here and there . . . some mere limbless trunks, blackened and bloody—some with the limbs remaining, but distorted, and the flesh hanging from the bones in strips. Here was a pile of undistinguishable fragments—here two sisters, one dead, the other in the last agonies—here a father and daughter—here two children whose names were known, but the parents could not distinguish one from the other. . . . Some had apparently died in great agony, from the contortions of their limbs, while the arms of some were folded as if in resignation to their fate.

Were it not for the familial references, readers might have taken this as a description of the carnage at Shiloh or Antietam. The next day, the *Post* reported that "[t]wo hundred feet from the laboratory was picked up the body of one young girl, terribly mangled; another body was seen to fly in the air and separate into two parts; an arm was thrown over the wall; a foot was picked up near the gate; a piece of skull was found a hundred yards away, and pieces of the intestines were scattered about the grounds." Newspapers repeatedly portrayed the scene of the arsenal disaster in ways similar to their depictions of battlefields. People read of the "charred remains of the victims" in Pittsburgh as they earlier read of the "half scorched" casualties at Pittsburg Landing (Shiloh). The dead arsenal girls reported as "lying about in rows" were like the fallen soldiers a battlefield correspondent recalled "lying in a row" in the aftermath of Shiloh.[11]

The friends and families of those killed in the arsenal disaster sensed these parallels with the front line with particular intensity. During the Civil War, families went to great lengths to find and bring home from the battlefield the remains of fallen soldiers. The inability to locate, identify, and transport deceased loved ones disrupted nineteenth-century conventions of mourning and made acceptance of the loss more difficult for the families. In the immediate aftermath of the arsenal explosions, Pittsburghers pored over the updated lists of arsenal casualties just as they had learned to do during the Peninsula Campaign. Arsenal employees took on the role of a local regiment at the front as anxious civilians now watched for the name of a laborer daughter rather than a soldier son. The proximity of this home-front battlefield did not, however, ensure that friends and family could be certain in every case of their loved one's fate. That of Susan McCreighton, for example, was undetermined for some time following the disaster. When her mother pleaded for the "satisfaction of seeing the body coffined," officials brought her to the arsenal to view a body supposed to be Susan's. The corpse's face was damaged beyond recognition but, examining the torn remnants of clothing, Mrs. McCreighton immediately realized that this was not her daughter and began frantically searching the arsenal grounds for "the body she so longed to have discovered and interred as she desired."[12]

In all, forty-five of the seventy-eight killed could not be identified. Their families were denied the comfort of private burial ceremonies. Instead, as was often the practice on battlefields, the remains of these unknown Pittsburghers were interred together in a mass grave. The director of the Allegheny Cemetery provided a plot and appropriate services "as a testimony of the earnest sympathy of the managers of the cemetery for this most afflicting dispensation to the families of so many of our citizens."[13]

Community leaders organized charitable endeavors similar to those for soldiers in battle. The day after the explosion, Mayor B. C. Sawyer requested that every business in Pittsburgh close at noon as a "fitting tribute" in response to "the sudden and terrible death of so many . . . whilst in the service of our country." He also called a public meeting to raise funds for the families of the killed and injured. In October, the *Gazette* published an appeal on behalf of Eliza Donnell, a widow whose daughter Sally was killed in the explosions, leaving Mrs. Donnell "entirely alone in her bereavement and in indigent circumstances." About that same time, fifty-five citizens from nearby Indiana County contributed thirty-six dollars for the sufferers in Pittsburgh.[14]

On the first anniversary of the disaster, a committee met at Robinson's Hall near the arsenal to discuss plans to erect a marker over the unidentified casualties in Allegheny Cemetery. The resulting monument, dedicated that same year, memorialized the tragedy not as the greatest industrial accident of the war but as a sacrifice for the Union war effort: "Tread softly, this is consecrated dust. Forty five pure patriotic victims lie here as a sacrifice to freedom and civil liberty. . . . These are patriots' graves, friends of humble, honest toil. These were your peers. Fervent affection kindled these hearts, honest industry employed these hands." While families privately mourned the loss of so many, publicly it was incorporated into the narrative of the community's participation in the war.[15]

The arsenal tragedy was woven into the larger experience of loss in Civil War Pittsburgh. A total of 25,930 men from Allegheny County served in the Union army, of whom 2,449, or 9.4 percent, died in service. An 1873 pamphlet on the history of Allegheny Cemetery said of Pittsburgh's Civil War dead: "Indeed, there are but few family circles in the large population of the two adjoining cities of Pittsburgh and Allegheny, whose hearts and sympathies

FIG. 12. Allegheny Arsenal Exterior and Gate. Library of Congress.

are not drawn with deep and sorrowful interest to this sacred spot by the fond memories of some one or more loved ones, who have been removed from their midst by the hand of death, and who now sleep beneath its quiet and peaceful shades." When two of Pittsburgh's most celebrated regiments returned home after the war, each with only around a hundred remaining men, the *Gazette* remarked that "[t]hey return to us few in numbers, but they are worthy remnants of two of the best regiments that ever left the State in defense of the nation."[16]

News of the death of soldiers from the community was a daily part of life on the Pittsburgh home front, as it was for other communities across the nation. Spared the pain of heavy casualties at Bull Run and Shiloh, Pittsburghers felt that pain for the first time in the late spring of 1862. Nine Pennsylvania regiments were recruited primarily or in large part in Allegheny County. The first major battle for any of them was during the Peninsula Campaign. Half of the 61st Pennsylvania Infantry Regiment was recruited in and around Pittsburgh. Its colonel, Oliver Hazard Rippey, was born in Pittsburgh in

1825. A veteran of the Mexican War, Rippey was often mentioned and much acclaimed in the city's newspapers. On May 31, 1862, his regiment suffered immense losses at the Battle of Fair Oaks. Twenty-four of its soldiers were killed, one of them Rippey. Every other field officer became a casualty as well. Lieutenant Colonel S. C. Speer, Major S. J. Sweet, and Adjutant W. G. Miller were wounded, and Major George Smith was captured. All together the regiment lost eighteen officers and 245 enlisted men killed, wounded, or captured: 46 percent of the 574 who went into battle. This was the greatest loss of any Allegheny County regiment in a single battle during the war. Other regiments with large numbers of Pittsburgh soldiers also suffered heavy losses that day. The 103rd Infantry had eighty-four casualties and the 101st lost a third of its number.[17]

In the wake of every battle, civilians on the home front endured harrowing uncertainty and tormenting misinformation or fragmented reports. Within days of Fair Oaks, sketchy reports of terrible losses among Pittsburgh regiments reached home. The *Post* reported on June 3 that "the details of killed, wounded and missing in Saturday's desperate battle near Richmond are very anxiously looked for here, as there are several western Pennsylvania regiments known to have been engaged." That same day, the *Gazette* told of rumors that local infantry regiments including the 61st, 62nd, 63rd, and 102nd had been "cut to pieces" and noted that the "most intense excitement and painful anxiety has been everywhere manifested in this community." No list of casualties would be available for one or two days, the newspaper added, but it would be published as soon as possible. "Of course it is impossible to allay apprehensions in the minds of those who have friends and relations in the army. . . . [T]he suspense will be painful indeed, until the facts are fully developed."[18]

As the days passed, the severity of the community's loss became clear. On June 5, Lieutenant W. L. Gould of Company C, 61st Regiment, wounded at Fair Oaks, arrived in Pittsburgh and was interviewed by the *Gazette*, providing details of the fate of several local soldiers. The families of Sergeant Joseph P. Orr, a jeweler from Allegheny, and Alexander McDonald, a glassblower from South Pittsburgh, learned of their deaths through this report. Private Henry C. Davis had been reported killed but Gould could not confirm this. All of the officers of Company F, readers learned, were killed in the battle.[19]

The next day, the remains of Colonel Rippey arrived in Pittsburgh and were brought to the home of his father-in-law, A. B. Curling. While the great majority of enlisted men's families were unable to bury their deceased loved ones, every effort was made to bring home the bodies of high-ranking officers. The *Post* reported that Rippey's corpse was found two days after the battle, lying in the arms of one of his fallen soldiers, a Private Anderson from Pittsburgh; the two had undoubtedly died together. It was also reported that three color bearers were shot trying to protect the regimental flag that was sent home with Rippey's body. Rippey was laid to rest accompanied by a military honor guard and a civilian procession.[20]

Some thought the colonel's funeral honors inadequate. On June 9, the *Post* published a letter complaining about the meager military presence at the service. "The first field officer from Pittsburgh who has fallen," said the writer, deserved more; had the Home Guards not been so ridiculed in the press for parading rather than going off to war, he added, it certainly would have contributed to a more fitting tribute. When the remains of the next field officer from Pittsburgh killed in battle were returned to the city, community organizers made better efforts. Major Frank B. Ward of the Anderson Cavalry was buried on January 20, 1863, his coffin escorted to the cemetery from his parents' home in Allegheny City by four companies of the 15th Pennsylvania Reserves, a brass band, and a large following of civilians.[21]

As the war progressed and more of the war dead came home, the community continued efforts to properly memorialize them. The body of Lieutenant Scott C. McDowell of the 62nd Regiment arrived in Pittsburgh on March 4, 1864, eight months after he was killed and buried at Gettysburg. The Committee on Home Defense arranged for a company at nearby Camp Copeland to serve as the honor guard at McDowell's reinterment. Less than a week later, Pittsburghers watched another soldier's funeral procession after the remains of Lieutenant Alexander McCord were brought home. While most families of deceased soldiers were not able to have this closure, the return of the remains of the fallen for local burial became common enough in Pittsburgh by then that W. C. Conn gave up the livery stable business in favor of the funeral business. Conn's timing was fortuitous, for in the months ahead Pittsburgh would endure another wave of staggering losses in its local regiments.[22]

In the spring of 1864, Ulysses S. Grant, now commanding all Union armies, began his Overland Campaign in the Eastern theater, forcing Robert E. Lee's Rebel army southward through Virginia. This campaign, which would end in the siege of Petersburg, generated horrific casualties on both sides. In the days following the campaign's opening battle, the Wilderness, Pittsburghers became engrossed in reports from the front line. A mixture of excitement about Grant's engagement of Lee's army and anxiety over initial reports of the high casualties among Pittsburgh regiments gripped the city. Newspapers reported unprecedented demands for extras and clergymen discarded planned sermons, replacing them with prayers for Grant's success and for the local families of the fallen.[23]

On the evening of May 7, Secretary of War Edwin Stanton telegraphed Thomas Howe to inform him that General Alexander Hays, the most esteemed of Pittsburgh's soldiers, was killed on the first day of the Battle of the Wilderness and asked Howe to inform Hays's wife. Stanton could not confirm the whereabouts of Hays's body at this time but assured Howe of its return to Pittsburgh as soon as possible. On May 12, the city was informed that Hays's remains would arrive the following day. The *Post* encouraged Pittsburghers to "unite in doing honor to the deceased hero." Community leaders sought to ensure a commemoration truly worthy of their local hero. Soldiers on furlough were strongly encouraged to show up in uniform and join the funeral cortège. Home Guard officers set up a station at Wilkins Hall where they distributed weapons and uniform items to soldiers who needed them for the ceremony. On Saturday, May 14, at two o'clock in the afternoon, the funeral procession departed from the First Presbyterian Church, where Hays's body had lain in state, guarded by soldiers, all morning long and Pittsburghers by the thousands lined up to view it.[24]

Again, Pittsburghers agonized as reports of heavy casualties in their local regiments reached the city. Accompanying the news of General Hays were accounts of terrible losses in the 61st Regiment on the Wilderness battlefield. These accounts of the fate of common soldiers, unlike that of General Hays, were terse and unadorned. Pittsburghers learned of their loved ones from reports such as this: "George Palton, arm; John Harper, neck; Peter Bradley, head, dead." Ordinary and prominent citizens alike received the news they had hoped never to hear. William Robinson, who served as the first mayor of Allegheny City and who went by the title of "General" for his leadership of the local militia, received a telegram on May 10 informing him that his grandson had been killed on the second day of the Wilderness. John Harper learned that his son Albert had been wounded.[25]

As the Overland Campaign progressed, the bodies of other prominent officers arrived in the city for burial. Each time a similar pattern was followed, drawing so many Pittsburghers into an act of mourning that served to memorialize their own fallen loved ones along with the notables: public notification, a call for soldiers in the city to participate, a funeral procession with a military honor guard, and a contingent of citizens. Colonel James C. Hull was born in Pittsburgh in 1828. At age seven, he became the ward of Alexander Hays, then followed him to Mexico in the 1840s as a member of his company, the Pittsburgh Independent Blues. On May 22, 1864, Captain

W. J. Moorhead wrote from Virginia to inform Pittsburgh that "Colonel Hull, late of the 62nd Regiment, died of his wounds today. I will send his body to-morrow evening. He was a brave Christian soldier, and died the death of the righteous. Let proper military honors be paid him." The soldiers of the 62nd took up a collection to pay for transporting the body. Pittsburgh newspapers called on the discharged soldiers of the regiment to muster once again at the Girard House to form a military detail for the funeral. The *Gazette* urged a memorialization of Hull befitting "his memory, . . . his sorrow-stricken family and friends, and . . . the holy cause in which he laid down his life." Not long after this, when the remains of Lieutenant Colonel William H. Moody returned to Pittsburgh, the veterans of the deceased's regiment were again summoned to the Girard House. The *Daily Commercial* printed Moody's reported last words, imbuing his death with meaning while underscoring the personal cost: "he was satisfied to die for his country. . . . [H]is only concern was for his mother and sister for whom he was the sole supporter."[26]

At times that spring, the remains of lower-ranking officers were also brought home. "Another gallant officer gone," the *Commercial* reported after the death of Lieutenant Frank Martin. His body was delivered by train and conveyed to his mother's house near the Allegheny Arsenal. A week later, Pittsburghers read of the return of Captain W. W. Dyer, who died of wounds received at the Battle of North Anna River. His funeral procession also set out from a private residence, this one in Allegheny's Second Ward. However, the losses that touched the mass of Pittsburghers most directly were those of common soldiers. As the casualties among Grant's forces mounted, Governor Curtin gave a speech in Philadelphia that was printed in the Pittsburgh papers: "My friends, if there is a man before me worthy of sincere reverence and respect, it is the private soldier of the Republic. He is the true nobleman of this land. He falls with an unrecorded name. . . . His friends are not gratified by magnificent pageants at his funeral; he is buried at Gettysburg, where there are one thousand graves of the unknown." On rare occasions, enlisted soldiers' bodies were returned home to Pittsburgh for burial. Private R. Bruce Young of the 102nd Regiment died of wounds received at the Wilderness. A military honor guard escorted Young's funeral procession from his home to Mount Union Cemetery outside Allegheny City. Three weeks later, the *Post* reported on the upcoming funeral of Corporal John Mackin, which "[s]oldiers, friends and relatives will no doubt attend and [thus] do honor to one who has served his country since August, 1862." Soldiers' funerals in the city, whether those of renowned commanders or humble enlisted men, were shared with the larger community. They presented moments when community leaders could attach meaning to such loss. For the families of fallen soldiers who could not be brought home, these funerals provided the opportunity to honor their own loved ones through the ceremonies for others.[27]

On December 7, 1905, twenty-eight veterans of the 101st Regiment gathered for the dedication of the Pennsylvania monument at Andersonville, Georgia. Among them were seven Pittsburghers who survived imprisonment there during the war. The 101st along with the 103rd had a distinctive experience among Pittsburgh regiments. Like others, these units suffered staggering casualty rates, but a large proportion of their losses was incurred not when they were serving in the field but when they were languishing in a prisoner of war camp. As the 101st's historian, John A. Reed, wrote, "There is glory in dying on the field of conflict amid shot and shell and the shout of victory and the urging forward of those in command, but we faced slow death by starvation, scurvy and gangrene . . . which awful condition took more strength and courage than to face death in a hundred battles. Our losses in killed in battle are small compared with the famous fighting regiments, but our losses in camp and hospital and in the charnel house of Andersonville . . . show a sacrifice of life equal to [that of] any regiment of like numbers in the Civil War." A total of 176 soldiers from the 101st and 103rd regiments died in Andersonville. On April 20, 1864, these two regiments were serving as garrison troops at Plymouth, North Carolina, when they were attacked by Confederate forces and captured. A. S. Billingsly, chaplain of the 101st, was immediately released and transported to Annapolis, Maryland, from where he wrote to the *Gazette*, providing a list of casualties. "Both these regiments were recruited in Allegheny and adjoining counties," the *Gazette* reported, "and their friends here have been exceedingly anxious to hear from them."[28]

Only days after the news of the regiments' capture came, Pittsburgh papers published the U.S. Senate's "Report on the Condition of the Returned Prisoners," based on the examination of a number of prisoners of war released by the Rebels. For the first time, the Northern public was made aware by official publication of the conditions endured by Union prisoners. The report painted an alarming picture for Pittsburghers who had recently learned of their soldiers' imprisonment: "Rebel authorities have determined to subject our soldiers and officers who fall into their hands to physical and mental suffering impossible to describe, many presenting now the appearance of living skeletons, little more than skin and bones, some maimed for life." The report also recounted the Confederate practice of robbing soldiers of all valuables and much clothing upon their capture. When the released prisoners arrived at Annapolis, their clothes, hair, and bodies were infested with lice. This "Rebel barbarity" could only be for the purpose of reducing Union soldiers "by privations and exposures to such a condition that they will never be able to render effective service in the field."[29]

Reports about prisoners of war continued to come into the city. On September 2, four exchanged prisoners arrived at Annapolis from Andersonville. They had prepared a petition urging the president to take steps to end the suffering of their fellow soldiers. This was printed in the Pittsburgh papers, further exciting the families of captured men. The statement asserted that two-thirds of the Andersonville prisoners were without shelter, prisoners' rations consisted solely of semi-cooked cornmeal and "rancid and rusty bacon," and the water was "literally poisonous, being taken from a muddy oozing stream." A ray of hope appeared in November, however, after Colonel W. H. Lehman of Allegheny City, commander of the 103rd Regiment, was released from prison and wrote optimistically to the *Daily Commercial*, saying that he expected the rest of the regiment's prisoners exchanged soon.[30]

Pittsburghers continued to learn of the hardships of prisoners of war through the personal accounts of local soldiers released from imprisonment. Some of these stories were printed in the newspapers to raise awareness of the captives' suffering. Privates James Logan Alter and Samuel Long of the 101st were taken prisoner with the rest of the regiment at Plymouth. After Long was paroled, he visited the Alter family to tell them how James had suffered, was hospitalized, and ultimately succumbed to his afflictions. Charles C. Lang, who graduated from Pittsburgh High School in 1860 and subsequently studied medicine before enlisting as a hospital steward, returned home and shared his story after more than a year of imprisonment at Andersonville.[31]

In December, many Pittsburghers who had been waiting anxiously for news of their imprisoned loved ones finally received some. Newspapers published a list of 122 soldiers of the 103rd Regiment who were reported to have died in Rebel prisons, but, while many thus learned the sad fate of their loved one, others found their soldier's name on the list only to learn later that it was an error, for forty of the soldiers named were in fact still living. The surviving imprisoned soldiers of the 101st and 103rd finally began to be released en masse that December and continued to come home through March 1865. The following May, the extent of the loss suffered in Andersonville started to become clear. Official Confederate records, leaked to Southern newspapers, were reprinted in the North. According to the account published in the *Gazette*, 12,878 Union soldiers died at Andersonville. The mortality reached a ghastly peak on August 23, 1864—four months after the Pittsburgh regiments were captured—when 127 prisoners died. Captain John Donaghy, the artist who enlisted after the firing on Fort Sumter, returned home from Confederate imprisonment in January 1865 and resumed painting. He closed his memoirs with a heartfelt reminder of the suffering of Pittsburgh soldiers in captivity: "And now comes the saddest item in all my story[:] of the thirty-three enlisted men of my company who were captured at Plymouth—the men who had stood all the service of our three years, and to whom I had become attached as though they were of my own family—but nine of them lived to reach their homes. The others left their bones at Andersonville."[32]

On January 1, 1864, the *Post* offered some thoughts on the twelve months past and the twelve ahead: "Another year has gone, and 1864 has begun its, to us, unseen and incomprehensible course. . . . With those who have lost relatives and friends in the field of battle, we heartily sympathize, and commend the widow and the orphan to the care of Him who 'tempers the wind to the shorn lamb.'" The deaths of 2,449 Allegheny County soldiers in service and the wounding of thousands more created needs that would far outlast the war. As Pittsburghers grappled with this terrible loss, many began to focus on the plight of disabled veterans and the survivors of the deceased. The *Post* called Pittsburghers to action, reminding them of the debt that every citizen owed to those who had sacrificed life or limb for their country: "Everyday the necessity grows stronger and it becomes most apparent that institutions . . . must be established for the maintenance and education of the children made orphans by the war. There are thousands of wounded and discharged soldiers. . . . [M]any are forever incapacitated for employment at all, and many more are so disabled as to be capable of only the lighter kinds of avocations. Are they to endure the uncertainties and chance assistance of the multitudes? Are they to go down to the grave with their marred limbs and honorable scars, wanting for bread?" In December 1863, the Allegheny Select and Common Council voted unanimously to appropriate five thousand dollars for the relief of the city's families suffering due to their loved one's service in the field. Newspapers in Pittsburgh lauded this and the similar actions of other cities and urged that even more be done. Following the great success of the Pittsburgh Sanitary Fair, the fair's executive committee decided to dedicate 25 percent of the proceeds toward the establishment of a hospital for wounded Pittsburgh soldiers and for the support of orphans of the city's fallen soldiers.[33]

In November 1864, a committee led by James P. Barr established the first institution incorporated by the Pennsylvania legislature to care for soldiers' orphans. Only children whose fathers were killed in the war or so badly wounded that they could no longer provide for their children were eligible for admission. The founders made it clear that this was not a common poorhouse, nor a "refuge or asylum." The children cared for in this home were not to be treated as "outcasts left to the cold charity of the world, or as orphans, in whose behalf can be pleaded only the ordinary motives of philanthropy or Christian love." This existed as more than another benevolent cause intended to elevate the station of those less fortunate. It was instead, as the *Post* declared, a manifestation of the sacred duty of every citizen to repay the wartime sacrifice of their fellow citizens in uniform by caring for their survivors: "[These children] have a special title on the nation, in whose defense they have been made fatherless, and which, in return for the life that has been preserved for it, should feel it a pride and honor to watch over and foster the young lives that its dying defenders have committed to its care." There was no civic duty more sacred than that "bequeathed thus by its dying defenders.... [T]hese CHILDREN OF THE REPUBLIC should be sheltered, fostered and educated by the nation." In Pittsburgh, this cause became a matter of local pride like other aspects of support for the war. When a committee sought to raise funds for an institution for soldiers' orphans in Philadelphia and encouraged Pittsburgh to do the same, the *Post* pointed out that Pittsburgh had already established such a home and supported it with funds from its Sanitary Fair, while Philadelphia had failed to commit one cent from its own fair for this purpose.[34]

Caring for soldiers' orphans became a high priority in Pittsburgh. It was significantly aided by the state government. On July 10, 1862, as Pittsburghers reeled from the shock of the Peninsula Campaign, community leaders convened a large public meeting to reenergize morale. Among the stirring speeches given that day, that of Governor Cutin evoked the greatest enthusiasm. He informed the crowd that he had just received a telegram from the president of the Pennsylvania Railroad offering fifty thousand dollars to help raise and equip more Pennsylvania troops. However, the governor lacked legislative authorization to spend this money on mobilization and therefore declined the offer. Instead, he arranged for the funds to be applied to caring for soldiers' orphans. In the summer of 1864, this program was inaugurated. In a speech at the Philadelphia Central Fair on June 7, Curtin added to his praise of the valor of the enlisted soldier a call to care for "his wife and orphans when he falls." In July, he appointed an agent to oversee the disbursement of funds for this purpose. This agent, Thomas Burrows, subsequently presented to the legislature his plan for a state system of soldiers' orphan schools. It was quickly approved and signed into law. Under the plan, these schools would accept children who met the following criteria: under fifteen years of age, a Pennsylvania resident, and the child of a soldier killed in the war and currently dependent on the labor of a mother or on charity. Applications were submitted to the director of common schools in the child's home district and then forwarded to the state superintendent of the new Bureau of Soldiers' Orphans Schools. Accepted children would receive care and instruction that would not only ensure their health and safety but also inculcate civic virtue and Christian morals. Boys would learn mechanical trades and also be trained in military drill and gymnastics; girls would learn domestic skills and practice calisthenics. The organizers of this state system intended education at these institutions to be a badge of distinction, not of shame.[35]

This new state system absorbed the already-established orphans' home in Pittsburgh. On December 13, 1864, Burrows visited Pittsburgh to accept applications. He met with the mothers or guardians of soldiers' orphans from Allegheny County. Several children from Pittsburgh subsequently enrolled in the city's own home but several others were placed in other schools throughout the state. Community leaders and state officials were deeply concerned about the future of these children. If these orphans of the nation's fallen heroes were to descend into destitution or grow up into irresponsible adults, the honor of Northern society would be tarnished.[36]

As the war came to a close, advocates for the cause of soldiers' orphans redoubled their efforts. For the first July Fourth celebration since the end of the war, the staff of the Pittsburgh Soldiers' Orphans' Home put on a fireworks display on the grounds of the home, which was on Bluff Street overlooking the Monongahela River. Charles Knap, who as head of the Fort Pitt Foundry had been so active producing cannons and munitions, now served as the president of the home. At this time, the home was filled to capacity with over thirty children, but applications continued to come in. The *Post*, whose editor James P. Barr was instrumental in establishing the home, reminded the public that victory in war did not mean the end of their responsibilities: "Amid the general joy, let us not forget the claims the gallant dead have upon our gratitude and generosity, [for] they have left widows and orphans, in the great majority of cases without a dollar to provide even the necessities."[37]

The care of soldiers' orphans in Allegheny County expanded in the years immediately following the war. At the close of 1866, Pittsburgh and Allegheny City had five institutions for this purpose. In addition to the Soldiers' Orphans' Home, Pittsburgh boasted the Orphan Asylum and the Episcopal Church Home. Allegheny City housed the Pittsburgh and Allegheny Or-

phan Asylum and the Home for the Friendless. Community leaders subsequently established several more institutions under the state Bureau of
Soldiers' Orphans Schools, including the Church Home, St. Paul's Roman
Catholic Orphan Asylum, and the Protestant Orphan Asylum of Pittsburgh
and Allegheny. W. A. Passavant founded the Orphan's Farm School on four
hundred acres north of Pittsburgh in Zelienople.[38]

The state plan did not address the needs of every soldiers' orphans. In July
1865, the *Post* received a letter from a Pittsburgher asking if any of the new
institutions for the care of war orphans would accept black children. The answer was, unfortunately, no. The initial plan provided that these orphans be
temporarily placed with other black orphans at the long-established Home
for Colored Children in Maylandville outside of Philadelphia and also at the
state Asylum for the Blind, Deaf, Dumb, and Feeble. Not until 1867 were the
regulations amended to provide a separate school for black soldiers' orphans.
In 1868, the doors of this institution opened and twenty-two orphans were
transferred from Maylandville.[39]

Soldiers' orphans became the focus of benevolence that the community
could not bestow on their fallen fathers. This endeavor was deemed necessary
for the honor of the community; caring for the survivors was just as essential
a part of patriotic duty as satisfying quotas for volunteers, meeting the terms
of contracts and requisitions for war materiel, and rendering aid to soldiers.
Some months after the war ended, the *Harrisburg Telegraph* celebrated the
accomplishments of these schools and extolled them as a symbol of the righ-
teousness of the Northern war effort: "Today there is not a soldiers' orphan
in the broad state of Pennsylvania, who, needing a home, is unprovided with
that and [with] the amplest means of deriving an education. . . . The states
through whose tremendous folly and damnable treason these children were
orphanized [sic], never at any time provided for the education of the poor
man's children. . . . This is the difference between a free state and a slave
state."[40]

CONCLUSION

The connection between the home front and the soldiers who fight our wars has been profoundly important throughout American history. The ability of our government to wage war effectively is predicated on the support of the civilian populace. The presence or absence of that support has shaped not only the outcome of wars but also foreign policy, ideas of citizenship, and the people's relationship with the government. Historian Andrew Bacevich argues that, in modern times, the American people have become so disconnected from their military and so little affected by the cost of our wars that the government has essentially been given free rein to keep the nation in a perpetual state of military conflict. The government now sustains support for war—or simply forestalls opposition to it—by separating the people from the conflict rather than mobilizing the home front.[1]

In the Civil War, however, this was not the case. The Northern war effort was sustained by linking the people to the war and nowhere was this more true than in Pittsburgh. Pittsburghers viewed the Civil War as their own cause because it was interpreted to fit their existing ideologies and because opportunities were created for them to directly participate in the prosecution of the war.

Three themes are apparent in every aspect of mobilization on the Pittsburgh home front. First was the practice of drawing on Pittsburghers' strong sense of localism. Mobilization was driven by the desire of Pittsburgh's citizens to surpass the efforts of other cities and to avoid the stain of local shame. Even the most nationalistic responses were characterized by an emphasis on local pride. This began with the people's reaction to the rebellion of the Southern states. The foiling of the gun removal scheme and the initial surfeit of volunteers for the army were touted as triumphs of the city's loyalty to the Union. So too, the interdiction of contraband passing through the city and the outcry over deficient uniforms being manufactured there were matters of pride not just because they helped the war effort but because they kept Pittsburgh's reputation for Unionism from being tarnished. The draft was resisted so ardently not because Pittsburghers as a whole sought to avoid service but mainly because the necessity of a draft in their community reflected badly on their reputation as strong supporters of the war. Opposition to emancipation, while inspired by white supremacy, concentrated on the threat freed blacks would pose to local economic prosperity. Moreover, the people were inspired by the city's manufacturing identity as they prepared to defend it against an invading Rebel army and as they rose to the challenge of securing naval control of the western rivers. Criticism of the city's treatment of transient soldiers prompted the establishment of a local benevolent group whose efforts would surpass those of nationally based organizations in the city. Even the honoring of fallen soldiers became a matter of competition with other cities.

The second persistent theme was the drawing of parallels between the home front and the battle front. For Pittsburghers who could not, or would not, don a uniform, every effort was made to relate alternative actions to military service. The construction of local forts using volunteer labor was in part intended to bestow on men not in the army a kind of public recognition akin to that lavished on the army volunteers. Home guardsmen and militia members drilled not only to develop readiness for battle but to convince their neighbors that they were worthy of the same accolades. In the case of the Ellet ram fleet, civilian workers of Pittsburgh actually engaged the enemy in battle. Volunteers in the benevolent societies on the Pittsburgh home front equated their endeavors with those of benevolence workers with the armies at the front. The deaths of civilians in the Allegheny Arsenal tragedy were reported and memorialized in terms of battlefield sacrifice.

Finally, in mobilizing to support the Union war effort, Pittsburghers drew on past experiences and existing traditions. They celebrated the city's military volunteers with the same sorts of martial pageantry and civic ritual with which they had honored veterans of earlier wars and national heroes. In rooting out treason in their city, organizing home defense, memorializing the deaths of local soldiers, and raising funds to avert the draft, community leaders continued the custom of reliance on civilian committees rather than local government to achieve results. The tradition of benevolent work for charity and social reform strongly influenced Pittsburghers' care of wounded and transient soldiers and the widows and orphans of the fallen. The city's history of opposition to antebellum proslavery measures primed many Pittsburghers to accept emancipation—though not racial equality—with minimal disruption to the city's mobilization.

Popular support manifested in significant contributions to the total Union war effort. The most tangible and quantifiable is the traditional mobilization of men and materiel sent forth to form and equip the armies required to fight and win the war. The soldiers contributed by Allegheny County account for only 1 percent of all soldiers who served in the Union army, but all of the 2.6 million who served throughout the war came from hundreds of such county-sized mobilization, facilitated by the efforts of local civilian committees, community leaders, and the energy and influence of ordinary citizens who committed themselves to a cause and pulled others along with them. The weapons, munitions, and supplies contributed to the federal armies from Pittsburgh represented a much greater share of the total. Pittsburgh's location, natural resources, and connections of rivers and railroads made it one of the principal centers of manufacturing and commerce well before the war. When hostilities commenced, the city's industrial leaders, supported by an eager workforce and wartime tariffs, transformed and expanded their production capacity to meet the demands of the war.

Just as noteworthy, if not as direct a contribution, was the movement that I refer to as benevolent mobilization. The activities of the national aid societies such as the U.S. Sanitary Commission and the U.S. Christian Commission have been well documented, but the innerworkings of their local chapters, as well as those of the smaller-scale community-based initiatives, are equally important to understanding how citizens provided care and comfort to soldiers on a scale that was unprecedented in the history of war and society. The contribution rendered in the maintenance of the physical and mental health of the tens of thousands of soldiers who received care in Pittsburgh is immeasurable.

The final significant contribution Pittsburgh made to the Union war effort is in the consistent, overarching support of the policies enacted by the Lincoln administration throughout the war. Pittsburgh was not without its dissenters, particularly during the secession crisis in the winter of 1860–61. And there were of course many whose voices we have no record of who detested the war or at least wanted nothing to do with it. However, the voices promoted mobilization amidst ever increasing demands for more men, cautioned vigilance against treason, advocated care for weary and wounded transient soldiers, demanded proper honors rendered for the fallen, and urged the acceptance of emancipation as an inevitable and just objective of the Union war effort. They also dominated so that no opposition movement could ever materialize in forms of civil disobedience, violence, or even consequential abstention from contributing. Apathy, malingering, and desertions did not prevent the city's quota of men from being mustered. The throngs of soldiers in the city, continued loss of life, and threat of invasion did not quell the community's resolve. White supremacy did not thwart the acceptance of emancipation as a policy and objective of the war. In the end, the city's record of support for the war effort shaped a collective memory that was shared for generations as a shining chapter of patriotism and unity.

More research is needed into the wartime experience of other urban areas to fully understand how distinctive or representative Pittsburgh is. Certainly, there are examples to support both arguments. The overwhelming endorsement of Lincoln's prosecution of the war and the economic prosperity the city enjoyed prevented any substantial incidents of civil unrest or labor strikes that occurred in many other Northern cities. No other community seems to have mobilized such a large number of its citizenry to defend against an enemy attack believed to be imminent. And, no other community experienced an industrial accident during the war on the scale of the Arsenal tragedy.

Other aspects of the Pittsburgh home front in the Civil War certainly mirror those of other cities. Most all Northern communities experienced a surge of war enthusiasm that carried forth the initial waves of volunteers in 1861. Cities across the North boasted chapters of the U.S. Sanitary Commission, the U.S. Christian Commission, and likely smaller local benevolent groups and every community suffered as families, congregations, and neighborhoods received the news of soldiers who died from disease or wounds. Pittsburgh was exemplary, but, like other Northern cities, its industrial production supplied the Federal war effort with the material that helped ensure final victory.

The experience of Pittsburgh in the Civil War reveals a number of important areas for further scholarship. More studies are needed to explore how the physical and human geography of urban areas and smaller communities shaped their interaction with the war. There is more to be learned about how cities negotiated changing war policies and objectives. Finally, far more research is needed into how communities rendered assistance to returning Civil War soldiers and how those initiatives created a legacy of enduring and expanding care for veterans of later wars.

The localism manifested in Pittsburghers' support for the war, the analogies they drew between their efforts and sacrifices at home and those of soldiers at the front, and the recourse to custom and tradition all strengthened the community's connection to the war. Rather than a distant conflict waged by strangers, the Union war effort was something the people of Pittsburgh participated in, actively raising and equipping the armies that preserved the Union, maintaining national morale, and providing for those who sacrificed life and limb and for their dependents. The Civil War became the most important event in the lives of not only the men who marched away to battle but of the men and women who remained at home.

NOTES

INTRODUCTION

1. *Pittsburgh Post-Gazette*, 25 January, 24 July, 16 August, and 10 October 1910.

2. *Post-Gazette*, 11–12 October 1910.

3. *Pittsburgh Press*, 11–12 October 1910.

4. Ginnette Aley and J. L. Anderson, eds. *Union Heartland: The Midwestern Home Front During the Civil War* (Carbondale: Southern Illinois University Press, 2013), 2–3.

5. Edward L. Ayers, *In the Presence of Mine Enemies: The Civil War in the Heart of America, 1859–1863* (New York: W. W. Norton, 2003), xviii-xx; Nicole Etcheson, *A Generation at War: The Civil War Era in a Northern Community* (Lawrence: University Press of Kansas, 2011; Christopher Phillips, *The Rivers Ran Backward: The Civil War and the Remaking of the American Middle Border* (New York: Oxford University Press, 2016); Stephen Rockenbach, *War upon Our Border: Two Ohio Valley Communities Navigate the Civil War* (Charlottesville: University of Virginia Press, 2016); Matthew E. Stanley, *The Loyal West: Civil War and Reunion in Middle America* (Urbana: University of Illinois Press, 2017).

6. Arnold Shankman, *The Pennsylvania Antiwar Movement, 1861–1865* (Rutherford, NJ: Fairleigh Dickinson University Press, 1980); Grace Palladino, *Another Civil War: Labor, Capital, and the State in the Anthracite Regions of Pennsylvania, 1840–1868* (Urbana: University of Illinois Press, 1990); Robert M. Sandow, *Deserter Country: Civil War Opposition in the Pennsylvania Appalachians* (New York: Fordham University Press, 2009); Melinda Lawson, *Patriot Fires: Forging a New American Nationalism in the Civil War North* (Lawrence: University Press of Kansas, 2002).

7. Earl J. Hess, *Liberty, Virtue, and Progress: Northerners and Their War for the Union* (New York University Press, 1988), 1; J. Matthew Gallman, *The North Fights the Civil War: The Home Front* (Chicago, IL: Ivan R. Dee, 1994); Gary Gallagher, *The Union War* (Cambridge, MA: Harvard University Press, 2011); Bridget Ford, *The Bonds of Union: Religion, Race, and Politics in a Civil War Borderland* (Chapel Hill: University of North Carolina Press, 2016); James Oakes, *Freedom National: The Destruction of Slavery in the United States, 1861–1865* (New York: W. W. Norton, 2013).

8. Paul A. Cimballa and Randall M. Miller, *The Northern Home Front During the Civil War* (Santa Barbara, CA: Praeger, 2017), xiii.

9. For an excellent study on these debates with the black northern community, see Brian Taylor, *Fighting for Citizenship: Black Northerners and the Debate over Military Service in the Civil War* (Chapel Hill: The University of North Carolina Press, 2020).

1. FOR THE VICTORY THAT MUST SOONER OR LATER CROWN THEIR EFFORTS

1. Eighth Census, 1860, Manuscript Returns of Free Inhabitants, Pittsburgh, Fourth Ward, Allegheny County, Pennsylvania, National Archives and Records Administration, Washington, D.C. [hereafter, NARA]; Larry Glasco, Historic Pittsburgh Census Data, 1860 census spreadsheet, University of Pittsburgh, University Library System, http://exhibit.library.pitt.edu/census/ [accessed December 1, 2014].

2. Sarah H. Killikelly, *The History of Pittsburgh: Its Rise and Progress* (Pittsburgh, PA: B. C. and Gordon Montgomery, 1906), 65–66.

3. Russel J. Ferguson, *Early Western Pennsylvania Politics* (PA: Pittsburgh Press, 1938), 12–13; Catherine E. Reiser, *Pittsburgh's Commercial Development, 1800–1850* (Harrisburg: Pennsylvania Historical and Museum Commission, 1951), 70; Killikelly, *History of Pittsburgh*, 86; *Pittsburgh Gazette*, 17 January 1789 [hereafter, *Gazette*].

4. Zadok Cramer, *The Ohio and Mississippi Navigator.* (Pittsburgh, PA: John Scull, 1802), 19–20.

5. Ferguson, *Early Western Pennsylvania Politics*, 13; Hugh Henry Brackenridge, *Gazette Publications* (Carlisle, PA: Alexander and Phillips, 1806), 7, 17; *Gazette*, 26 July 1786.

6. Reiser, *Pittsburgh's Commercial Development*, 70.

7. Richard C. Wade, *The Urban Frontier: The Rise of Western Cities, 1790–1830* (Cambridge: Harvard University Press, 1959), 342.

8. Reiser, *Pittsburgh's Commercial Development*, 2, 70–73. Matthew Stanley in *The Loyal West* contends that the old Northwest identified more with the South than North because of their shared agrarianism opposed to the industrialized economy of the Northeast. However, this separation between Midwest and Northeast was driven more by geography and eroded with the building of the Erie Canal and railroads which made overland shipping as viable as riverine.

9. William F. Trimble, "From Sail to Steam: Ship Building in the Pittsburgh Area, 1790–1865," *Western Pennsylvania Historical Magazine* 58 (1975): 147–48 [hereafter, *WPHM*]; Reiser, *Pittsburgh's Commercial Development*, 4–5, 29.

10. Trimble, "From Sail to Steam," 147–48, 154–57.

11. Arthur Cecil Bining, "The Rise of Iron Manufacturing in Western Pennsylvania," *WPHM* 16 (1933): 236–38; Zadock Cramer, *Pittsburgh Magazine Almanack* (Pittsburgh, PA: Cramer, Spear, and Eichbaum, 1812), 5–53.

12. Bining, "Rise of Iron Manufacturing," 245–47; Freeman Hunt, *The Merchants' Magazine and Commercial Review* (New York: Freeman Hunt, 1850), 688.

13. Margaret Elder, "Pittsburgh Industries that Used to Be," *WPHM* 12 (1929): 216; *Gazette*, 11 January 1820; Murray N. Rothbard, *The Panic of 1819: Reaction and Policies* (New York: Columbia University Press, 1962), 1–4, 93–94.

14. M. Flavia Taylor, "The Political and Civic Career of Henry Baldwin, 1799–1830," *WPHM* 24 (1941): 45; *Annals of Congress*, 16th Cong., 1st Sess., p. 1923; Bining, "Rise of Iron Manufactures," 243–45.

15. Trimble, "From Sail to Steam," 158; *Pittsburgh Daily Post* [hereafter, *Post*], 20 September 1842; *Erie Gazette*, 7 December 1843.

16. *Philadelphia Public Ledger*, 23 August 1849; *Gazette*, 22–24 November 1849.

17. Bining, "Rise of Iron Manufacturing," 253; Hunt, *Merchant's Magazine and Commercial Review*, 688.

18. Edward K. Muller, "Was Pittsburgh's Economic Destiny Set in 1815?," *Indiana Magazine of History* 105 (2009): 207.

19. John S. Rittenour, "Over the Old Roads to Pittsburgh," *WPHM* 4 (1921): 76–79; Killikelly, *History of Pittsburgh*, 131.

20. Diane Barnes, "Urban Rivalry in the Upper Ohio Valley: Wheeling and Pittsburgh in the Nineteenth Century," *Pennsylvania Magazine of History and Biography* [hereafter, *PMHB*] 123 (1999): 214–15; Rittenour, "Over the Old Roads to Pittsburgh," 82; Muller, "Was Pittsburgh's Economic Destiny Set in 1815?," 213.

21. William Kenneth Schusler, "The Railroad Comes to Pittsburgh," *WPHM* 43 (1960): 251–66; Charles Dickens, *American Notes* (New York: John W. Lovell, 1842), 727.

22. Muller, "Was Pittsburgh's Economic Destiny Set in 1815?," 215; Joseph S. Clark Jr. and Michael Schlatter, "The Railroad Struggle for Pittsburgh: Forty-three Years of Philadelphia-Baltimore Rivalry, 1838–1871," *PMHB* 48 (1924): 2–3.

23. M. B. Lowrie to Select and Common Council, 6 June 1830. Records of the Pittsburgh Select and Common Council, Senator John Heinz History Center [hereafter, *SJHHC*], Pittsburgh.

24. Clark and Schlatter, "Railroad Struggle for Pittsburgh," 1–6; *North American*, 5 and 19 March 1846; *Gazette*, 15 March 1846.

25. John P. Cowan, "Beginning of the Early Railroads in Pittsburgh," *WPHM* 12 (1929): 115; Clark and Schlatter, "Railroad Struggle for Pittsburgh," 11–12.

26. Schusler, "Railroad Comes to Pittsburgh," 256–58.

27. Nora Faires, "Immigrants and Industry: Peopling the 'Iron City,'" in *City at the Point: Essays on the Social History of Pittsburgh*, ed. Samuel P. Hays (Pittsburgh, PA: University of Pittsburgh Press), 5–6; Oscar Handlin, *Boston's Immigrants: A Study in Acculturation* (Cambridge, MA: Harvard University Press, 1957).

28. Nora Faires, "Immigrants and Industry," 7–8.

29. George H. Thurston, *Directory of Pittsburgh and Allegheny Cities, and the Adjoining Burroughs, 1861–1862* (Pittsburgh, PA: George H. Thurston, 1861), 450–52;

Walter D. Kamphoefner, Wolgang Helbich, and Ulrike Sommer, eds., *News from the Land of Freedom: German Immigrants Write Home* (Ithaca, NY: Cornell University Press, 1991), 62–94.

30. Stanton Belfour, "The Philanthropic Tradition in Pittsburgh," *WPHM* 37 (1954): 93; Papers of the Select and Common Council of Pittsburgh, Charities Committee, *SJHHC*, Pittsburgh, PA.

31. Lloyd L. Sponholtz, "Pittsburgh and Temperance, 1830–1854," *WPHM* 46 (1963): 360, 378.

32. *Ibid.*, 351.

33. R. A. B. Housman, *The Liquor Laws of Pennsylvania, with Annotations to January 1st, 1907* (Washington, D.C.: Office of the Librarian of Congress, 1907), 40–41, 54; Sponholtz, "Pittsburgh and Temperance," 353.

34. Sponholtz, "Pittsburgh and Temperance," 355–56; Marcus E. Cross, *The Mirror of Intemperance Reform* (Philadelphia, PA: John T. Lange, 1849), 101; John Boucher and John Jordan, *A Century and a Half of Pittsburgh and Her People*, 2 vols. (New York: Lewis Publishing Company, 1908), 1:526.

35. Sponholtz, "Pittsburgh and Temperance," 357–58; *Pittsburgh Daily Commercial Journal*, 16 September 1848; *Temperance Gem* (Allegheny, PA), 1 October 1851.

36. Harry M. Chalfant, *Father Penn and John Barleycorn* (Harrisburg, PA: Evangelical Press, 1920), 73; Asa E. Martin, "The Temperance Movement in Pennsylvania Prior to the Civil War," *PMHB* 49 (1925): 210; *Gazette*, 7 July 1848.

37. *Gazette*, 10 July and 14 October 1854; Martin, "Temperance Movement in Pennsylvania," 227.

38. J. Herron Foster, *A Full Account of the Great Fire at Pittsburgh.* (Pittsburgh, PA: J.W. Cook, 1845), 3–7. 38; Foster, *Full Account of the Great Fire*, 6; Charles F. C. Arensberg, "The Pittsburgh Fire of April 10, 1845," *WPHM* 28 (1945): 14.

39. Foster, *Full Account of the Great Fire*, 6–9; Arensberg, "Pittsburgh Fire," 14–18.

40. Arensberg, "Pittsburgh Fire," 19.

41. Edward M. Burns, "Slavery in Western Pennsylvania," *WPHM* 8 (1925): 204; Pennsylvania State Legislature, *Laws of the Commonwealth of Pennsylvania*, 4 vols. (Philadelphia, PA: John Bioren, 1810), 1, 492–96.

42. R. J. M. Blackett, "Freedom or the Martyr's Grave: Black Pittsburgh's Aid to the Fugitive Slave," *WPHM* (1978): 117–18.

43. Eric Ledell Smith, "The Pittsburgh Memorial: A Forgotten Document of Pittsburgh History," *Pittsburgh History* 80 (1997): 106–108; Records of the Constitutional Convention and the Council of Censors, 1837–1838, Pennsylvania Constitutional Convention, RG-5, Pennsylvania State Archives, Harrisburg.

44. William C. Nell, *The Colored Patriots of the American Revolution* (Boston, MA: Robert F. Walcut, 1855), 182–88; Catherine M. Hanchett, "George Boyer Vashon, 1824–1878: Black Educator, Poet, Fighter for Equal Rights-Part One," *WPHM* 68 (1985): 205–206.

45. Belfour, "Philanthropic Tradition in Pittsburgh," 95.

46. Blackett, "Freedom or the Martyr's Grave," 120.

47. Burns, "Slavery in Western Pennsylvania," 210; Killikelly, *History of Pittsburgh*, 182.

48. Paul Finkelman, *An Imperfect Union: Slavery, Federalism and Comity* (Chapel Hill: University of North Carolina Press, 1981), 11; *Post*, 28 January and 17–22 April 1847; *Pittsburgh Daily Commercial Journal* [hereafter, *Commercial Journal*], 7 July 1848; *Gazette*, 8 July 1848.

49. *Gazette*, 6 June and 30 September 1850; *Post*, 30 September 1850; *Commercial Journal*, 1 October 1850; Irene F. Williams, "The Operation of the Fugitive Slave Law in Western Pennsylvania from 1850 to 1860," *WPHM* 4 (1921): 152–53.

50. *Gazette*, 24–26 September 1850; *Liberator* (Boston), 4 October 1850; Williams, "Operation of the Fugitive Slave Law," 152.

51. *Gazette*, 14 March 1851; *Post*, 14 March 1851; Williams, "Operation of the Fugitive Slave Law," 154.

52. *Gazette*, 30 May and 12 August 1853; *Post*, 14 March 1851, 31 May 1853, and 14 March 1854; *Pittsburgh Evening Chronicle*, 12 August 1853.

53. Weston Arthur Goodspeed and Erasmus Wilson, *Standard History of Pittsburgh, Pennsylvania* (Chicago, IL: H.R. Cornell, 1898), 825; *Gazette*, 17 July 1855.

54. *Gazette*, 10, 24 January and 24 May 1854.

55. *Ibid.*, 23–24 May 1856.

56. *Ibid.*, 14 and 26 March 1857.

57. *Ibid.*, 19 May and 9 November 1860; Michael Holt, *Forging a Majority: The Formation of the Republican Party in Pittsburgh, 1848–1860* (New Haven, CT: Yale University Press, 1969), 263–67.

2. NOT ONLY BY EXPRESSIONS OF SENTIMENT, BUT BY THE EXERCISE OF PHYSICAL FORCE

1. Boucher and Jordan, *A Century and a Half of Pittsburgh*, vol. 2, 153; James Speers to James Buchanan, 24 December 1860, James Buchanan Papers, Historical Society of Pennsylvania, Philadelphia.

2. William Wilkins et al. to James Buchanan, 25 December 1860, quoted in *Gazette*, 27 December 1860.

3. *Pittsburgh Daily Dispatch* [hereafter, *Dispatch*], 25 December 1860; *Gazette*, 25 December 1860.

4. James McClelland Diary, 27 December 1860, McClelland Family Papers, *SJHHC*, Pittsburgh, PA; *Gazette*, 28 December 1860; *Post*, 28 December 1860; *Daily National Intelligencer* (Washington, D.C.), 1 January 1861.

5. John H. Niebaum, *History of the Washington Infantry* (Pittsburgh, PA: Bergun Print Co., 1931), 24.

6. *Chicago Tribune*, 28 December 1860; *New York Daily Tribune*, 29 December 1860.

7. *Gazette*, 4 January 1861.

8. *Post*, 28 December 1860.

9. Cimballa and Randal M. Miller, *The Northern Home Front during the Civil War*, 14; *Post*, 25 December 1860; Boucher and Jordan, *A Century and a Half of Pittsburgh*, vol., 151–52.

10. *Gazette*, 28 December 1860. Historians of Northern society in the Civil War typically see the firing on Fort Sumter as the catalyst for animosity toward the South. See Gallman, *North Fights the Civil War*, 4. Gallman argues that "[i]n many Northern eyes this [the firing on Fort Sumter] transformed the people of the infant Confederacy from wayward brother to audacious enemies." See also Hess, *Liberty, Virtue, and Progress*, 23. Hess claims that it was not secession that inspired unified ideological defiance to the South. Rather, it was the firing on Fort Sumter that "refocused the sectional debate and created a mighty consensus in favor of war."

11. *Gazette*, 28 December 1860 and 1 January 1861.

12. *Ibid.*; for a comprehensive study of Northern party politics during the Civil War, see: Adam I. P. Smith, *No Party Now: Politics in the Civil War North* (Oxford: Oxford University Press, 2006); Samuel W. Durant, et al., *History of Allegheny Co., Pennsylvania: With Illustrations Descriptive of Its Scenery, Palatial Residences, Public Buildings, Fine Blocks, and Important Manufactories* (Philadelphia, PA: L. H. Everts, 1876), 63; Boucher and Jordan, *A Century and a Half of Pittsburgh*, vol. 2, 153.

13. *Gazette*, 1 January 1861.

14. Goodspeed and Wilson, *Standard History of Pittsburgh, Pennsylvania*, 549; Jon Grinspan, "Young Men for War: The Wide Awakes and Lincoln's 1860 Presidential Campaign," *Journal of American History* 96, no. 2 (September 2009), 357–58; John Donaghy, *Army Experience of Captain John Donaghy* (De Land, FL: E. O. Painter Print Co., 1926), 3; George Thorton Fleming, *Program of the Exercises Attending and Addresses Delivered at Fifth Avenue High School: March 1, 1907* (Pittsburgh, PA: Central Board of Education, 1907), 22.

15. *Gazette*, 1 January 1861.

16. *Ibid.*; *Dispatch*, 3 January 1861; Michael Holt, *Forging a Majority*, 312; Avery Craven, *The Coming of the Civil War, Second* (New York: Charles Scribner's Sons, 1942), 428–29; Eric Foner, *Free Soil, Free Labor, Free Men: The Ideology of the Republican Party Before the Civil War* (New York: Oxford University Press, 1970).

17. *Gazette*, 4 January 1861.

18. Kenneth Stampp, *And the War Came*, 2nd ed. (Baton Rouge: Louisiana State University Press, 1970), 123–25, 143; *Daily Post*, 8 January 1861; *Daily Dispatch*, 16 February 1861.

19. J. W. F. White, "The Judiciary of Allegheny County," *PMHB* 7 (1883), 143–93; *San Diego Union*, 21 April 1899.

20. *Dispatch*, 19 February 1861.

21. *Ibid.*; *Gazette*, 19 February 1861. Several historians have found in communities across the North a precarious balance early in the secession crisis between the desire for peace through compromise and growing antipathy toward the South. See Nicole Etcheson, *A Generation at War*, 46–49; Stephen Rockenbach, *War upon Our Border*, 35–48; and Bridget Ford, *The Bonds of Union*, 251–52.

22. *Post*, 23 December 1861; *Gazette*, 23 February 1861; *Dispatch*, 23 February 1861.

23. *Gazette*, 2 March 1861. The *Gazette* on 23 February 1858 made a brief mention of a parade honoring Washington's birthday with little fanfare. Spectators were largely surprised by it. Attention to Washington's birthday continued to fall off over the next two years. In 1859, a small banquet was held at the newly opened Girard House but the newspapers mentioned no parade. In 1860, the *Gazette* mentioned no Washington's Birthday events. See George H. Thurston, *Allegheny County's Hundred Years* (Pittsburgh, PA: A.A. Anderson and Son, 1888), 71; Goodspeed and Wilson, *Standard History of Pittsburgh*, 549–51; *Pittsburgh Daily Gazette*, 2 March 1861.

24. *Dispatch*, 23 February 1861; *Gazette*, 23 February 1861; Cimbala and Miller, *The Northern Home Front During the Civil War*, 68–69.

25. J. Matthew Gallman has made a similar observation about Philadelphia's 1861 observance of Washington's birthday which coincided with a visit by President-Elect Lincoln. Gallman writes: "These two days, coming in the midst of the secession winter, fused the political concerns of the moment with familiar patriotic symbols and modes of celebration." See J. Matthew Gallman, *Mastering Wartime: A Social History of Philadelphia During the Civil War* MA: Cambridge University Press, 1990), 86.

26. *Post*, 23 February 1861.

27. *Ibid.*

28. *Ibid.*

29. *Ibid.*, 12 April 1861; Boucher and Jordan, *A Century and a Half of Pittsburgh*, vol. 2, 154; Goodspeed and Wilson, *Standard History of Pittsburgh*, 551.

30. Cimballa and Randal M. Miller, *The Northern Home Front during the Civil War*, 14–15. *Post*, 15 April 1861; *Gazette*, 15 April 1861.

31. 155th Pennsylvania Infantry Regiment, *Under the Maltese Cross, Antietam to Appomattox, the Loyal Uprising in Western Pennsylvania, 1861–1865: Campaigns 155th Pennsylvania Regiment* (Pittsburgh, PA: The 155th Regimental Association, 1910), 5–6; *Gazette*, 16 April 1861; William G. Johnston, *Life and Reminiscenses from Birth to Manhood of Wm. G. Johnston* (Pittsburgh, PA: Knickerbocker Press, 1901), 70; *Post*, 17 April 1861; James McClelland Diary, 15 April 1861; Donaghy, *Army Experience of John Donaghy*, 3. The firing on Fort Sumter had a transformative effect in cities across the North, galvanizing communities in their support to quickly put down the rebellion. See Cimbala and Miller, *The Northern Home Front During the Civil War*, 24–29 and Ayers, *In the Presence of Mine Enemies*, 143–47.

32. Boucher and Jordan, *A Century and a Half of Pittsburgh*, 154; *Dispatch*, 16 April 1861.

33. Gallagher, *Union War, passim*; Ford, *The Bonds of Union*, 251–56, 266–67.

34. *Gazette*, 16 April 1861.

35. Edgar Cowan, *Speeches of Maj. Wm. A. Stokes, U.S. Army, and Hon. Edgar Cowan, U.S. Senate: Delivered at the Union Convention, Westmoreand County, PA*, September 1861 (Pittsburgh, PA: Barr & Meyers, 1861).

36. Oakes, *Freedom National*, xxii–xxiv. Oakes's argument—that from the beginning of the war, the eradication of slavery was as essential an objective as was the preservation of the Union—is specific to the Republican party. Other historians have found more evidence of Republican leaders distancing their support of the war from the cause of emancipation. Edward Ayers states that "Northern leaders [as the war was beginning] expressed barely a word of concern for the millions of people currently enslaved." Nicole Etcheson argues that "to ward off the charge of abolitionism, Republicans [in Putnam County, Indiana] had flaunted their own racism." See Ayers, *In the Presence of Mine Enemies*, 148 and Etcheson, *A Generation at War*, 49.

37. *Post*, 17–18 April 1861. Other historians of northern society during the war have found similar evidence in other communities of this transformative effect of the firing on Fort Sumter. Edward Ayers writes that the Democratic paper in Chambersburg, Pennsylvania "exploded in headlines proclaiming its change of heart." See Ayers, *In the Presence of Mine Enemies*, 143–47 and Cimballa and Randal M. Miller, *The Northern Home Front During the Civil War*, 27. Stephen Rockenbach sees the consequences of the firing on Fort Sumter as a final but ineffective push for secessionism in Kentucky. See Rockenbach, *War upon Our Border*, 42.

38. *Post*, 17–18 April 1861.

39. *Ibid.*

40. *Gazette*, 16 and 20 April 1861; *Post*, 20 April 1861.

41. *The Rebellion Record of Allegheny County, from April, 1861, to October, 1862.* (Pittsburgh, PA: W.A. Lare and W.M. Hartzell, 1862), 12.

42. *Gazette*, 22 April 1861.

43. *Ibid.*

44. Rebellion Record of Allegheny County, 12; *Dispatch*, 29 April 1861.

45. *Dispatch*, 29 April 1861.

46. James McPherson, *Battle Cry of Freedom: The Civil War Era* (Oxford: Oxford University Press, 1988), 323–24.

47. *Quarter Sessions of Allegheny County*, no. 261, June 1861, Records of Quarter Session Court, 1799–1906, Allegheny County Court House, Pittsburgh, PA; George Bergner, *The Legislative Record: Containing Debates and Proceedings of the Session of 1862* (Harrisburg, PA: Telegraph Book Job Office, 1862), 907–18. Mark R.

Wilson, *The Business of Civil War: Military Mobilization and the State, 1861–1865* (Baltimore, MA: John Hopkins University Press, 2006), 39.

48. *Rebellion Record of Allegheny County*, 12. For an excellent study of Americans' expectations at the onset of the war that challenges the short war theory, see Jason Phillips, *Looming Civil War: How Nineteenth-century Americans Imagined the Future* (New York: Oxford University Press, 2018).

49. Mark R. Wilson, *The Business of Civil War*, 7–12.

50. Allan Nevins, *War for the Union: Vol. 1, 1861–1862: The Improvised War* (New York: Konecky and Konecky, 1971), 87–91; A. Howard Meneely, *The War Department, 1861: A Study in Mobilization* (New York: Columbia University Press, 1928), 13–31.

51. George H. Thurston, *Directory of Pittsburgh* (Pittsburgh, PA: George H. Thurston, 1861), 359–62.

52. Lorien Foote argues that the Union army represented northern society in miniature, "reflecting its culture and values and imbued with its strengths and weaknesses." See Lorien Foote, *The Gentlemen and the Roughs: Violence, Honor, and Manhood in the Union Army* (New York University Press, 2010), 1.

53. Niebaum, *History of the Washington Infantry*, 65; *The Rebellion Record of Allegheny County*, 4. While the Pittsburgh newspapers report daily on the activities of the militia companies during this period, none mentioned the offer made by the Hannibal Guards, nor did any local publication until the *Rebellion Record of Allegheny County* was published a few weeks after the Emancipation Proclamation was issued in 1863. See Jennifer R. Harbour, *Organizing Freedom: Black Emancipation Activism in the Civil War Midwest* (Carbondale: Southern Illinois University Press, 2020), 76.

54. Donaghy, *Army Experiences of Captain John Donaghy*, 3–5.

55. *Gazette*, 22 April 1861. Scholarship on the direct participation of women in the northern war effort produced a handful of excellent studies in recent decades. Catherine Clinton and Nina Sibler, in their edited collection *Divided Houses*, shows the diversity in women's wartime experiences based on region, race, and class. Jeanie Attie argues that women supported the war effort out of patriotic motivations through practical and literary labor. Judith Giesberg details the efforts of women on the northern home front in support of their own prosperity during the war as well as that of the Union cause. See Catherine Clinton and Nina Silber, eds., *Divided Houses: Gender and the Civil War* (New York: Oxford University Press, 1992); Jeanie Attie, *Patriotic Toil: Northern Women and the American Civil War* (Ithaca, NY: Cornell University Press, 1998); and Judith Giesberg, *Army at Home: Women and the Civil War on the Northern Home Front* (Chapel Hill: University of North Carolina Press, 2009).

56. *Gazette*, 24 April 1861.

57. *Post*, 23, 24 April 1861.

58. *Rebellion Record of Allegheny County*, 6.

59. *Ibid.*; *Dispatch*, 25 April 1861.

3. EVERY PROMINENT POINT WILL BRISTLE
WITH CANNON AND BAYONETS

1. *Rebellion Record of Allegheny County*, 21.

2. *Post*, 27 April 1861.

3. Timothy Justin Orr, "Cities at War: Union Army Mobilization in the Urban Northeast, 1861–1865" (Ph.D. diss., Pennsylvania State University, 2010), 76–77; *Post*, 27 April 1861.

4. *Gazette*, 29 April 1861.

5. *Ibid.*, 29 April 1861.

6. *Dispatch*, 29 April 1861; Samuel P. Bates, *History of the Pennsylvania Volunteers, 1861–65*, 5 vols. (Harrisburg: B. Singerly, 1869), vol. 2, 106.

7. *Post*, 1 May 1861.

8. *Rebellion Record of Allegheny County*, 21–22; *Post*, 1, 2, and 6 May 1861.

9. George H. Thurston, *Allegheny County's Hundred Years* (Pittsburgh, PA: A. A. Anderson and Son, 1888), 68.

10. *Ibid.*, 68–69.

11. A. A. Lambling and J. W. F. White, *Allegheny County: It's Early History and Subsequent Development* (Pittsburgh, PA: Snowden and Peterson, 1888), 104; *Rebellion Record of Allegheny County*, 14–16; Sewell E. Slick, "William Wilkins: Pittsburgher Extraordinary," *WPHM* 22 (1939): 217; George Thorton Fleming, *History of Pittsburgh and Environs*, 5 vols. (New York: American Historical Society, 1922), [ED: Which volume?]851–53.

12. Harper Family Papers, 1796–1882, *passim*, *SJHHC*.

13. William Wilkins to Major John Symington, 26 July 1861; John Harper to Albert Harper, 20 September 1862; and account book, Harper Family Papers.

14. *Rebellion Record of Allegheny County*, 13–14; Boucher and Jordan, *A Century and a Half of Pittsburgh*, 157.

15. John Harper to Albert Harper, 16 and 20 September 1862, Harper Family Papers; Durant, et al., *History of Allegheny Co.*, 69.

16. First Methodist Protestant Church, *Closing Services: First Methodist Protestant Church, Fifth Avenue Pittsburgh, May 11, 12, 13 and 15* (Pittsburgh, PA: Rawsthorne, 1892), 11.

17. John J. Matvia, "Riot at Camp Wilkins," unpublished manuscript, Civil War Collection, *SJHHC*; *Post*, 18 June 1861; *Dispatch*, 3 May 1861; Robert Rutland, "A Union Rookie at Camp Wilkins, 1861," *WPHM* 37 (1954): 60. *Gazette*, 18 June 1861; Matvia, "Riot at Camp Wilkins;" Luther C. Furst Diary, 18 June 1861, Harrisburg Civil War Round Table Collection, U. S. Army Military History Institute, Carlisle, PA.

18. Matvia, "Riot at Camp Wilkins."

19. Matvia, "Riot at Camp Wilkins"; *Post*, 18–21 June 1861; *Gazette*, 18–21 June 1861.

20. *Gazette*, 18 June 1861; Furst Diary, 19 June 1861.

21. *Dispatch*, 19–20 June 1861; Matvia, "Riot at Camp Wilkins."

22. Furst Diary, 1–20 May 1861. The presence of soldiers and camps in northern communities created a mixture of amicable and confrontational interactions across the North. See Cimbala and Miller, *The Northern Home Front During the Civil War*, 47–51.

23. Killikelly, *History of Pittsburgh*, 444.

24. Rutland, "Union Rookie at Camp Wilkins, 60–61.

25. John A. Cushing, *History of Allegheny County Pennsylvania* (Chicago, IL: A. Warner, 1889), 186; Boucher and Jordan, *A Century and a Half of Pittsburgh and Its People*, 156.

26. *Gazette*, 28 February and 9, 12 March 1861.

27. *Post*, 6, 9 June 1861.

28. *Gazette*, 9 September 1861.

29. *Ibid.*, 27 August 1862, 27 February 1864, and 27 February 1862; *Post*, 20 February 1862 and 5 May 1864; *Gazette,* 2 April 1864.

30. *Post*, 20 February 1862 and 5 May 1864; *Gazette,* 2 April 1864.

31. *Post*, 2 November 1863; *Gazette*, 16 July 1863; *Commercial Journal*, 7 September 1863.

32. *Gazette*, 12 December 1864.

33. *Ibid.*, 12 and 14 December 1864.

34. *Ibid.*, 14 December 1864.

35. *Ibid.*, 21 December 1864.

36. *Commercial Journal*, 23 and 28 February 1865.

37. *Post*, 28 December 1865; *Commercial Journal*, 28 December 1865.

38. *Post*, 24 April 1861.

39. *Gazette*, 8 September 1862.

40. John Harper to Albert Harper, 20 September 1862, Harper Family Papers; *Pennsylvania Daily Telegraph* (Harrisburg), 30 September 1862.

41. John I. Nevin Diary, 2 June 1863, Civil War Collection, *SJHHC*; *Gazette*, 5 June 1863.

42. Letters Received and Endorsements Sent, Department of the Monongahela, January 1863-October 1865, pp. 6, 22, 186, Record Group 98, Records of United States Army Commands, 1784–1821, NARA; United States War Department, *The War of the Rebellion: A Compilation of the Official Records of the Union and Confederate Armies* [hereafter, *O.R.*] (70 vols. In 128 pts., Washington, D.C.: Government Print Office, 1880–1901), Series One, vol. 27, 32.

43. *O.R.*, Series One, vol. 21, 36, 55.

44. *Ibid.*, vol. 27, 54; Durant, et al., *History of Allegheny Co.*, 65.

45. *O.R.*, Series One, vol. 27, 77–80, 161.

46. *Ibid.*, 113; Thurston, *Allegheny County's Hundred Years*, 77; Durant, et al., *History of Allegheny Co.*, 64.

47. McClelland Diary, 15 June 1863; John Harper to Albert Harper, 16 June 1863,

Harper Family Papers; Frances Bruce to John McAllister, 16 June 1863, Civil War Collection, *SJHHC*; Durant, et al., *History of Allegheny Co.*, 64; *Post*, 18 June 1863.

48. John Harper to Albert Harper, 16 and 19 June 1863, Harper Family Papers.

49. *Gazette*, 23 June 1863; John P. Cowan, "Fortifying Pittsburgh in 1863: Historic Document Gives Interesting Record of the Men Who Worked on Construction of Coal Hill Fort," *WPHM* 2 (1919): 59–64; Boucher and Jordan, *A Century and a Half of Pittsburgh and Its People*, 181; John Harper to Albert Harper, 25 June 1863, Harper Family Papers.

50. *Gazette*, 19 and 27 June 1863.

51. *Gazette*, 20 and 23 June 1863.

52. John Harper to Albert Harper, 19, 22, 24, and 25 June 1863, Harper Family Papers.

4. THE COUNTRY HAS A RIGHT TO THE SERVICES OF HER CITIZENS

1. *Gazette*, 24 July and 5 August 1862.

2. *Ibid.*, 25 September 1862.

3. 25 September 1862, 8 August 1862; *Post*, 15, 18 August and 25 September 1862; *Commercial Journal*, 11 August 1862.

4. *Gazette*, 14 January 1862; *Post*, 6 June 1862.

5. *Post*, 5 May 1862; *Gazette*, 2 May 1862.

6. *Post*, 25, 26, 30 September, 6 October, and 5 December 1862; Ayers, *In the Presence of Mine Enemies*, 320, 361.

7. *Post*, 11 October 1862; Paul D. Escott, *The Worst Passions of Human Nature: White Supremacy in the Civil War North* (Charlottesville: University of Virginia Press, 2020), 55–57, 68–72; Edward L. Ayers, *The Thin Light of Freedom: The Civil War and Emancipation in the Heart of America* (New York: W. W. Norton, 2017), 286–287; Rockenbach, *War upon Our Border*, 98; Phillips, *The Rivers Ran Backward*, 224; Cimbala and Miller, *The Northern Home Front During the Civil War*, 134.

8. *Post*, 10 September 1862.

9. *Post*, 24, 25 July and 4 August 1862.

10. *Gazette*, 7 and 21 August 1862; *Post*, 17 July and 8 August 1862.

11. Bell Irvin Wiley, *The Life of Billy Yank: The Common Soldier of the Union* (Baton Rouge: Louisiana State University Press, 1952), 48–49; Cibala and Miller, *The Northern Home Front During the Civil War*, 137–38.

12. *Post*, 17 July and 4 August 1862; *Gazette*, 2 August 1862.

13. *Post*, 26 July and 4, 9, 18 August 1862; *Gazette*, 8 August 1862.

14. *Gazette*, 10, 17, and 18 September 1862; James W. Geary, *We Need Men: The Union Draft in the Civil War* (Dekalb: Northern Illinois University Press, 1991), 35–36; Cimbala and Miller, *The Northern Home Front during the Civil War*, 140–42.

15. *Post*, 25 August 1862.

16. Geary, *We Need Men*, 35; *Gazette*, 27 August and 10, 14 October 1862; *Post*, 24 September, 8 October 1862.

17. *Post*, 12 March 1863; *Gazette*, 30 May 1863.

18. *Post*, 5 January and 20 February 1863.

19. *Ibid.*, 8 and 9 July 1863; James Fry to Edwin Stanton, 3 May 1863, General Records of the Provost Marshal General's Office (PMGO), Washington, D.C., and of the Enrollment Division, AGO, 1861–89, Records of the Provost Marshal General's Bureau, Record Group 110, NARA.

20. *Gazette*, 9 July 1863; *Post*, 14 and 18 July 1863; Cimbala and Miller, *The Northern Home Front during the Civil War*, 140; Geary, *We Need Men*, 105–7.

21. *Post*, 20 July 1863; *Gazette*, 21 and 23 July 1863.

22. *Post*, 20 July 1863; *Gazette* 18 and 21 July 1863; Geary, *We Need Men*, 214; Medical Register of Examinations of Recruits and Substitutes, Twenty-Second District, Pennsylvania, Records of the Provost Marshal General's Bureau, Record Group 110, NARA.

23. *Gazette*, 18 July and 9, 24 September 1863.

24. RG 94, Records of the Adjutant General's Office, M1817, M1659, M1820, and M1821, M1822, M1823 NARA, Washington, D.C.; Robert S. Levine, *Martin R. Delany: A Documentary Reader* (Chapel Hill: University of North Carolina Press, 2003), 383–84; Taylor, *Fighting for Citizenship*, 74.

25. *Post*, 30 September and 17 October 1863; *Gazette*, 30 September 1863; *Commercial Journal*, 9 September 1863.

26. *Post*, 19, 20 October, 10 November, and 16, 19 December 1863; *Post*, 19 October and 23 December 1863.

27. Medical Register of Examinations of Recruits and Substitutes, Twenty-Second District, Pennsylvania; *Gazette*, 4 and 20 January 1864; *Commercial Journal*, 9, 11 January and 7 June 1864; RG 94, Records of the Adjutant General's Office, M1823, NARA, Washington, D.C.

28. *Gazette*, 28 January 1864.

29. *Commercial Journal*, 16 and 19 February 1864; *Gazette*, 17 February 1864; *Post*, 22 February 1864. *Daily Commercial*, 22 February 1864.

30. *Gazette*, 7 and 16 March 1864; *Post*, 28 May and 3 June 1864; *Commercial Journal*, 6 June 1864; *Gazette*, 15–16 June 1864.

31. *Gazette*, 14 March 1864; *Commercial Journal*, 23 July 1864; *Post*, 13 June 1864.

32. *Gazette*, 20 July 1864; Geary, *We Need Men*, 139; *Congressional Globe*, 38th Cong., 1st Session: 3485–91; *Post*, 13 June 1864.

33. *Commercial Journal*, 10 and 27 August 1864; *Gazette*, 11 August 1864.

34. RG 94, Records of the Adjutant General's Office, M1994, M589, NARA, Washington, D.C.; Ninth Census, 1870, Manuscript Returns of Free Inhabitants, McKeesport, Allegheny County, 17.

35. *Commercial Journal*, 20 August 1864; *Gazette*, 31 August 1864; *Post*, 7 September 1864.

36. *Gazette*, 14, 20 and 24 September 1864.

37. *Post*, 31 August and 9 September 1864; *Gazette*, 8 September and 19 October 1864.

38. Norman C. Brillhart, "The Election of 1864 in Western Pennsylvania," *WPHM* 8, no. 1 (January 1925): 34–35; *Gazette*, 22 November and 8 December 1864.

39. *Post*, 26 November and 22 December 1864; *Commercial Journal*, 1 December 1864.

40. *Commercial Journal*, 26 January 1865; *Post*, 16 February 1865; *Gazette*, 17 February, 8 March, and 13 April 1865.

5. YOUR PATRIOTISM, AS WELL AS YOUR HONOR

1. *Dispatch*, 6 June 1861.

2. Thurston, *Directory of Pittsburgh and Allegheny Cities*, 341–49; Boucher and Jordan, *A Century and a Half of Pittsburgh and Its People*, 156.

3. William Wilkins, et al., *Does the Country Require a National Armory and Foundry West of the Allegheny Mountains* (Pittsburgh, PA: W. S. Haven, 1862), 4–7; Correspondence and Reports Relating to the Choice of a Site for a Western Armory, 1835–1862, Record Group 156, Records of the Office of the Chief of Ordnance, Special File, 1812–1862, NARA.

4. Wilkins, *Does the Country Require a National Armory and Foundry West of the Allegheny Mountains*, 57–60.

5. Register of Contracts, 1819–70, pp. 32, 87, 180–81, RG 92, Records of the Office of the Quartermaster, NARA; Register of Contracts, vol. 15, pp. 38–39, RG 74, Records of the Bureau of Ordnance, NARA.

6. Register of Contracts, Vol. 15, pp. 32, 38–39, 54–55, RG 74, Records of the Bureau of Ordnance; Banner Cotton Mills to John Symington, 7 March 1862, RG 156, Records of the Office of the Chief of Ordnance, Special File.

7. "Extraordinary Prosperity of our Railroads," *Scientific American* 5 (1861): 219; *Post*, 30 September 1863 and 29 March 1864; *Commercial Journal*, 7 July 1864; *Gazette*, 19 September 1864.

8. *Post*, 4 May 1864. On the role of women in Northern war industries, see also Giesberg, *Army at Home*; and Rachel Filene Seidman, "A Monstrous Doctrine? Northern Women on Dependency During the Civil War," in Paul A. Cimbala and Randall M. Miller, eds., *An Uncommon Time: The Civil War and the Northern Home Front* (New York: Fordham University Press, 2002), 170–88.

9. Reports on the Manufacture of Heavy Ordnance, 1841–1862, Box 28, RG 156, Records of the Office of the Chief of Ordnance; Andrew E. Masich, "Rodman's Big Gun," *WPHM* 98 (2015): 22–24; "Manufacture of Mammoth Cannon," *Scientific American* 2 (1860): 17–32.

10. Charles Knap to A. A. Harwood, 24 June, 24 August, and 7, 9, 11 September

NOTES TO PAGES 103–107 ★ 177

1861, Letters Received from Inspectors of Ordnance, 1861–1864, Box 5, Records of the Bureau of Ordnance; *O.R.*, Series One, vol. 22, 295–96; A. B. Dyer to J. W. Ripley, 19 December 1861, Reports on the Manufacture of Heavy Ordnance, 1841–1862, Records of the Office of the Chief of Ordnance, Special File.

11. Charles Knap to A. Dahlgren, 21 November 1862 and J. M. Berrien to A. Dahlgren, 10 January 1861, Letters Received from Inspectors of Ordnance, 1861–1864, Box 5, Records of the Bureau of Ordnance.

12. J. M. Berrien to A. Dahlgren, 12, 13, and 15 January 1863, Letters Received from Inspectors of Ordnance, 1861–1864, Box 5, Records of the Bureau of Ordnance; A. Dahlgren to J. M. Berrien, 15 June 1863, Letters and Telegrams Sent to Inspectors, Box 2, p. 267, Records of the Bureau of Ordnance.

13. Wilson, *The Business of the Civil War*, 118–19, 122; Extreme Proofing of the XV Inch Gun, Fort Pitt Foundry, October 1862–January 1869, Records of the Bureau of Ordnance.

14. U.S. Vessels Built at Cincinnati, Mound City, Pittsburgh, and St. Louis, 1862–1873, RG 45, Naval Records Collection of the Office of Naval Records and Library, Box 25, NARA.

15. *Ibid*; Circular Letters Sent to Contractors, June 1863-July 1864, March to June 1865, Box 1, Records of the Office of the General Superintendent of Ironclads, RG 19, Records of the Bureau of Ships.

16. Alban Stimers to Snowden and Mason, 31 August, 28 December 1863, and 5 January 1864, Circular Letters Sent to Contractors, June 1863-July 1864, March to June 1865, Box 1, Records of the Office of the General Superintendent of Ironclads, RG 19, Records of the Bureau of Ships. See also William H. Roberts, *Civil War Ironclads: The U.S. Navy and Industrial Mobilization* (Baltimore, MA: Johns Hopkins University Press), 2002.

17. Alban Stimers to Snowden and Mason, 14 December 1863 and W. E. Roe to Alban Stimers, 4 and 25 February 1864, Circular Letters Sent to Contractors, Records of the Office of the General Superintendent of Ironclads, RG 19, Records of the Bureau of Ships.

18. F. H. Gregory to J. B. Hull, 24 March 1864, U.S. Vessels Built at Cincinnati, Mound City, Pittsburgh, and St. Louis, 1862–1873, Box 25, RG 45, Naval Records Collection of the Office of Naval Records and Library; *Gazette*, 2 October 1865; Letters Received Concerning the *Manayunk* and the *Umpqua*, January 1865-July 1866, Records of the Office of the General Inspector of Ironclads, RG 19, Records of the Bureau of Ships.

19. Gene D. Lewis, *Charles Ellet Jr., 1810–1862: The Engineer as Individualist* (Urbana: University of Illinois Press, 1968), 21–25; John S. Van Voorhis, *The Old and New Monongahela* (Pittsburgh, PA: Nicholson, 1893), 420.

20. Howard P. Nash, *Naval History of the Civil War* (South Brunswick, NY: A. S. Barnes, 1972), 28; Charles Ellet Jr., *Coastal Defenses, or the Substitution of Steam Battering Rams for Ships of War* (Philadelphia, PA: John C. Clark and Son, 1855).

21. James M. McPherson, *War on the Waters: The Union and Confederate Navies, 1861–1865* (Chapel Hill: University of North Carolina Press, 2012), 72–73; Charles Henry Ambler, *A History of Transportation in the Ohio Valley* (Glendale, CA: Arthur H. Clark, 1932), 250–51; *O.R.*, Series Three, vol. 2, 792; United States Navy Department, Official Records of the Union and Confederate Navies [hereafter, *O.R.N.*] (31 vols., Washington: Government Printing Office, 1894–1922), Series One, vol. 23, 315–86; *Lancaster Intelligencer*, Lancaster, PA, 18 March 1862; *Republican Compiler*, Gettysburg, PA, 31 March 1862; *Philadelphia Press*, 6 February 1862; *Gazette*, 4 April 1862.

22. *O.R.N.*, Series One, vol. 22, 680–81; *Dispatch*, 28 March 1862.

23. *O.R.N.*, Series One, vol. 22, 680–82.

24. *Gazette*, 17–29 April and 7 May 1862.

25. Lewis Clark Walkinshaw, *The Annals of Southwestern Pennsylvania* (4 vols., New York: Lewis Historical Publishing, 1939), vol. 4, 246; Eighth Census, 1860, Manuscript Returns of Free Inhabitants, First Ward, Allegheny City, Allegheny County, PA, 571, and Franklin Township, Allegheny County, PA, 307; Samuel Evans, *Allegheny County Pennsylvania, in the War for the Suppression of the Rebellion, 1861–1865: Roll of Honor, Defenders of the Flag* (Pittsburgh, PA: Board of Managers, Soldiers and Sailors Memorial Hall, 1924), 30.

26. *Philadelphia Press*, 9 June 1862; *Argus* (Memphis), 6 June 1862.

27. *O.R.N.*, Series One, vol. 23, 118–21.

28. *Philadelphia Press*, 9 June 1862; McPherson, *War on the Waters*, 89; *Gazette*, 3 July 1862.

29. *Gazette*, 12 June 1862; *American Presbyterian* (Philadelphia), 1 November 1866.

30. George H. Thurston, *Directory of Pittsburgh and Allegheny Cities, 1861–62* (Pittsburgh, PA: G. H. Thurston, 1870); Sarah H. Killikelly, *The History of Pittsburgh*, 192–94, 222; John W. Leonard, *Pittsburgh and Allegheny Illustrated Review: Historical, Biographical, and Commercial* (Pittsburgh, PA: J. M. Elstner, 1889), 25; and Pittsburgh and Allegheny County Almanac, 1867 (Pittsburgh, PA: Woods and Co., 1867), 85.

6. THE VOLUNTARY AND SPONTANEOUS ACTION OF THE PEOPLE

1. Funeral program and pass, Ellen R. Murdock Watson Papers, *SJHHC*; Fleming, *History of Pittsburgh and Environs*, vol. 6, 47; 155th Regimental Association, *Under the Maltese Cross*, 41–42; *Gazette*, 16 October 1913; *Detroit Free Press*, 16 October 1913.

2. McPherson, *Battle Cry of Freedom*, 481; Robert H. Bremner, *The Public Good: Philanthropy and Welfare During the Civil War Era* (New York: Albert A. Knopf, 1980), 62, 72–74.

3. Dorothy Daniel, "The Sanitary Fair," *WPHM* 41 (1958):146; McPherson,

Battle Cry of Freedom, 480–81; "Health in the Camps," *Atlantic Monthly* 49 (1861): 579; Cimbala and Miller, *The Northern Home Front During the Civil War*, 74–75.

4. Lemuel Moss, *Annals of the United States Christian Commission* (Philadelphia, PA: J. B. Lippincott, 1868), 155.

5. Boucher and Jordan, *A Century and a Half of Pittsburgh and Its People*, 187; Charles Janeway Stillwell, *History of the United States Sanitary Commission, the General Report of Its Work During the War of the Rebellion* (New York: Hurd and Houghton, 1868), 141; Moss, *Annals of the United States Christian Commission*, 219; Thomas Bakewell, et al., First Report, Address, and Proceedings of the Pittsburgh Sanitary Committee (Pittsburgh, PA: W. S. Haven, 1868), 1–2.

6. Bakewell, et al., *First Report, Address, and Proceedings*, 1–2.

7. Brunot Family Papers, *passim*, SJHHC.

8. Bakewell, First Report, Address, and Proceedings of the Pittsburgh Sanitary Committee, 6–7; Boucher and Jordan, *A Century and a Half of Pittsburgh and Its People*, 180.

9. *Gazette*, 28 April 1862.

10. *Ibid.*, 6 May 1862 and 28 April 1861.

11. Bakewell, First Report, Address, and Proceedings of the Pittsburgh Sanitary Committee, 6–7; *O.R.*, Series Two, vol. 4, 332–33, 307.

12. *Gazette*, 16 June 1862.

13. Sanitary Commission Bulletin 2 (1864):193; Bakewell, First Report, Address, and Proceedings of the Pittsburgh Sanitary Committee, 3.

14. Bakewell, First Report, Address, and Proceedings of the Pittsburgh Sanitary Committee, 4–5; Bremner, *Public Good*, 43–46.

15. Bakewell, First Report, Address, and Proceedings of the Pittsburgh Sanitary Committee, 3–5.

16. Sanitary Commission Bulletin 2 (1864):645, 1 (1863): 58–59; Bakewell, First Report, Address, and Proceedings of the Pittsburgh Sanitary Committee, 3–4.

17. William Todd, *The Seventy-Ninth Highlanders, New York Volunteers in the War of the Rebellion, 1861–1865* (Albany, NY: Brandow, Barton, 1886), 434; Minnesota State Legislature, Minnesota in the Civil and Indian Wars, 1861–1865 (St. Paul, MN: Pioneer Press, 1890), 509.

18. Boucher and Jordan, *A Century and a Half of Pittsburgh and Its People*, 156; Cushing, *History of Allegheny County*, 186; Grand Army of the Republic, Department of Pennsylvania, Proceedings of the 28th Annual Encampment of the Department of Pennsylvania, Grand Army of the Republic (Pittsburgh, PA: H. D. W. English, 1894), 38; *Rebellion Record of Allegheny County*, 41.

19. Grand Army of the Republic, Department of Pennsylvania, Proceedings of the 28th Annual Encampment, 38.

20. Fleming, *History of Pittsburgh and Its Environs*, 170–71; Seventh Census, 1850, Manuscript Returns of Free Inhabitants, Ohio Township, Allegheny County, PA, 382; Thurston, *Directory of Pittsburgh and Allegheny Cities, 1861–62*, 11, 452;

Samuel Minis Evans, *Allegheny County, Pennsylvania, in the War for the Suppression of the Rebellion, 1861–1865* (Pittsburgh, PA: Board of Managers Soldiers and Sailors Memorial Hall, 1924), 26.

21. Thurston, *Directory of Pittsburgh and Allegheny Cities, 1861–62*, 329, 357; Walkinshaw, *Annals of Southwestern Pennsylvania*, vol. 2, 348; Thurston, *Allegheny County's First Hundred Years*, 238; Eliot E. Swift, *Brief Biographies of Ruling Elders in the First Presbyterian Church, Allegheny, During the First Fifty Years of Its History . . .* (Pittsburgh: Jackson and McEwen, 1880), 8; Eight Census, 1860, Manuscript Returns of Free Inhabitants, First Ward, Allegheny, Allegheny County, PA, 669; *Rebellion Record of Allegheny County*, 41.

22. Joseph Albree Papers, *passim*, *SJHHC*; Eight Census, 1860, Manuscript Returns of Free Inhabitants, Fourth Ward, Allegheny, Allegheny County, PA, 844.

23. Scrapbook, Joseph Albree Papers; Eighth Census, 1860, Manuscript Returns of Free Inhabitants, Plum Township, Allegheny County, PA, 953, and Second Ward, Pittsburgh, Allegheny County, PA, 365; Seventh Census, 1850, Manuscript Returns of Free Inhabitants, First Ward, Pittsburgh, Allegheny County, PA, 27.

24. Scrapbook, Joseph Albree Papers; *Rebellion Record of Allegheny County*, 41; Grand Army of the Republic, Department of Pennsylvania, Proceedings of the 28th Annual Encampment, 38.

25. Grand Army of the Republic, Department of Pennsylvania, Proceedings of the 28th Annual Encampment, 40–42; *Rebellion Record of Allegheny County*, 42.

26. Scrapbook, Joseph Albree Papers.

27. William P. Weyman to Joseph Albree, 13 November 1862, Joseph Albree Papers.

28. Edward O. Lord, *History of the Ninth Regiment New Hampshire Volunteers in the War of the Rebellion* (Concord, NH: Republican Press Associations, 1895), 647.

29. William P. Weyman to Joseph Albree, 13 November 1862, Joseph Albree Papers.

30. William P. Weyman to Abraham Lincoln, 27 January 1864, Abraham Lincoln Papers, Library of Congress, Washington, D.C.

31. Josiah Copely, *Gathered Sheaves* (New York: Anson D. F. Randolph, 1886), 80–81.

32. *Ibid.*, 81–82.

33. William P. Weyman to Joseph Albree, 13, 19 November 1862, Joseph Albree Papers.

34. Grand Army of the Republic, Department of Pennsylvania, Proceedings of the 28th Annual Encampment, 46; Moss, *Annals of the United States Christian Commission*, 346.

35. *Ibid.*, 153, 155, 347–48.

36. *Ibid.*, 260–61.

37. *Presbyterian Banner*, 4 February 1863; G. H. Gerberding, *Life and Letters of W. A. Passavant, D. D.* (Greenville, PA: Young Luther, 1906), 307.

38. Pittsburgh Sisters of Mercy, *Memoirs of the Pittsburgh Sisters of Mercy* (New York: Devin-Adair, 1918), 254; *Altoona Tribune*, 15 November 1862. The Pittsburgh order of the Sisters of Mercy was known for its charitable works in the city well before the war. The Sisters of Mercy was established in Dublin, Ireland in 1831 and the Pittsburgh order was founded in 1843. It maintained a staff of eight nuns at the Stanton Hospital until the end of the war, caring for thousands of wounded soldiers.

39. Moss, *Annals of the United States Christian Commission*, 174.

40. *Ibid.*, 261.

41. *Gazette*, 18 July and 30 September 1862.

42. *Ibid.*, 2; December 1862 and 26 November 1864.

43. Scrapbook, Joseph Albree Papers; *Gazette*, 26 November 1862.

44. *Gazette*, 26 November 1862.

45. Mary A. Livermore, *My Story of the War: A Woman's Narrative of Four Years Personal Experience* (Hartford, OH: A. D. Worthington, 1896), 412–14; Cimbala and Miller, *The Northern Home Front During the Civil War*, 75–76.

46. Grand Army of the Republic, Department of Pennsylvania, Proceedings of the 28th Annual Encampment, 46.

47. Charles W. Dalinger, "The Pittsburgh Sanitary Fair," *WPHM* 2 (1929): 99–100; *Gazette*, 2 June 1864.

48. *Gazette*, 1 June 1864; Dahlinger, "Pittsburgh Sanitary Fair," 100; Sanitary Fair notes, Brunot Family Papers.

49. Sanitary Fair notes, Papers of the Brunot Family.

50. Sanitary Fair pamphlet, James Veech Papers, *SJHHC*.

7. UNITE IN DOING HONOR TO THE DECEASED HERO

1. Thurston, *Directory of Pittsburgh and Allegheny Cities, 1862–1863*, 28.

2. *Dispatch*, 18 and 19 September 1862; *Post*, 20 September 1862.

3. *Post*, 20 September 1862.

4. Tom Powers and James Wudarczyk, "Behind the Scenes of the Allegheny Arsenal Explosion," *Pennsylvania Legacies* 13 (2013): 43–45; John Symington to James W. Ripley, 2 October 1861, Allegheny Arsenal Records, National Archives, Philadelphia, PA.

5. Eighth Census, 1860, Manuscript Returns of Free Inhabitants, Ligonier, Westmoreland County, PA, 577; Ninth Ward, Pittsburgh, Allegheny County, Pennsylvania, 486; and Borough of Lawrenceville, Allegheny County, PA, 63; Thurston, *Directory of Pittsburgh and Allegheny Cities, 1862–1863*, 65.

6. *Post*, 20 September 1862.

7. *Gazette*, 11 November 1862.

8. *Boston Transcript*, 11 January 1860; *Boston Herald*, 11 January 1860; *New York Herald*, 4 February 1860.

9. *Lowell Daily Citizen and News*, 7 February 1860; *Harper's Weekly*, 28 January and 20 July 1860.

10. *Post*, 18 September 1862; R. Lea, *Sermon Commemorative of the Great Explosion at the Arsenal* (Pittsburgh, PA: W. S. Haven, 1862), 5.

11. *Post*, 18 September 1862; *Pittsburgh Evening Chronicle*, 18 September 1862; *Gazette*, 22 April and 18 September 1862; *Pennsylvania Daily Telegraph*, 19 September 1862; Giesberg, *Army at Home*, 69.

12. Drew Gilpin Faust, *This Republic of Suffering: Death and the American Civil War* (New York: Vintage Books, 2008), 127–30; *Gazette*, 19 September 1862.

13. *Gazette*, 18 September 1862.

14. *Ibid.*, 11 and 16 October 1862.

15. William E. Gienapp, *This Fiery Trial: The Speeches and Writing of Abraham Lincoln* (Oxford: Oxford University Press, 2002), 220.

16. Durant, *History of Allegheny County*, 216–42; *Allegheny Cemetery: Historical Account of Incidents and Events Connected with Its Establishment* (Pittsburgh, PA: Bakewell Marthens, 1873), 48; Gazette, 23 June 1865.

17. Durant, *History of Allegheny County*, 208; *Post*, 5 June 1862; A. T. Brewer, *History of the Sixty-first Regiment, Pennsylvania Volunteers, 1861–1865* (Pittsburgh, PA: Art Engraving and Printing, 1911), 26, 147.

18. *Post*, 3 June 1862; *Gazette*, 3 June 1862.

19. *Gazette*, 6 June 1862.

20. *Post*, 7, 9 June and 27 December 1862; Ida Bright Holmes, "The Civil War Letters of James Rush Holmes," *WPHM* 44 (1961): 105; Brewer, *History of the Sixty-first Regiment*, 26; *Gazette*, 7 August 1862.

21. *Post*, 7, 9 June, 27 December 1862, and 21 January 1863.

22. *Gazette*, 5 and 10 March 1864; *Post*, 17 March 1864.

23. *Commercial Journal*, 9 May 1864.

24. *Ibid.*, 9 and 12–13 May 1864; *Post*, 12 and 16 May 1864.

25. *Gazette*, 12 May 1864; *Commercial Journal*, 13 May 1864.

26. *Commercial Journal*, 9 June 1864; *Gazette*, 9–10 June 1864.

27. *Commercial Journal*, 10 June 1864; *Gazette*, 24 May and 17 June 1864; *Post*, 17 June 1864.

28. John A. Reed, *History of the 101st Regiment Pennsylvania Veteran Volunteer Infantry, 1861–1865* (Chicago, IL: L. S. Dickey, 1910), 73, 38–39; Goodspeed and Wilson, *History of Allegheny County*, 235–37; *Post*, 27 April 1864; *Gazette*, 6 May 1864.

29. *Gazette*, 12 May 1864; United States Congress, Joint Committee on the Conduct of the War, *Report on the Condition of the Returned Prisoners* (1864), 2, University of California Libraries, Americana Collection.

30. *Altoona Tribune*, 3 September 1864; *Commercial Journal*, 22 November 1864.

31. *Commercial Journal*, 3 November 1864; Reed, *History of the 101st Regiment Pennsylvania Veteran Volunteer Infantry*, 51; *Biographical Review Vol. 24 Contain-*

ing Life Sketches of Leading Citizens of Pittsburgh (Boston, MA: Biographical Review, 1897), 238.

32. *Commercial Journal*, 21 December 1864; Gazette, 9 May 1865; Donaghy, *Army Experience of John Donaghy*, 243–44.

33. *Post*, 1 January, 16 April 1864; *Gazette*, 28 December 1863; *Commercial Journal*, 27 January 1864.

34. James Laughery Paul, *Pennsylvania Soldiers' Orphan Schools* (Philadelphia, PA: Claxton, Remsen and Haffelfinger, 1876), 50; *Post*, 27 April, 2, 14 December 1864, and 11 November 1865.

35. *Commercial Journal*, 10 June and 25, 27 July 1864; Paul, *Pennsylvania Soldiers' Orphan Schools*, 33–34, 44.

36. *Post*, 12 and 14 December 1864; Paul, *Pennsylvania Soldiers' Orphan Schools*, 301–305.

37. *Post*, 6 April and 6 July 1865.

38. Paul, *Pennsylvania Soldiers' Orphan Schools*, 109, 301–305, 339–47, 376–77, 518.

39. *Post*, 26 July 1865; Paul, *Pennsylvania Soldiers' Orphan Schools*, 124.

40. *Harrisburg Telegraph*, 20 March 1866.

CONCLUSION

1. Andrew J. Bacevich, *Breach of Trust: How Americans Failed Their Soldiers and Their Country* (New York: Henry Holt, 2013), 13–14.

BIBLIOGRAPHY

MANUSCRIPTS

Albree, Joseph. Papers.

Allegheny Arsenal Records.

Brunot Family Papers.

Buchanan, James. Papers. Historical Society of Pennsylvania.

Civil War Collection.

Eighth Census, 1860. Manuscript Returns of Free Inhabitants.

Furst, Luther C. Diary. U.S. Army Military History Institute, Carlisle, Pennsylvania.

Harper Family Papers.

McClelland Family Papers.

McClelland, James. Diary.

National Archives and Records Administration, Washington, D.C.

Naval Records Collection of the Office of Naval Records and Library.

Nevin, John I. Diary.

Ninth Census, 1870. Manuscript Returns of Free Inhabitants.

Pennsylvania State Archives, Harrisburg.

Records of the Adjutant General's Office.

Records of the Bureau of Ordnance, Register of Contracts.

Records of the Bureau of Ships.

Records of the Constitutional Convention and the Council of Censors, 1837–1838. National Archives and Records Administration, Philadelphia, Pennsylvania.

Records of the Office of the Chief of Ordnance, Special File, 1812–1862.

Records of the Office of the General Inspector of Ironclads.

Records of the Office of the General Superintendent of Ironclads.

Records of the Pittsburgh Select and Common Council.

Records of the Provost Marshal General's Bureau.

Records of Quarter Session Court, 1799–1906. Allegheny County Court House, Pittsburgh, Pennsylvania.

Records of the Quartermaster Bureau, Register of Contracts, 1819–70.

Records of United States Army Commands, 1784–1821.

Seventh Census, 1850, Manuscript Returns of Free Inhabitants.

Senator John Heinz History Center, Pittsburgh, Pennsylvania.

University of California Libraries. *Report on the Condition of the Returned Prisoners.*

NEWSPAPERS

Altoona Tribune.
American Presbyterian (Philadelphia).
Argus (Memphis).
Boston Herald.
Boston Transcript.
Chicago Tribune.
Daily National Intelligencer (Washington, D.C.).
Detroit Free Press.
Erie Gazette.
Harrisburg Telegraph.
Lancaster Intelligencer (Lancaster, PA).
Liberator (Boston).
Lowell Daily Citizen and News (Lowell, MA).
New York Herald.
North American (Philadelphia).
Pennsylvania Daily Telegraph (Harrisburg).
Philadelphia Press.
Philadelphia Public Ledger.
Pittsburgh Daily Commercial Journal.
Pittsburgh Daily Dispatch.
Pittsburgh Daily Gazette.
Pittsburgh Daily Post.
Pittsburgh Evening Chronicle.
Pittsburgh Post-Gazette.
Presbyterian Banner (Pittsburgh).
Republican Compiler (Gettysburg, PA).
San Diego Union.
Temperance Gem (Allegheny, PA).

PERIODICALS

Annals of Congress.
Atlantic Monthly.
Congressional Globe.
Harper's Weekly.
Sanitary Commission Bulletin.
Scientific American.

BOOKS

155th Pennsylvania Infantry Regiment. *Under the Maltese Cross, Antietam to Appomattox, the Loyal Uprising in Western Pennsylvania, 1861–1865: Campaigns 155th Pennsylvania Regiment.* Pittsburgh, PA: 155th Regimental Association, 1910.

Aley, Ginnette, and J. L. Anderson, eds. *Union Heartland: The Midwestern Home Front During the Civil War.* Carbondale: Southern Illinois University Press, 2013.

Allegheny Cemetery: Historical Account of Incidents and Events Connected with Its Establishment. Pittsburgh, PA: Bakewell & Marthens, 1873.

Ambler, Charles Henry. *A History of Transportation in the Ohio Valley.* Glendale, CA: Arthur H. Clark, 1932.

Attie, Jeanie. *Patriotic Toil: Northern Women and the American Civil War.* Ithaca, NY: Cornell University Press, 1998.

Ayers, Edward L. *In the Presence of Mine Enemies: The Civil War in the Heart of America, 1859–1863.* New York: W. W. Norton, 2003.

Bacevich, Andrew J. *Breach of Trust: How Americans Failed Their Soldiers and Their Country.* New York: Henry Holt, 2013.

Bates, Samuel P. *History of the Pennsylvania Volunteers, 1861–65.* 5 vols. Harrisburg, PA: B. Singerly, 1869.

Bergner, George. *The Legislative Record: Containing Debates and Proceedings of the Session of 1862.* Harrisburg, PA: Telegraph Book Job Office, 1862.

Biographical Review Vol. 26 Containing Life Sketches of Leading Citizens of Pittsburgh. Boston, MA: Biographical Review Publishing Company, 1897.

Boucher, John, and John Jordan. *A Century and a Half of Pittsburgh and Her People.* 2 vols. New York: Lewis Publishing, 1908.

Boucher, John Newton, and John W. Jordan. *A Century and a Half of Pittsburgh.* New York: Lewis Publishing, 1908.

Brackenridge, Hugh Henry. *Gazette Publications.* Carlisle, PA: Alexander and Phillips, 1806.

Bremner, Robert H. *The Public Good: Philanthropy and Welfare During the Civil War Era.* New York: Albert A. Knopf, 1980.

Brewer, A. T. *History of the Sixty-first Regiment, Pennsylvania Volunteers, 1861–1865.* Pittsburgh, PA: Art Engraving and Printing, 1911.

Chalfant, Harry M. *Father Penn and John Barleycorn.* Harrisburg, PA: Evangelical Press, 1920.

Cimball, Paul A. and Randall M. Miller. *The Northern Home Front During the Civil War.* Santa Barbara, CA: Praeger, 2017.

Clinton, Catherine and Nina Silber, eds. *Divided Houses: Gender and the Civil War.* New York: Oxford University Press, 1992.

Copely, Josiah. *Gathered Sheaves.* New York: Anson D. F. Randolph, 1886.

Cowan, Edgar. *Speeches of Maj. Wm. A. Stokes, U.S. Army, and Hon. Edgar Cowan, U.S. Senate: Delivered at the Union Convention, Westmoreland County, PA, September, 1861.* Pittsburgh, PA: Barr & Meyers, 1861.

Cramer, Zadok. *The Ohio and Mississippi Navigator.* Pittsburgh, PA: John Scull, 1802.

Craven, Avery. *The Coming of the Civil War.* 2nd ed. New York: Charles Scribner's Sons, 1942.

Cross, Marcus E. *The Mirror of Intemperance Reform.* Philadelphia, PA: John T. Lange, 1849.

Cushing, John A. *History of Allegheny County Pennsylvania.* Chicago, IL: A. Warner, 1889.

Donaghy, John. *Army Experience of Captain John Donaghy.* De Land, FL: E. O. Painter, 1926.

Durant, Samuel W., et al. *History of Allegheny Co., Pennsylvania: with Illustrations Descriptive of Its Scenery, Palatial Residences, Public Buildings, Fine Blocks, and Important Manufactories.* Philadelphia, PA: L. H. Everts, 1876.

Ellet, Charles, Jr. *Coastal Defenses, or the Substitution of Steam Battering Rams for Ships of War.* Philadelphia, PA: n.p., 1855.

Etcheson, Nicole. *A Generation at War: The Civil War Era in a Northern Community.* Lawrence: University Press of Kansas, 2011.

Evans, Samuel Minis. *Allegheny County, Pennsylvania, in the War for the Suppression of the Rebellion, 1861–1865.* Pittsburgh, PA: Board of Managers, Soldiers and Sailors Memorial Hall, 1924.

Faust, Drew Gilpin. *This Republic of Suffering: Death and the American Civil War.* New York: Vintage Books, 2008.

Ferguson, Russel J. *Early Western Pennsylvania Politics.* PA: Pittsburgh Press, 1938.

Finkelman, Paul. *An Imperfect Union: Slavery, Federalism and Comity.* Chapel Hill: University of North Carolina Press, 1981.

First Methodist Protestant Church. *Closing Services: First Methodist Protestant Church, Fifth Avenue, Pittsburgh, May 11, 12, 13 and 15, 1892.* Pittsburgh, PA: Rawsthorne, 1892.

Fleming, George Thorton. *History of Pittsburgh and Environs.* 6 vols. New York: American Historical Society, 1922.

Fleming, George Thorton. *Program of the Exercises Attending and Addresses Delivered at Fifth Avenue High School: March 1, 1907.* Pittsburgh, PA: Central Board of Education, 1907.

Foner, Eric. *Free Soil, Free Labor, Free Men: The Ideology of the Republican Party before the Civil War.* New York: Oxford University Press, 1970.

Foote, Lorien. *The Gentlemen and the Roughs: Violence, Honor, and Manhood in the Union Army.* New York University Press, 2010.

Ford, Bridget. *The Bonds of Union: Religion, Race, and Politics in a Civil War Borderland.* Chapel Hill: University of North Carolina Press, 2016.

Foster, J. Herron. *A Full Account of the Great Fire at Pittsburgh.* Pittsburgh, PA: J. W. Cook, 1845.

Gallagher, Gary. *The Union War.* Cambridge, MA: Harvard University Press, 2011.

Gallman, Matthew. *The North Fights the Civil War: The Home Front.* Chicago, IL: Ivan R. Dee, 1994.

Geary, James W. *We Need Men: The Union Draft in the Civil War.* Dekalb: Northern Illinois University Press, 1991.

Gerberding, G. H. *Life and Letters of W. A. Passavant, D. D.* Greenville, PA: Young Luther, 1906.

Gienapp, William E. *This Fiery Trial: The Speeches and Writings of Abraham Lincoln.* Oxford: Oxford University Press, 2002.

Giesberg, Judith. *Army at Home: Women and the Civil War on the Northern Home Front.* Chapel Hill: University of North Carolina Press, 2009.

Goodspeed, Weston Arthur, and Erasmus Wilson. *Standard History of Pittsburgh, Pennsylvania.* Chicago, IL: H. R. Cornell, 1898.

Grand Army of the Republic, Department of Pennsylvania. *Proceedings of the 28th Annual Encampment of the Department of Pennsylvania, Grand Army of the Republic.* Pittsburgh, PA: H. D. W. English, 1894.

Hess, Earl J. *Liberty, Virtue, and Progress: Northerners and Their War for the Union.* 2nd ed. New York: Fordham University Press, 1997.

Holt, Michael. *Forging a Majority: The Formation of the Republican Party in Pittsburgh, 1848–1860.* New Haven, CT: Yale University Press, 1969.

Housman, R. A. B. *The Liquor Laws of Pennsylvania, with Annotations to January 1st, 1907.* Washington, D.C.: Office of the Librarian of Congress, 1907.

Johnston, William G. *Life and Reminiscenses from Birth to Manhood of Wm. G. Johnston.* Pittsburgh, PA: Knickerbocker Press, 1901.

Kamphoefner, Walter D., Wolgang Helbich, and Ulrike Sommer, eds., *News from the Land of Freedom: German Immigrants Write Home.* Ithaca, NY: Cornell University Press, 1991.

Killikelly, Sarah H. *The History of Pittsburgh: Its Rise and Progress.* Pittsburgh, PA: B. C. and Gordon Montgomery, 1906.

Lambling, A. A., and J. W. F. White. *Allegheny County: Its Early History and Subsequent Development.* Pittsburgh, PA: Snowden and Peterson, 1888.

Lea, Rev. R. *Sermon Commemorative of the Great Explosion at the Allegheny Arsenal, at Lawrenceville, Pennsylvania on September 17th, 1862.* Pittsburgh, PA: W. S. Haven, 1862.

Levine, Robert S. *Martin R. Delany: A Documentary Reader.* Chapel Hill: The University of North Carolina Press, 2003.

Lewis, Gene D. *Charles Ellet Jr., 1810–1862: The Engineer as Individualist.* Urbana: University of Illinois Press, 1968.

Livermore, Mary A. *My Story of the War: A Woman's Narrative of Four Years' Personal Experience.* Hartford, OH: A. D. Worthington, 1896.

Lord, Edward O. *History of the Ninth Regiment New Hampshire Volunteers in the War of the Rebellion.* Concord, NH: Republican Press Associations, 1895.

McPherson, James M. *Battle Cry of Freedom: The Civil War Era.* Oxford: Oxford University Press, 1988.

McPherson, James M. *War on the Waters: The Union and Confederate Navies, 1861–1865.* Chapel Hill: University of North Carolina Press, 2012.

Meneely, A. Howard. *The War Department, 1861: A Study in Mobilization.* New York: Columbia University Press, 1928.

Minnesota State Legislature. *Minnesota in the Civil and Indian Wars, 1861–1865.* St. Paul, MN: Pioneer Press, 1890.

Moss, Lemuel. *Annals of the United States Christian Commission.* Philadelphia, PA: J. B. Lippincott, 1868.

Nash, Howard P. *Naval History of the Civil War.* South Brunswick, New York: A. S. Barnes, 1972.

Nell, William C. *The Colored Patriots of the American Revolution.* Boston, MA: Robert F. Walcut, 1855.

Nevins, Allan. *War for the Union: Vol. 1, 1861–1862: The Improvised War.* 2nd ed. New York: Konecky and Konecky, 1971.

Niebaum, John H. *History of the Washington Infantry.* Pittsburgh, PA: Bergun, 1931.

Oakes, James. *Freedom National: The Destruction of American Slavery.* New York: W. W. Norton, 2013.

Palladino, Grace. *Another Civil War: Labor, Capital, and the State in the Anthracite Regions of Pennsylvania, 1840–1868.* Urbana: University of Illinois Press, 1990.

Paul, James Laughery. *Pennsylvania Soldiers' Orphan Schools.* Philadelphia, PA: Claxton, Remsen and Haffelfinger, 1876.

Phillips, Christopher. *The Rivers Ran Backward: The Civil War and the Remaking of the American Middle Border.* New York: Oxford University Press, 2016.

Phillips, Jason. *Looming Civil War: How Nineteenth-century Americans Imagined the Future.* New York: Oxford University Press, 2018.

Pittsburgh Sisters of Mercy. *Memoirs of the Pittsburgh Sisters of Mercy.* New York: Devin-Adair, 1918.

Rebellion Record of Allegheny County, from April, 1861, to October, 1862. Pittsburgh, PA: W. A. Lare and W. M. Hartzell, 1862.

Reed, John A. *History of the 101st Regiment Pennsylvania Veteran Volunteer Infantry, 1861–1865.* Chicago, IL: L. S. Dickey, 1910.

Reiser, Catherine E. *Pittsburgh's Commercial Development, 1800–1850.* Harrisburg: Pennsylvania Historical and Museum Commission, 1951.

Rockenbach, Stephen. *War upon Our Border: Two Ohio Valley Communities Navigate the Civil War.* Charlottesville: University of Virginia Press, 2016.

Sandow, Robert M. *Deserter Country: Civil War Opposition in the Pennsylvania Appalachians*. New York: Fordham University Press, 2009.

Shankman, Arnold. *The Pennsylvania Antiwar Movement, 1861–1865*. Rutherford, NJ: Fairleigh Dickinson University Press, 1980.

Smith, Adam I. P. *No Party Now: Politics in the Civil War North*. Oxford: Oxford University Press, 2006.

Stampp, Kenneth. *And the War Came*. 2nd ed. Baton Rouge: Louisiana State University Press, 1970.

Stanley, Matthew E. *The Loyal West: Civil War and Reunion in Middle America*. Urbana: University of Illinois Press, 2017.

Stillwell, Charles Janeway. *History of the United States Sanitary Commission, the General Report of Its Work During the War of the Rebellion*. New York: Hurd and Houghton, 1868.

Swift, Eliot E. *Brief Biographies of Ruling Elders in the First Presbyterian Church, Allegheny, During the First Fifty Years of Its History*. Pittsburgh, PA: Jackson and McEwen, 1880.

Taylor, Brian. *Fighting for Citizenship: Black Northerners and the Debate over Military Service in the Civil War*. Chapel Hill: The University of North Carolina Press, 2020.

Thurston, George H. *Allegheny County's Hundred Years*. Pittsburgh, PA: A. A. Anderson and Son, 1888.

Thurston, George H. *Directory of Pittsburgh and Allegheny Cities, 1861–62*. Pittsburgh, PA: G. H. Thurston, 1861.

Thurston, George H. *Directory of Pittsburgh and Vicinity for 1859–60*. Pittsburgh, PA: George H. Thurston, 1859.

United States War Department, *The War of the Rebellion: A Compilation of the Official Records of the Union and Confederate Armies*. 70 vols. In 128 pts. Washington, D.C.: n.p., 1880–1901.

Van Voorhis, John S. *The Old and New Monongahela*. Pittsburgh, PA: Nicholson, 1893.

Wade, Richard C. *The Urban Frontier: The Rise of Western Cities, 1790–1830*. Cambridge, MA: Harvard University Press, 1959.

Walkinshaw, Lewis Clark. *The Annals of Southwestern Pennsylvania*. 4 vols. New York: Lewis Historical Publishing, 1939.

Wiley, Bell Irvin. *The Life of Billy Yank: The Common Soldier of the Union*. Baton Rouge: Louisiana State University Press, 1952.

Wilkins, William, et al. *Does the Country Require a National Armory and Foundry West of the Allegheny Mountains; If It Does, Where Should They be Located?* Pittsburgh, PA: W. S. Haven, 1862.

Wilson, Mark R. *The Business of the Civil War: Military Mobilization and the State, 1861–1865*. Baltimore, MD: The Johns Hopkins University Press, 2006.

ARTICLES AND ESSAYS

Arensberg, Charles F. C. "The Pittsburgh Fire of April 10, 1845." *Western Pennsylvania Historical Magazine* 28 (1945): 11–19.

Barnes, Diane. "Urban Rivalry in the Upper Ohio Valley: Wheeling and Pittsburgh in the Nineteenth Century." *Pennsylvania Magazine of History and Biography* 123 (1999): 201–26.

Belfour, Stanton. "The Philanthropic Tradition in Pittsburgh." *Western Pennsylvania Historical Magazine* 37 (1954): 91–105.

Bining, Arthur Cecil. "The Rise of Iron Manufacturing in Western Pennsylvania." *Western Pennsylvania Historical Magazine* 16 (1933): 235–56.

Blackett, R. J. M. "Freedom or the Martyr's Grave: Black Pittsburgh's Aid to the Fugitive Slave." *Western Pennsylvania Historical Magazine* 61 (1978): 117–34.

Brillhart, Norman C. "The Election of 1864 in Western Pennsylvania." *Western Pennsylvania Historical Magazine* 8, no. 1 (January 1925): 26–36.

Burns, Edward M. "Slavery in Western Pennsylvania." *Western Pennsylvania Historical Magazine* 8 (1925): 204–14.

Clark, Joseph S., Jr., and Michael Schlatter. "The Railroad Struggle for Pittsburgh: Forty-three Years of Philadelphia-Baltimore Rivalry, 1838–1871." *Pennsylvania Magazine of History and Biography* 48 (1924): 1–38.

Cowan, John P. "Beginning of the Early Railroads in Pittsburgh." *Western Pennsylvania Historical Magazine* 12 (1929): 112–29.

Cowan, John P. "Fortifying Pittsburgh in 1863: Historic Document Gives Interesting Record of the Men Who Worked on Construction of Coal Hill Fort." *Western Pennsylvania Historical Magazine* 2 (1919): 59–64.

Dalinger, Charles W. "The Pittsburgh Sanitary Fair." *Western Pennsylvania Historical Magazine* 12 (1929): 97–101.

Daniel, Dorothy. "The Sanitary Fair." *Western Pennsylvania Historical Magazine* 41 (1958): 145–62.

Elder, Margaret. "Pittsburgh Industries that Used to Be." *Western Pennsylvania Historical Magazine* 12 (1929): 211–25.

Grinspan, Jon. "Young Men for War: The Wide Awakes and Lincoln's 1860 Presidential Campaign." *Journal of American History* 96, no. 2 (September 2009): 357–78.

Hanchett, Catherine M. "George Boyer Vashon, 1824–1878: Black Educator, Poet, Fighter for Equal Rights—Part One." *Western Pennsylvania Historical Magazine* 68 (1985): 333–49.

Holmes, Ida Bright. "The Civil War Letters of James Rush Holmes." *Western Pennsylvania Historical Magazine* 44 (1961): 105–27.

Martin, Asa E. "The Temperance Movement in Pennsylvania Prior to the Civil War." *Pennsylvania Magazine of History and Biography* 49 (1925): 195–230.

Masich, Andrew E. "Rodman's Big Gun." *Western Pennsylvania Historical Magazine* 98 (2015): 20–31.

Muller, Edward K. "Was Pittsburgh's Economic Destiny Set in 1815?" *Indiana Magazine of History* 105 (2009): 203–18.

Powers, Tom, and James Wudarczyk. "Behind the Scenes of the Allegheny Arsenal Explosion." *Pennsylvania Legacies* 13 (2013): 42–55.

Rittenour, John S. "Over the Old Roads to Pittsburgh." *Western Pennsylvania Historical Magazine* 4 (1921): 76–83.

Rutland, Robert. "A Union Rookie at Camp Wilkins, 1861." *Western Pennsylvania Historical Magazine* 37 (1954): 56–60.

Schusler, William Kenneth. "The Railroad Comes to Pittsburgh." *Western Pennsylvania Historical Magazine* 43 (1960): 251–66.

Seidman, Rachel Filene. "A Monstrous Doctrine? Northern Women on Dependency During the Civil War." In *An Uncommon Time: The Civil War and the Northern Home Front,* edited by Paul A. Cimbala and Randall M. Miller. New York: Fordham University Press, 2002.

Slick, Sewell E. "William Wilkins: Pittsburgher Extraordinary." *Western Pennsylvania Historical Magazine* 22 (1939): 217–36.

Smith, Eric Ledell. "The Pittsburgh Memorial: A Forgotten Document of Pittsburgh History." *Pittsburgh History* 80 (1997): 106–11.

Sponholtz, Lloyd L. "Pittsburgh and Temperance, 1830–1854." *Western Pennsylvania Historical Magazine* 46 (1963): 347–79.

Taylor, M. Flavia. "The Political and Civic Career of Henry Baldwin, 1799–1830." *Western Pennsylvania Historical Magazine* 24 (1941): 37–50.

Trimble, William F. "From Sail to Steam: Ship Building in the Pittsburgh Area, 1790–1865." *Western Pennsylvania Historical Magazine* 58 (1975): 147–67.

White, J. W. F. "The Judiciary of Allegheny County." *Pennsylvania Magazine of History and Biography* 7 (1883): 163–93.

Williams, Irene F. "The Operation of the Fugitive Slave Law in Western Pennsylvania from 1850 to 1860." *Western Pennsylvania Historical Magazine* 4 (1921): 150–60.

DISSERTATIONS AND THESES

Orr, Timothy Justin. "Cities at War: Union Army Mobilization in the Urban Northeast, 1861–1865." Ph.D. diss., Pennsylvania State University, 2010.

WEBSITES

Civil War Photos. "Portrait of Pennsylvania Representative James Kennedy Moorhead." Accessed October 13, 2022. https://civilwarphotos.net/files/cartes_de_visite_images/c174.jpg.

Condon, Rich. "'A Vigorous Defense'—Pittsburgh's Forgotten Civil War Fortifications." Pennsylvania in the Civil War. Accessed October 13, 2022. https://
www.penncivilwar.com/post/a-vigorous-defense.

———. "The Tragedy at Allegheny Arsenal—'A Horrid Moment of a Most Wicked
Rebellion." American Battlefield Trust. Accessed October 13, 2022.

Glasco, Larry. Historic Pittsburgh Census Data, 1860 census spreadsheet. University
of Pittsburgh, University Library System. http://exhibit.library.pitt.edu
/census/ [accessed December 1, 2014]. https://www.battlefields.org/learn
/articles/tragedy-allegheny-arsenal-horrid-moment-most-wicked-rebellion.

Naval History and Heritage Command. "Colonel Ellett's Ram Fleet on the
Mississippi." Accessed October 13, 2022. https://www.history.navy.mil
/content/history/nhhc/our-collections/photography/numerical-list-of
-images/nhhc-series/nh-series/NH-59000/NH-59007.html.

———. "The Total Annihilation of the Rebel Fleet by the Federal Fleet under
Commodore Davis." Accessed October 13, 2022. https://www.history.navy
.mil/content/history/nhhc/our-collections/photography/numerical-list-of
-images/nhhc-series/nh-series/NH-42000/NH-42367.html.

INDEX

Page numbers in **boldface** refer to illustrations.